D1789621

The Finale Projects

THE finale® PROJECTS

THE NEW APPROACH TO LEARNING finale

TOM CARRUTH

GIA PUBLICATIONS, INC.
CHICAGO

finale

Finale trademark owned by MakeMusic, Inc. Used with permission of MakeMusic, Inc.

G-7203
GIA Publications, Inc.
7404 S. Mason Ave., Chicago, IL 60638
www.giamusic.com

ISBN: 978-1-57999-696-3

Copyright © 2008 GIA Publications, Inc.
All rights reserved.
Printed in the United States of America.

CONTENTS

PREFACE

1988: Finale was introduced to the world, and Tom Johnson and Tom Carruth were introduced to each other at a Finale dealer training session in Minneapolis. Tom Johnson has been the product specialist for Finale since that day, attending countless conventions and teaching countless clinics, and has become the face many people associate with Finale. Tom Carruth has taught many Finale clinics and used Finale professionally since Finale 1.0. Today they both work for MakeMusic Inc., the creators of Finale, and have teamed up to teach a new approach to Finale.

Finale has gone through so many changes since that 1.0 version. The collaborative concepts of Carruth and Johnson have produced this manual to help users understand the direction that Finale has taken and the direction it will continue. Although many users have "their way" of doing things, this book is designed to teach the most consistent, intuitive, and easiest method for using Finale.

Based on a project-oriented approach that has been proven effective in many clinic situations, this book can teach you the most effective approach to practical, everyday, and not so everyday needs of Finale.

CHAPTER 1

GETTING ACQUAINTED WITH FINALE

CONCEPTS USED IN THIS BOOK

Within this book there are a couple of things to remember:

1. Modifier keys are always listed this way: Windows/Macintosh. For example, you will see the text **Ctrl/Command** many times. This means that for Windows, use the **Ctrl** key; for Macintosh, use the **Command** key.

Windows Ctrl key

2. Keystrokes in commands are set in a contrasting font. If you should use the 'A' key, it will be set as **A**. A capitalized letter does not mean you use the **Shift** key. If you are to use the **Shift** key, that will be noted.

Macintosh Command key

3. The key shown is used to help you remember the intuitive logic behind using that key. For example, you will learn about *zoom in* and *zoom out*. This is accessed from the hyphen key (–) and the equal sign key (=), but the plus key (+) is shown rather than the = key. This is not meant to indicate the **Shift** key should be used to access the +; it simply means the + is to zoom in and – is to zoom out.

4. Another set of standard commands listed in the book are *right-click* and *control-click*. On a standard mouse there are two buttons: left and right. Generally the left button is used. In many places in Finale the right button is used to activate a contextual menu. Not all Macintosh mice have a right button. You can use a two-button mouse on a Macintosh, or you can hold the **Control** button while clicking. **Note:** Some Macintosh mice are deceiving: they appear to have only one button, but by tapping the top of the mouse, a right-click can be achieved.

5. Standard path text format is used when directing you to a menu command. For example, *Plug-ins* menu/*TG tools/Modify Rests* means to click on the *Plug-ins* menu at the top of the screen, then click on the submenu *TG tools*, which reveals another submenu containing *Modify Rests*. That is the command you ultimately click to perform the function.

EXTRA CREDIT SECTION ✓

BACK TO THE PROJECT ↺

6. The projects in this book will teach you many powerful features of Finale. Information not required by a project but still valuable and worth knowing is set in a section marked *Extra Credit*. This is followed by a *Back to the Project* marker.

Included with this book is a CD-ROM containing PDF files of the completed projects. You will find them in a folder on the CD-ROM named *Project PDF Files*. Open and print these files. Refer to these printed versions to better understand the end result as you work through a project.

STARTING FINALE

When you first launch Finale, the *Launch* window is displayed. From here you can start a new document from the *Setup Wizard*, a blank default document, or a template.

From the *Launch* window you can also open existing documents, quickly return to previously opened documents, and more.

1. Open the project file *Be Still My Soul*, found on the CD-ROM.

2. The default view in Finale 2006 and higher is the Studio View, which will be discussed later. It looks similar to this illustration:

Studio View

3. If this view is presented when you open the project file, click on the *View* menu and select *Page View*.

4. Now, from the *Edit* menu on Windows or the *Apple/Preferences* menu on Macintosh, select *Program Options* and change the default view to *Page View*. Now close these options.

VIDEO CLIP 1:1

FINALE INTRODUCTION AND NAVAGATION

VIDEO INSTRUCTION

Many people (like myself) learn better with visual demonstrations than with textual descriptions of tasks to be performed, so on the CD-ROM you will also see an application named *Project Video Demonstration*.

Double-click this to open a menu of videos that show how to compete the projects in each chapter. Once the menu appears, click once on a chapter title to open a submenu of videos. Click once on a video title to start it.

You can watch the entire video without stopping, or, using the playback controls in the lower right of the window, you can stop and start the video, doing each task as shown.

Remember that this video window can be maximized, as most windows on your computer screen can. Doing this will enlarge the video for better viewing.

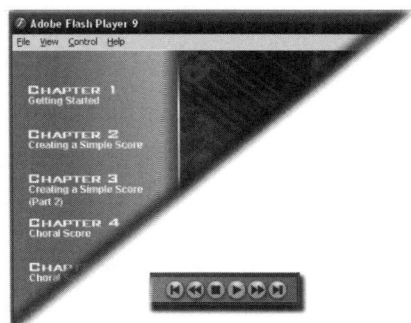

Video interface and transport controls.

MOVING THE SCORE

Unless you have a large screen you probably cannot see the entire page.

1. On Windows, hold down the right mouse button and drag the page in any direction to see the page. Avoid clicking on a staff; click in the white space of the page instead.

2. On Macintosh, hold down both **Command** and **Option**, then press and hold the mouse button and drag the page.

3. You can also use the **Page Up** and **Page Down** keys to view the score.

4. If your mouse has a scroll wheel, you can use that to move the page up and down.

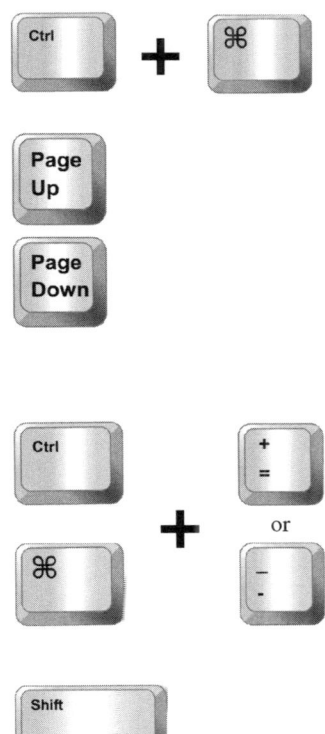

ZOOMING IN AND OUT

When working with details in Finale, it is helpful to *zoom in*. When working with page layout, *zoom out* is helpful.

1. You can hold down **Ctrl/Command** and use the **+** and **–** keys to zoom in and out.

2. To zoom into a specific place in the score, on Windows hold down **Shift** and right-click on the score where you want to zoom in. This is **Command-Shift-click** on the Macintosh.

Teacher, I Have a Question

Is there a way to change my screen to see more music?

Yes, you can change your computer's screen resolution. *If you are using a shared computer, do not do this without consulting with other users, or in a school setting, a lab tech or teacher.* On Windows, close Finale and return to the desktop. Right-click the desktop and select *Properties*. Select *Settings*. Change the desktop size to a higher number (1024 x 786 or higher). On Macintosh, select the monitor resolution from the pull-down menu at the top of the screen, or set this by going to *Apple menu/System Preferences/Displays*.

CHANGING PAGES

To change pages, do one of the following:

1. Click the page up and down arrows in the lower left hand corner of the screen.

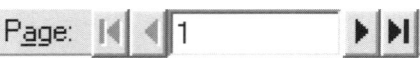

2. Press **Ctrl/Command–Page Down** to go to the next page; press **Ctrl/Command–Page Up** for the previous page.

TOOLS

Across the top and along the side of the screen, you will see palettes containing icons that represent different tools. These tools let you quickly get to the functions that you need in Finale. You will notice that they can be dragged and reshaped to optimize screen space. From the *Windows* menu you can access more tools that might be helpful for you to have quickly available if you would like. On Windows, you can also customize the tools within each palette to optimize space.

NOTE

When using a shared computer, it is not advisable to customize Finale without consulting other users, or, in a school setting, a lab tech or teacher.

CHAPTER 2

CREATING A
SIMPLE SCORE

Concepts covered in this chapter:

- Setting up the score
- Inputing notes, rests, and triplets
- Editing and altering notes
- Changing time and key signatures
- Copying and pasting music
- Re-pitching music

PROJECT FILE: SIMPLE SONG

If you have not already printed out this file, find the file on the included CD. Find "Simple Song on the accompanying CD and print it. You will need to refer to this score to as you re-create it in this project. **Each of the projects have PDF files you will want to have at your access to see the score referred to in each of the following projects in this book.**

SETTING UP THE SCORE

At this point you should be in *Page View*. If not, select *Page View* from the *View menu*. Review Chapter 1 to learn how to set *Page View* as the default view.

Note to Finale 2008 users: The *Setup Wizard* was changed dramatically in Finale 2008. Due to the new design, instructions for Finale 2008 users will be given in a separate section below. Disregard this information section and skip to Setting up the Score: Finale 2008.

1. From the *Launch* window, select *Setup Wizard*.

2. In the provided text fields, type the title, composer and copyright information as shown on the example. Note that you can change page size and orientation, but there is no need to in this score.

3. Click *Next*.

VIDEO
CLIP 2:1
SETTING UP THE SCORE

4. Select *SmartMusic SoftSynth* from the dropdown menu at the top of the dialog.

Document Setup Wizard

5. Now select the instruments. This is a Flute and Clarinet duet. Select the woodwind group from the list to the left. Now double-click *Flute* and double-click *Clarinet in Bb* from the list in the center.

6. Click *Next*.

7. Set the meter and key. The meter is already set to common time. Choose the concert key of F using the scroll buttons, clicking **Down Arrow** once for one flat.

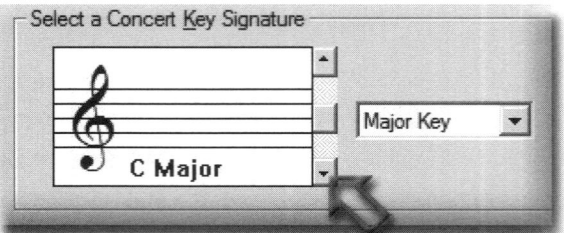

Key Signature dialog

8. Click *Next*.

9. Click on *Specify Pickup Measure*. This score starts with three eighth notes in the pickup measure. Specify the size of the pickup measure by selecting a note value that is the sum of the note durations in the pickup measure. In this example, click on the dotted quarter note value, since it is the sum of three eighth notes.

Specify pickup measure dialog

10. Click *Finish*.

SETTING UP THE SCORE: FINALE 2008

VIDEO
CLIP 2:1
SETTING UP THE SCORE

As stated above, the *Setup Wizard* in Finale 2008 is completely different from previous versions of the program. If you are using Finale 2008, follow these instructions. If not, you should have followed the instructions above and are not ready to go on to the next section, *Format the Number of Measures in a System.*

1. From the *Launch* window (the first window you encounter when you launch Finale), select *Setup Wizard.*

2. In this dialog, you can select an ensemble from the window pane on the left and a document style on the right. This song is very simple, we will select the instrumentation manually. For this project, select document style *Engraved Style (Maestro Font)*. Now click *Next.*

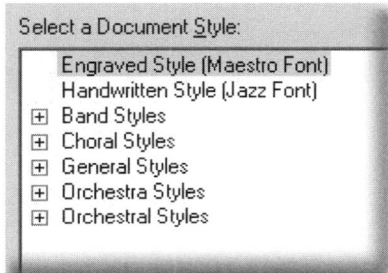

Select an Ensemble and Document Style dialog

3. In this dialog, make sure the *Instrument Set* is set to *SmartMusic SoftSynth* for this project. If it is not selected, click on the dropdown menu next to *Instrument Set* and select this option.

Instrument Set dropdown menu

4. From this page you can also setup instrument staves. Click on *Woodwinds* in the far left window pane.

5. In the pane to the right of *Woodwinds,* select *Flute,* then click *Add.* You could also double-click on *Flute* to add it to the score.

6. Select *Clarinet in B♭.* Add it to the score as you did with *Flute.*

7. Now click *Next* to go to the *Score Information* page.

8. On this page you can enter the name of the song, composer, and other text items that will appear on the score. Type **Simple Song** in the *Title* field and click *Next* to go to the *Score Settings* page.

9. On this final page you can select time and key signatures and set a pickup measure if needed. This score is in common time, which should already be selected. If not, click the common time symbol between 4/4 and 3/8.

10. In the *Key Signature* section, click on the down arrow key next to key signature illustration to add a flat for the key of F major.

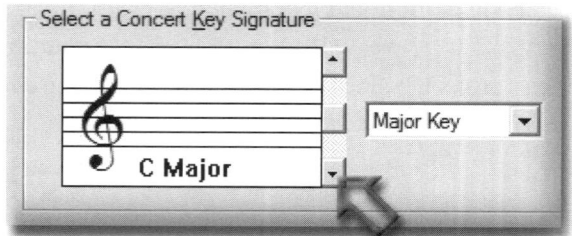

The Key Signature dialog

11. This song does start with a pickup measure of three eighth notes, so the pickup measure needs a dotted-quarter-note beat. Click the checkbox by *Specify Pickup Measure* to select it and then select the dotted-quarter-note icon in this area of the dialog.

The Specify Pickup Measure dialog

12. A new feature in Finale 2008 allows you to specify the number of measures. This is optional, since it is easy to delete measures, but you may want to enter **12** measures.

13. Click *Finish*.

FORMATTING THE NUMBER OF MEASURES IN A SYSTEM

Generally you can just start inputting notes and let Finale decide how many measures will fit in each system based on content. But for this exercise, select four measures in each system.

1. From the main tool palette, select the *Mass Edit* tool. If using Finale 2008, there is no *Mass Edit* tool. Press the **Esc** key to activate the *Selection* tool. All *Mass Edit* functions in this book are accessed from the *Selection* tool in Finale 2008.

2. Click to the left of the Flute staff. This selects from measure 1 to the end of the score.

3. In Finale 2006 and 2007, right-click on the highlighted measures if you have a two-button mouse, or, on Macintosh, press and hold **Control** and click (hereafter referred to as **Control–click**) on the highlighted measures.

4. In the contextual menu, click *Fit Music*. This item is in the *Utilities* menu on Finale 2008 and can also be accessed by typing **Shift–Command-M** (on Macintosh) or **Ctrl–M** (on Windows).

5. Enter **4** measures per system and click *OK*.

NOTE

Next you are going to input notes. If you are using a laptop, you will need to change the note entry key commands to the laptop set. Otherwise, go directly to *Inputting Notes*.

SELECTING THE LAPTOP SET

1. Click on the *Simple Note Input* tool in the *Simple Note* palette. This puts you into simple note input mode.

2. From the *Simple* menu at the top of the screen, select *Simple Entry Options/Edit Keyboard Shortcuts*.

3. Now in the *Name* dropdown menu select *Laptop Shortcut Table*. Click *OK* to return to the score.

Mass Edit and Selection tools

Control key

Simple Note Entry tool

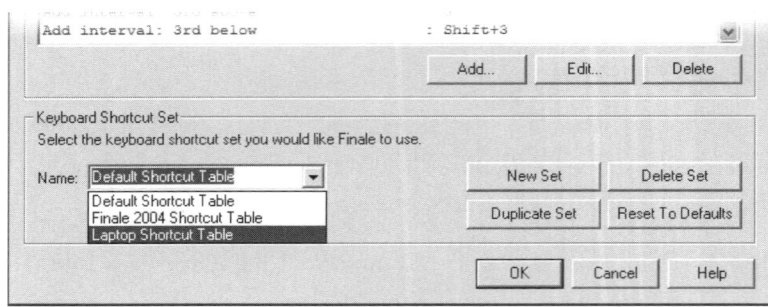

Selecting the Laptop Shortcut Table

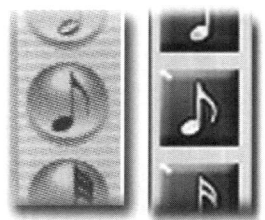

Simple Note Entry tool

Entering the first three notes

INPUTTING NOTES

Before starting, you may want to zoom in on the top system. On Windows, hold **Shift** and right-click on the top system. On Macintosh, **Command-Shift-click** the top system.

1. Click on the eighth note icon in the note palette. You will see an eighth note cursor in the first measure (pickup measure).

2. Type the letters **G**, **A**, and **B** for the first three notes. The cursor will now advance to the next measure. If not, you have a problem.

Teacher, I Have a Problem

Did you forget to set the pickup measure? If so, in Finale 2006, click on the *Options* menu, or, in Finale 2007–2008, the *Document* menu, and select *Pickup Measure*. Select the dotted-quarter note as the pickup measure size. Now go back to step one and input the notes.

3. In the next measure, type the number **5** on the numpad, or if using a laptop, the number **5** in the number row. Notice the note caret changes to a quarter note. Now type the letter **C** to input that note.

4. Type a period (**.**) to add the dot to the quarter note.

5. Type the number **4** (numpad–**4**, or on a laptop, number row–**4**). Notice that the cursor value is now an eighth note and the eighth note icon is selected in the note palette. Try each of the numbers 1–8 to see the corresponding note values. You can always tell which value you select from the note caret and the note palette. Select the eighth note again (**4**) and type **G**, **A**, and **B**.

Full-sized Keyboard Map uses the Numpad

With the laptop map selected, use these number keys

6. Select the quarter note (**5**) and type **D**.

7. **Rests.** The next measure starts with a quarter rest. The quarter value should still be selected, so type **0** (numpad–**0** or laptop–**0**) to input a rest of the currently selected duration (**0** for zero notes).

8. Select sixteenth note (**3**) and type the note names for the next four notes: **F**, **D**, **B**, and **C**.

Here are graphics depicting all of the numpad and laptop numrow note duration assignments:

Numpad note duration assignments

Numrow note duration assignments

Teacher, I Made a Mistake

Anytime you need to fix a duration, use the **Left Arrow** key to select the note or rest. You can use **Left Arrow** and **Right Arrow** keys to select notes backwards or forwards. Once selected, you can type the correct pitch, change the octave, or move the note to the correct pitch with the **Up Arrow** and **Down Arrow** keys. Press the **Right Arrow** key until you return to the note caret to input more notes.

9. **Ties.** Type **T** for tie, then select quarter note (**5**) and type **C**.

10. Press the **Right Arrow** key to move to the next measure. Notice that Finale fills in the necessary rests.

11. Select eighth note (**4**) and type **D** and **A**.

12. **Shift the Octave**. *Now* hold **Shift** and press the **Up Arrow** key to shift the cursor up an octave. Type **F**, then input the rest (**0**).

   a. When typing notes, Finale will always select the pitch closest to the current cursor position. So, if you had typed **F** before shifting the cursor up an octave, you would have selected the F an octave too low.

Teacher, I Made a Mistake

Suppose you typed the **F** key before you **Shift**-ed the cursor up an octave. Now the F pitch is in the wrong octave. Hold **Alt/Option** and press **Shift** to "alter" the note by shifting it up or down an octave using the **Up Arrow** or **Down Arrow** key. Notice that this will also change the note caret so that the next note to input will be in the same range.

13. **Saving the file**. It is always a good idea to save your work frequently. Computer glitches can happen.

   a. Type **Ctrl/Command–S**. The first time you do this Finale will ask for a filename.

   b. Type **Ctrl/Command–S** anytime you want to save your work. This will overwrite the last saved version.

14. **Triplet**. The next figure is an eighth-note triplet.

   a. Put in the first eighth note (**D**).

   b. Now type **9** on the numpad or laptop **9**.

  c. The number 9 is the last note value and represents triplet and other tuplet values. (Here is a logical way to think of this key: Most of the time, you will use this for triplets, which is a set of three notes, and nine is divisible by three.)

  d. Finish typing the remaining notes in the triplet. This automatically changes the remaining rests in the triplet to the pitches you type or play.

15. **Auto Tie**. Type an eighth note **F** *then* change the note value to a quarter note (**5**). Type **D**. Notice that Finale automatically creates the tie over the barline for you.

16. **Accidentals**. Change the note value to eighth (**4**), and type **0** to input the eighth rest followed by a **D**.

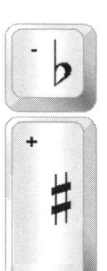

  a. Type **+** on the numpad or laptop number row to place a sharp on the note.

  b. Input the next note (**A**) and flat this note by typing **−**.

  c. Finish inputting the notes in this measure.

  d. Notice that once an accidental has been placed, it is in effect throughout the measure. Type **+** to raise any note one-half step or **N** (for *n*atural) to change a note to a natural, as in the last note of the triplet.

USING MIDI TO INPUT PITCHES

If you have a MIDI keyboard interfaced with your computer, you can use it to input pitches rather than typing letter keys. In the case of a MIDI keyboard, simply play the correct pitch on the MIDI keyboard rather than typing letter keys for pitches.

  Finish measure five using the information you have learned. You can either type the pitches or use a MIDI keyboard for the pitches.

VIDEO
CLIP 2:3

SIMPLE NOTE ENTRY
(PART 2)

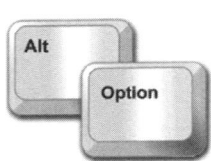

**Hold down the Alt/
Option key and type G**

**Hold down the Ctrl/
Command key and type G**

**Hold down the Alt/
Option key and type K**

Teacher, I Have a Problem

I played an A♭ on the MIDI keyboard but got a G♯ instead! When using a MIDI keyboard you may intend an A♭ but get a G♯. This behavior can be set in *Enharmonic Spellings*. For now, a simple way to change a few notes enharmonically is to select the note, then type **Alt/Option–E** (for *e*nharmonic).

USING THE ALT/OPTION AND CTRL/COMMAND KEYS

Grace Notes. The first note in measure 6 is a grace note.

1. Input the D eighth note as you normally would.

2. **Alter a Note**.

   a. The **Alt/Option** key is used to alter notes.

   b. To change from a regular eighth note to a grace note, Type **Alt/Option–G** (for *g*race note).

3. Now input the next two notes.

4. **Lock-in Functions** (or sticky keys).

   a. For the sixteenth grace notes, instead of altering them from regular notes to grace notes, we will lock in the grace note function. Type **Ctrl/Command-G**.

5. Now change the note value to a sixteenth note (**3**) and type the notes.

6. When you are finished typing the grace notes, type **Ctrl/Command–G** to exit sticky grace notes or lock-in mode. Another way to exit lock-in mode is to press a duration key twice. Since the next note is a dotted quarter, press **5** twice to select quarter and exit lock-in mode.

7. Finish inputting the notes in measure 6.

Altering the Key Signature. There are several ways to change the key signature. We will use the logic we have already learned, using **Alt/Option** to alter things.

1. Before inputting the first note in measure 7, type **Alt/Option–K** (for *k*ey signature).

2. You are prompted for a shortcut key. If you knew that key, you could press it now. The shortcut key for two sharps is the number **2** in the numrow.

    a. If you do not know the shortcut, simply press **Enter** and select the new key from the *Key Signature* dialog.

Tuplets other than Triplets. In measure 8 we start with five eighth notes in the space of four eighth notes.

1. Input the first eighth note as we did when we created the triplet.

2. Type **Alt/Option–9** for tuplet. Now we can alter the tuplet definition.

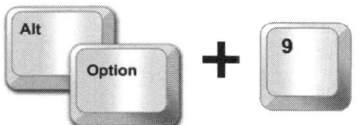

Hold down the Alt/ Option key and type 9

3. In the dialog that appears type **5** in the first text field and **4** in the *In the space of* field. (**Note**: You can always use the **Tab** key to cycle through value boxes in a dialog.)

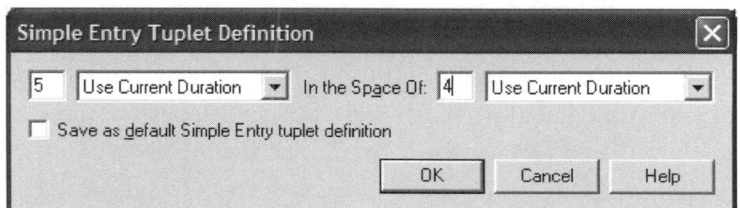

Simple Entry Tuplet Definition dialog

4. Press **OK** or **Enter**.

5. Now finish the remaining notes in the tuplet and complete measure 7. Again, the rests added to the tuplet will be changed to notes simply by typing or playing the notes as you normally would.

6. In measure 8, hold **Alt/Option–K** and set the key back to F major. The shortcut key for one flat is the key below numrow **1**, which is the **Q** key. Use that key or press **Enter** and alter the key signature using the *Key Signature* dialog.

7. Input the first two notes in measure 8: C and A.

Triplets with Mixed Durations. In measure 8 we have an eighth-note triplet that starts with a quarter note. We will see if we can do this with what we have learned.

1. To tell Finale that we want an eighth-note triplet, input an eighth note for the first note of the triplet. Select eighth note (**4**) and input the D.

2. Now type **9** for triplet as before.

3. Before going on, alter (**Alt/Option**) the first note to be a quarter note. Type **Alt/Option–5**.

4. Now use the **Right Arrow** key to select the eighth rest and type or play the pitch for that note.

5. Finish measure 8.

6. This is a good place to save your work. Type **Ctrl/Command–S** (for *save*).

EXTRA CREDIT
SECTION

MORE ON TRIPLETS WITH MIXED DURATIONS

If the score you are working on has multiple triplets of the same size but mixed duration, you can change the tuplet definition before inputting tuplets. This will allow you to input tuplets of mixed durations without having to alter notes after putting them in. For example, consider the musical example below. Note that all of the triplets are three eighths in the space of two eighths. Some start or end with a quarter note. To input this quickly:

Triplets of mixed durations

1. Input either quarter or eighth note.

2. Now type **Alt/Option–9** (for "alter the tuplet definition") on the numpad or numrow.

3. The *Simple Entry Tuplet Definition* dialog will display. Change the values to *3 Eighth(s) In the Space of 2 Eighth(s)*.

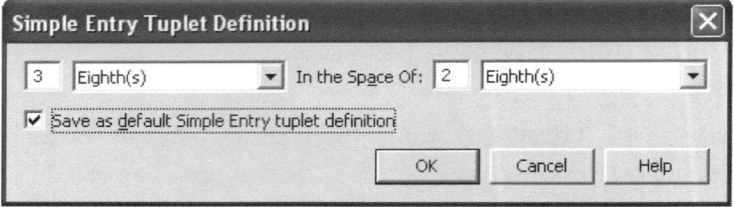

Simple Entry Tuplet Definition dialog

4. Check the box next to *Save as default Simple Entry tuplet definition*. Click *OK*.

5. Notice the note you input has been changed to a triplet. Select the new duration value (**4** for eighth, **5** for quarter) and input the next note in the triplet.

6. Now you can select either eighth or quarter note to start the triplet and Finale will know it is an eighth-note triplet.

7. You can also lock in triplets (Finale calls this *sticky triplets* in *Simple* entry mode). Type **Ctrl/Command–9** (for tuplet). Now you can input several consecutive tuplets without having to press **9** for each one. To exit this mode, type a new duration key (**1–8**) twice to exit tuplet lock-in or sticky triplet mode.

8. After you are finished using this current tuplet definition, you may want to set the tuplet definition back to the regular default mode. This setting will carry over to other files you are working on.

    a. Type a note.

    b. Type **Alt/Option–9** to enter the *Tuplet Definition* dialog.

    c. Now change the settings back to *3* [Use Current Duration] *In the Space Of: 2* [Use Current Duration].

    d. Check the box next to *Save as default Simple Entry tuplet definition*. Click *OK*.

BACK TO THE **PROJECT**

Altering the Time Signature. Use **Alt/Option** to alter the time signature as you did the key signature.

1. Type **Alt/Option–T** (for *t*ime signature).

2. The shortcut key for 3/4 time is **3**. Or you can always press **Enter** and set the time signature in the *Time Signature* dialog. You will get some practice using this dialog in the next measure.

Hold down the Alt/
Option key and type T

Altering the Clef. Although not part of this project, you can also alter the clef by typing **Alt/Option–C** (for *c*lef). Simply have the first note in the new clef selected before typing this key combination.

Cautionary Accidentals. In measure 9 we have a cautionary accidental.

1. Input the G. By default, this will be G♮ because it is in the next measure.

2. Type **P** to *p*arenthesize and force an accidental to appear.

3. Finish the inputting the notes in this measure.

Altering and Hiding the Time Signature. In measure 10, we need to take one-and-a-half beats out of the measure to compensate for the pickup measure at the beginning of the score.

1. Type **Alt/Option–T** (for *t*ime signature) as we did above.

2. Press **Enter** to access the *Time Signature* dialog.

3. Change the number of beats to five, using the scroll arrow on the right to increase the number of beats.

4. Next to *Beat Duration,* change the size of the beats to display eighth notes by clicking the left scroll arrow twice.

5. We do not want this new time signature to show in the score. Click *Options* on Windows or *More Choices* on Macintosh.

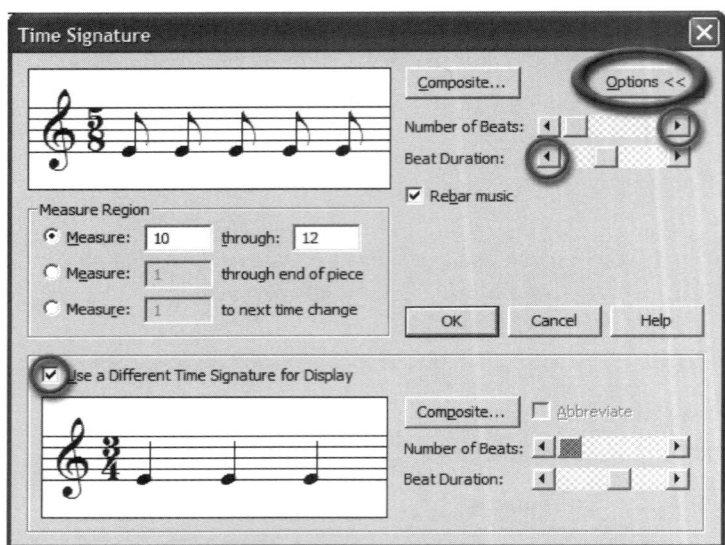

The Time Signature dialog

6. Select *Use a Different Time Signature for Display.* Note the displayed time signature is already set to 3/4. Since this is what we want Finale to show, a time signature change will not display at all, because the previous measure is already in 3/4.

7. Click *OK* to exit.

Articulations in Note Entry. There are several ways to add articulations for one note or several notes. In this case we want a fermata on the last note.

1. After inputting the last note, Type **Alt/Option–A** to alter the note with an articulation.

Hold down the Alt/ Option key and type A

2. A *Waiting for input* dialog appears. Type **F** (for *fermata*).

    a. **Note**: In certain versions of Finale 2006 the **F** key was not assigned to the fermata symbol. Typing **F** will instead open the *Articulation Selection* dialog. Here you can select the articulation you like. Double-click the fermata symbol.

    b. You can also open the *Articulation Selection* dialog by pressing **Return** if you do not know the correct shortcut key.

COPYING, PASTING AND RE-PITCHING

Since the Clarinet is rhythmically identical to the Flute part, copy the Flute to the Clarinet part. Then we only have to change the pitches.

1. If you cannot see the top of the score, press **Page Up.**

2. **Copy**. Select the *Mass Edit* tool. (In Finale 2008, press **Esc** to go to the *Selection* tool.)

3. Click to the left of the Flute staff. This selects (or highlights) the Flute staff from measure 1 to the end of the score.

4. Click in the pickup measure of the Flute part and drag the mouse to the pickup measure in the Clarinet part until you see the Clarinet part highlighted as in the graphic below.

Dragging the selection

5. Now release the mouse. This copies the Flute notes to the Clarinet part. Since the Clarinet is a transposing instrument, Finale automatically displays the notes a step higher.

6. Re-pitch. In the note palette, select the *Re-pitch* tool.

7. Click on the first note in the Clarinet part to highlight it.

8. Type **F**, then press **Right Arrow**. Repeat this procedure for G and A. Press **Right Arrow** to advance to the next measure. (This is only necessary for pickup measures.)

VIDEO CLIP 2:4

FORMATTING, COPY/PASTE, AND REPITCH

Mass Edit and Selection tools

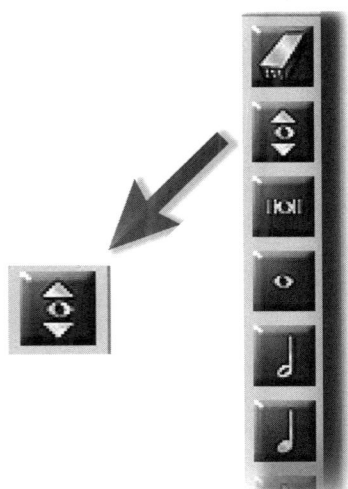

The Re-pitch tool

9. Using letter keys or the MIDI keyboard, re-pitch the rest of the notes to the correct pitch. Finale will automatically select the next note for re-pitch, skipping over rests.

10. The *Re-pitch* tool may not work for grace notes. Use the **Right Arrow** key to select each grace note, then use the **Up Arrow** and **Down Arrow** keys to re-pitch them.

11. When typing to re-pitch, remember to shift the octave before re-pitching. If you forget to do this, the fastest way to fix this is to type **Shift–Alt/Option–Up Arrow** or **Shift–Alt/Option–Down Arrow** to alter a note by an octave. You can also use the **Left Arrow** and **Right Arrow** keys to select a note, then type **Shift–Up Arrow** or **Shift–Down Arrow** to change the octave. Use the **Right Arrow** key to return to the cursor position for new notes. Also, the octave position for the cursor might not be where you want it. That is why it is best to type **Shift–Alt/Option–Up Arrow** or **Shift–Alt/Option–Down Arrow**, since this moves both the last note entered and the note caret or cursor to the correct octave.

12. **Note**: You may have a problem in measure 6 after copying the music. There is a chance that the dotted quarter note turned into a quarter tied to an eighth.

   a. Press **Esc** a couple of times to access the *Selection Tool*.

   b. Double-click on the notehead of the unwanted eighth note. Press **Delete** to remove it.

   c. Press **Left Arrow** to select the quarter note.

   d. Type **T** to toggle off the tie.

   e. Type a period (.) to add a dot to the quarter note.

DELETING UNUSED MEASURES

This song has only eleven measures, including the pickup measure. We need to delete all other measures.

1. Press **Page Down** to move to the bottom of the page.

2. Select the *Mass Edit* tool. (In Finale 2008, press **Esc** to go to the *Selection* tool.)

Mass Edit and Selection tools

3. Click on measure 12 (the first empty measure). In Finale 2008, double-click measure 12 to select the entire measure stack.

4. Type **Shift–Right Arrow**. (In Finale 2008, type **Shift–End**.) This selects from measure 12 to the end of the score.

5. To delete the measures, press **Delete**.

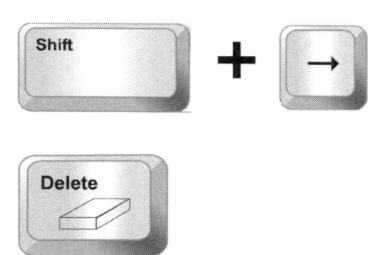

ADJUSTING MEASURES PER SYSTEM

To better balance the music spacing, it is advisable to move measure 7 to the third system.

1. Using the *Mass Edit* tool (the *Selection* tool in Finale 2008), click on measure 7.

2. Press **Down Arrow** to move the measure down to the next system.

Mass Edit and Selection tools

CHAPTER 3

ADDING PERFORMANCE MARKINGS

Concepts covered in this chapter:
- Articulations
- Expressions
- Phrase Markings (shapes)
- Editing and deleting items
- Formatting pages
- Printing

PROJECT FILE: SIMPLE SONG WITH PERFORMANCE MARKINGS

INPUTTING ARTICULATIONS

There are several ways to input articulations. In the previous chapter, we added a fermata on the last note. This is an articulation. We will start by adding articulations in note entry mode. As you input notes, you can add articulations as we did previously. Since we already have the notes in our score, we will select a note and add an articulation to it.

1. **The Selection Tool.** Press **Esc** twice. You will be prompted many times throughout this book to press **Esc**. This activates the *Selection* tool, which allows you to edit items and activate other tools from this tool. The item you click with the *Selection* tool determines available options. You can drag or delete items, and right-click (or **Control-click** for a single-button mouse) for more options. You can also double-click on an item to activate its native tool. For example, double-clicking a notehead enters *Simple Note Entry* mode. In Finale 2008, the *Selection* tool also performs all of the *Mass Edit* functions, as you have already learned. It also performs many of the *Staff*, *Repeat*, and *Measure* tool functions.

VIDEO
CLIP 3:1

ADDING PERFORMANCE
MARKINGS (PART 1)

**The Escape key
and Selection tool**

2. Double-click on the first notehead in measure 1 (the C in the first full measure, not the pickup measure).

   a. Since the *measure map* doesn't consider the pickup measure to be measure 1, we will consider the first full measure to be measure 1 throughout this book when the score starts with a pickup measure.

3. You are now in *Simple Note Entry* mode with the C highlighted.

4. **Simple Entry Articulation Input.** Type **Alt/Option–A** to alter the note with an articulation. Now Finale will display a *Waiting for Input* message.

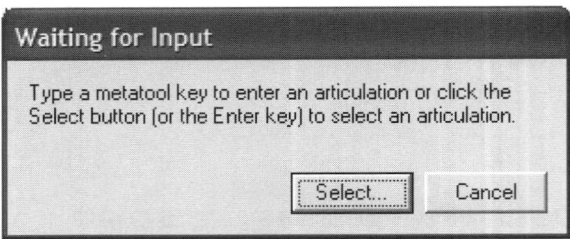

The Waiting for Input dialog

5. Finale is waiting for you to tell it what articulation you want. Generally you can guess what key to hit for the desired articulation, e.g., **A** for accent, **S** for staccato, etc. In this case, type **A** for accent.

6. Now put an accent in the Clarinet part. Type **Ctrl/ Command– Down Arrow**. This moves you to the Clarinet staff, and selects the dotted quarter note.

7. Now repeat steps three and four to input an accent on this note.

Hold down the Ctrl/ Command key and press the Down Arrow key

EXTRA CREDIT SECTION

You can also lock in articulation mode while inputting notes. Try this exercise:

1. Type **Ctrl/Command–Up Arrow** to return to the Flute staff.

2. Press **Right Arrow** to select the eighth note (G). Now Press **Delete** to delete the note. Press **Delete** three more times to remove the notes A, B, and D.

3. The first note is now highlighted, since there are no other notes in the measure. Type **4** for eighth note duration. Press **Right Arrow** to activate the note caret.

Hold down the Ctrl/ Command key and press the Up Arrow key

4. Before inputting these notes, we want to lock in articulation mode.

5. In chapter three we locked in grace notes. So, as you will recall, the lock in key is **Ctrl** for windows and **Command** for Macintosh. You can hold **Ctrl/Command** *and* **Shift**, then press **Alt/Option** and **A** together for articulations.

   Note: **Ctrl/Command–A** is used for *Select All*. This is the best key combination because it is most consistent with the logic we have been learning and still allows these keys to be used for standard Windows and Macintosh functions.

6. Now a message appears asking what articulation you want. Type **S** for staccato. A staccato is placed on the note caret.

7. Now type or play the notes to input them again. A staccato appears on each note.

8. As with the grace note lock in function, exit this mode by typing the same keys you did to enter it: **Ctrl/Command–Shift + Alt/Option–A**.

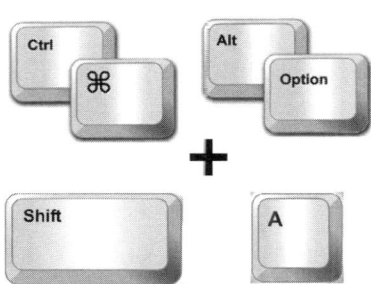

Hold Ctrl/Command and Shift together, then press Alt/Option and A together

The *Extra Credit* section teaches a fast way to input articulations *as* you input notes. But we have already input the notes for this score, so let's simply apply articulation to the existing notes. To do this, we will use the *Articulation* tool. It is easy, but slower, to drag your mouse over to the *Articulation tool* and click on it. Here is a faster way.

1. Press **Esc** twice. This activates the *Selection* tool.

2. With the *Selection* tool, double-click on an existing articulation, such as one of the accents. This selects the *Articulation* tool, and keeps you focused where you are working in the score, rather than searching the tool palette for the *Articulation* tool.

Now that the *Articulation* tool is selected, we will learn how to use it.

1. In measure 2 of the Flute staff, there is an accent on the first sixteenth note and staccatos on the next two notes. Press and hold **A** (for accent) and click on the first sixteenth note.

2. Press and hold **S** (for staccato) and click on the second and third notes.

BACK TO THE
PROJECT

The Escape key and Selection tool

The Articulation tool

Hold down the Ctrl/Command key and type Z

3. Press and hold **T** (for *t*enuto) and click on the first note in measure 3. We got a trill instead of a tenuto! What is the key for tenuto?

4. Undo the last command by typing **Ctrl/Command–Z**. This is the standard keyboard shortcut for the *Undo* command used in most programs.

5. Since we do not know the key for tenuto, click on the note without holding any key down. This will display the *Articulation Selection* dialog.

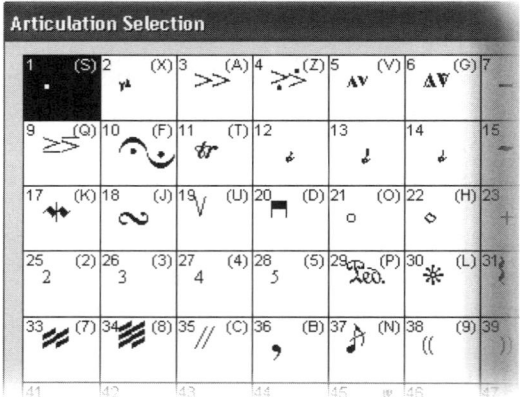

The Articulation Selection dialog

6. Here you could simply double-click on the desired articulation, but note the letter (or number) in parentheses in each box. That is the assigned key for that articulation. Note that tenuto is **E** (the second letter in *t*enuto) rather than **T**. So next time you need a tenuto, you will know to use **E**. Double-click on the tenuto.

7. Finish the articulations in measure 3 of the Flute staff.

Teacher, I Have a Question

My staccato marks look like little boxes! Do not be alarmed. While in articulation mode, all articulations have a handle on them for moving or deleting. Once you exit articulation mode, this handle will disappear and you will see your staccato marks.

Mass Articulation Input. In measure 1 of the Clarinet staff, you could press and hold **S** and then click on each note to add staccatos, but there is a faster way.

1. Press and hold **S** (for staccato), but do not click on the notes.

2. Drag a box around the notes you want to apply staccatos to and then release the mouse.

3. Now, finish adding articulations to measure 3 of the Flute part. Do not finish the Clarinet staff right now; we will save that for another function.

Dragging with the Articulation tool

An optional way to do this is to *not* hold down a key while dragging a box around a group of notes. Try this exercise:

1. Without holding down any keys, drag a box around measures 4 and 5 in the Flute staff. When you release the mouse, the *Apply Articulation* dialog appears.

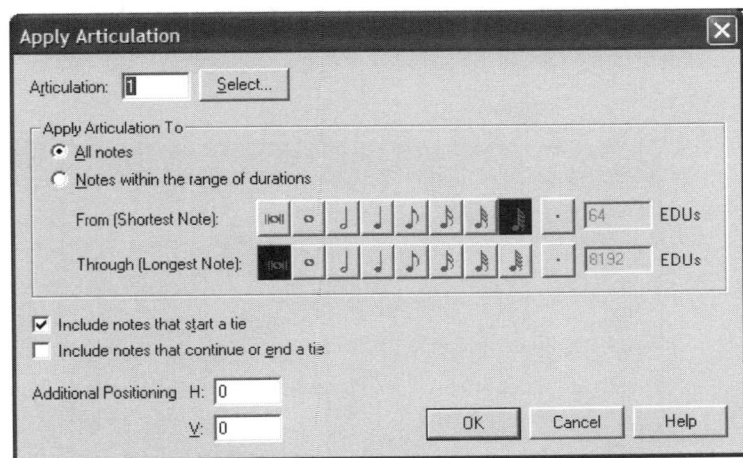

The Apply Articulation dialog

2. Click on *Select* to select an articulation from the *Articulation Selection* dialog—the staccato mark, in this case. Once you select an articulation and click *Select*, you will return to the *Apply Articulation* dialog. Here you can select a range of note durations to which to apply the articulation. For example, you may want staccatos on all sixteenth and eighth notes in an area, but not quarter notes.

   a. Click *Notes within the range of durations*.

   b. Now click sixteenth note on the *From (Shortest Note)* row, and eighth note on the *Through (Longest Note)* row.

   c. Click *OK*.

COPYING ARTICULATIONS

Since the articulations in the Clarinet part are identical to ones in the Flute part, copy them from the Flute part. Keep in mind that we could have put the articulations on the Flute part before we copied the notes to the Clarinet part and re-pitched them. But since we didn't, we will copy them now.

Mass Edit and Selection tools

1. Select the *Mass Edit* tool. (In Finale 2008, press **Esc** to go to the *Selection* tool.) This is generally the tool we use to select an area to edit.

2. Select measures 1 through 5. Click on the first measure (not the pickup measure), then press and hold **Shift**, and then click on measure 5.

3. We are going to use a contextual menu. *Right-click* (**Control-click** on Macintosh) in the highlighted area.

4. In the contextual menu, select *Items to Copy*. The *Items to Copy* dialog displays. In Finale 2008, this is called the *Edit Filter* dialog.

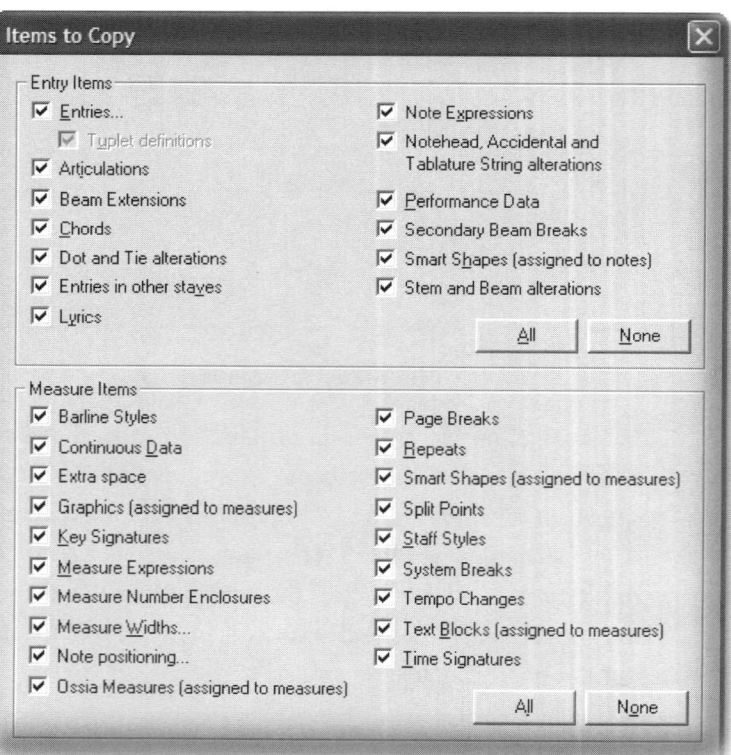

The Items to Copy dialog

5. Here you can select any item that you want to copy. There is another box, similar to this for *Items To Clear*. Click on *None* for both *Entry Items* and *Measure Items*. (In Finale 2008, this dialog is not divided into *Entry Items* and *Measure Items*).

6. Under *Entry Items* (under *Markings* in Finale 2008), click on *Articulations*, then click *OK*.

7. Click in the first measure of the highlighted area and drag it to the first measure in the Clarinet part and release. Now all of the articulations in the Flute part are in the Clarinet part.

8. Keep this in mind: to copy other items in the score, you will need to go back and reset the *Items to Copy* (or *Edit Filter*) dialog.

   a. In Finale 2008, you can retain filter settings and still be able to copy all items. Simply de-select the *Use Filter* command in the contextual menu.

Teacher, I Have a Question

What if I do not like the articulation key assignments? With the *Articulation* tool selected, you can change key assignments by doing this:

1. Press and hold **Shift**, then type the key you want to assign.

2. The *Articulation Selection* dialog opens.

3. Click on the articulation you want, then click *Select*.

This key is now assigned to the selected articulation for this score. We will do this later on.

ADDING EXPRESSIONS

As with articulations, expressions can be added using several methods. For this project, we will use the *Note Entry* method as we did with articulations.

1. Press **Esc** to go to the *Selection* tool.

2. Double-click on the first note in the Flute part. This will select the first note.

3. Type **X** (for expression; sorry, **E** is a pitch key).

The Escape key and Selection tool

4. If you knew the correct shortcut key for *mf*, you could type it now, but since you do not, just press **Return** to display the *Expression Selection* dialog.

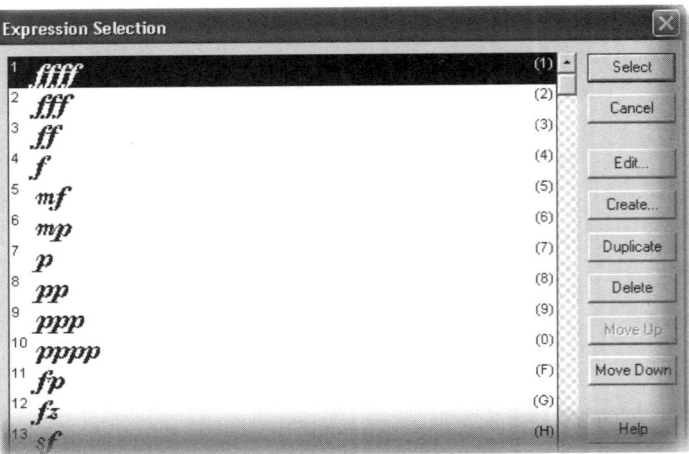

The Expression Selection dialog

5. The numbers and letters in parentheses are the assigned keys for these items. Note the **5** in parentheses to the right of the *mf*. That is the *Metatool* key (Finale's term for certain shortcut keys) to input *mf*. In fact, most of the dynamic markings are numbered 1–0, 1 being the loudest and 0 the softest. It is interesting that **4** is *for*te. This makes it a bit easier to remember.

6. You can either double-click on the expression (*mf* in this case), or use the **Up Arrow** or **Down Arrow** keys to select an expression, then press **Enter** to select it.

7. Type **Ctrl/Command–Down Arrow** to select the first note in the Clarinet part. Repeat steps 3–6.

8. Select the first note in measure 9 of the Flute staff. You can use the *Selection* tool to select a note, but since you have already chosen the *Simple Note Entry* tool, simply hold **Ctrl/Option** and click on the note.

9. Type **X**, then **R** for *rit.*

ADDING SLURS, HAIRPINS AND OTHER SHAPES

Now we will input some slurs. Click on the *Smart Shapes* tool in the main tool palette. Of course, we could use the *Selection* tool, but we do not have any shapes in the score to click on right now. A palette of shapes that you can input displays.

VIDEO
CLIP 3:1

ADDING PERFORMANCE
MARKINGS (PART 2)

The Smart Shapes tool

The Smart Shapes palette

1. The *Slur* tool should already be selected. If it is not, click it to select it.

2. Double-click the first note in measure 3 to add a slur from it to the next note.

3. Double-click the grace note in measure 6 to add a slur.

4. In measure 6 we slur over several notes. To do this, double-click on the first note (not the grace note), as we did before, *but do not release the mouse button*. If you do, undo that function (**Ctrl/Command–Z**).

5. While holding down the mouse button, drag to highlight the last note in the slur. (This is called a double-click-and-drag.) Release the mouse button.

Dragging to create a simple slur

Teacher, I Have a Question

I can't double-click the grace note! The grace note is pretty small, and so you may not be able to accurately double-click it. If not, remember in chapter one that we discussed how to zoom in and out. On Windows, press and hold **Shift** and then right-click near the grace note. On Macintosh, this is **Command–Shift** and click. To zoom back out, use **Ctrl/Command** and the minus (–) key.

Now we will add the crescendo marks.

1. Click on the *Crescendo* tool.

2. In measure 5, position the cursor where you want to start the crescendo. Make sure the cursor arrow is pointing up to the Flute staff. (This ensures that the symbol is attached to the Flute staff instead of the Clarinet staff.)

3. Double-click-and-drag to the end of this measure. Release the mouse.

4. To input the decrescendo, you could click on the proper tool, but it is faster to do the following:

   a. Position the cursor where the decrescendo ends. Again, make sure the cursor arrow is pointing up to the Flute staff.

The Crescendo tool

b. Double-click-and-drag to the left. Once the decrescendo is the right length, release the mouse.

Teacher, I Have a Question

Are there shortcut keys for shapes? Yes, there are. You can hold down a shortcut key, then double-click-and-drag as before. Here is a chart showing some of the shortcuts for shapes:

S	Slur
<	Decrescendo (the comma key, without **Shift**)
>	Crescendo (the period key, without **Shift**)
8	*8va*
L	Line
T	Trill
G	Glissando, etc.

Go to the *Help* menu and select *User Manual/Keyboard Shortcuts*, then scroll down to *Smart Shapes* to see them all.

The Escape key and Selection tool

EDITING AND POSITIONING ITEMS

Most of the items we have added to the score are placed appropriately, but we may want to move, edit, or delete them.

1. Press **Esc** to activate the *Selection* tool.

2. Now you can click on an expression, articulation, or shape and drag it to the desired place.

3. Once you click on an item, you can use the arrow keys to nudge an item to the desired place.

4. Once you click on an item, you can press **Delete** to delete it from the score.

Previously we entered a specific tool using the *Selection* tool. You can enter a specific tool by double-clicking on an item associated with that tool. For example:

1. Press **Esc** (twice if you are in *Simple Note Entry* mode) and double-click on an articulation.

2. With the articulation tool selected, you will notice a small box, called a handle, on each articulation.

An articulation with handle highlighted

3. Drag a box around several articulations to select the handles.

    a.   You can delete these now by pressing **Delete**.

    b.   You can move them by dragging one of the selected articulations (click and hold on a selected handle), or using the arrow keys to nudge the articulations.

4. Press **Esc** to return to the *Selection* tool.

5. Double-click on the crescendo in the measure 5.

6. Notice the handles on each of the hairpins. You can easily align these hairpins.

    a.   Drag a box around the handles of both hairpins in the Flute staff.

    b.   Right-click (**Control-click** on Macintosh) the handle of the hairpin that is positioned correctly.

    c.   From the contextual menu, select *Align Horizontally*.

    d.   With the handles still selected, press **Up Arrow** to nudge the hairpins closer to the staff if desired.

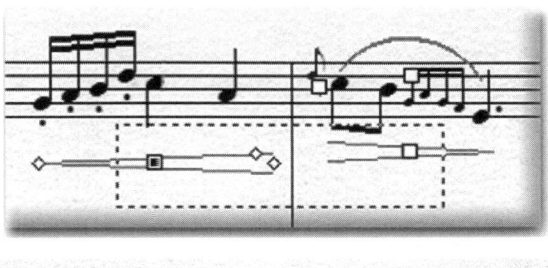

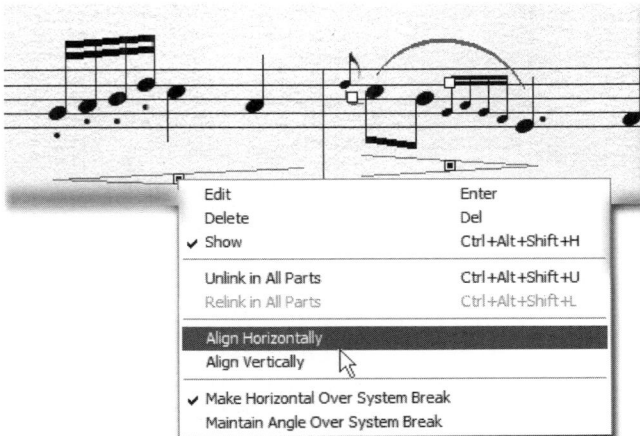

COPYING SHAPES

As we did with articulations, we can also set our copy filter for shapes. In fact, we could copy the articulation, shapes and expressions from the Flute staff to the Clarinet staff all at the same time. But then we wouldn't have had all this great experience in learning how to do it separately!

Mass Edit and Selection tools

1. Select the *Mass Edit* tool. (In Finale 2008, press **Esc** to go to the *Selection* tool.) Click to the left of the Flute staff. This selects the Flute staff from measure 1 to the end.

2. Select the contextual menu (**Right-click/Control-click**) in the highlighted area and select *Items to Copy* (*Use Filter* in Finale 2008).

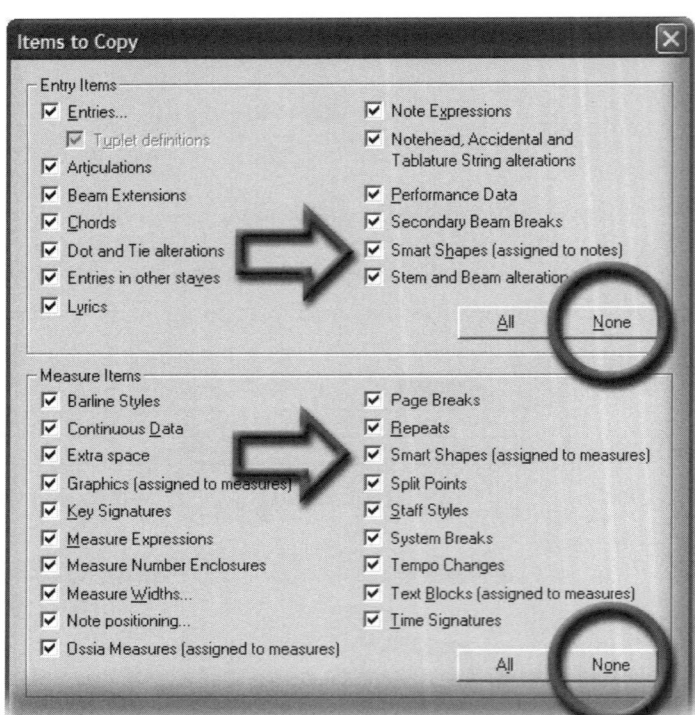

The Items to Copy dialog

3. Click on *None* for both *Entry Items* and *Measure Items*. (In Finale 2008, there is only one *None* button).

4. Under *Entry Items*, select *Smart Shapes (assigned to notes)*. Slurs are shapes that are assigned to notes. (In Finale 2008, this is in the *Markings* area of the *Edit Filter* dialog.)

5. Under *Measure Items* (under *Markings* in Finale 2008), select *Smart Shapes (assigned to measures)*. Hairpins are shapes that are assigned to measures.

6. You could also select articulations and expressions assigned to notes to copy them as well.

7. Click *OK*.

8. Click in the pickup measure of the Flute staff, drag it down to the Clarinet staff, and release.

Playback controls

You might want to listen to your score playback. Be aware, this is a strange song! Click on the *Play* icon in the playback controls to hear the score play. Note that Finale responds to the performance markings that you have added.

Teacher, I Have a Question

In other programs I use **Ctrl/Command–C** *for copy and* **Ctrl/Command–V** *for paste. Can I use that in Finale?* The answer is yes, you can. After setting the *Items to Copy* filter, type **Ctrl/Command–C** to copy these items. Now click to the left of the Clarinet staff to select it and type **Ctrl/Command–V** to paste. This is not as fast, but can be useful when copying from one page to another or one document to another.

CHAPTER 4

SETUP AND NOTE ENTRY FOR A CHORAL/PIANO SCORE

Concepts covered in this chapter:

- Using Templates
- Adding Intervals
- Text Inserts
- Changing the Key
- Layers and Voices
- Staff Styles
- Using MIDI in Real-time to input notes
- Quantization and other real-time clean-up features
- Tapping the rhythm, then re-pitching notes.
- Optimizing Staves

PROJECT FILE: BE STILL MY SOUL

This is an alteration of an arrangement of this piece. This is to be used for the educational purposes of this book and not to be performed in this form.

CREATING THE SCORE FROM A TEMPLATE

1. From the *Launch* window, select *Templates*.

2. Select the *Choral Templates* folder.

3. Select the template file *SATB (4 staff) with piano*.

4. Click *Open*.

This score starts with Piano only, then moves to SATB in closed score. Later in the score, the choral part is in open score with Piano. So the total number of staves we need for this score is six: SATB and grand staff Piano. Later, we will hide or optimize the empty, unused staves to utilize the space on the page as effectively as possible.

VIDEO
CLIP 4:1

SETTING UP
A CHORAL SCORE

Since we start with a pickup measure, and we did not use the *Setup Wizard*, we will select *Pickup Measure* from the *Options* menu. In Finale 2007 and 2008, this item is in the *Document* menu.

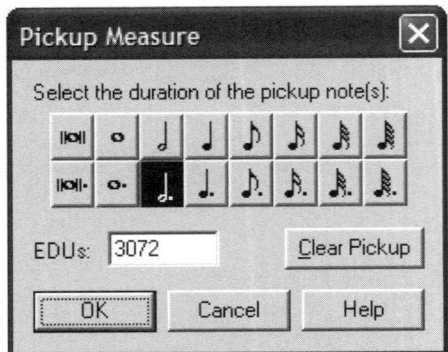

The Pickup Measure dialog

1. **Pickup Measure.** Select *Pickup Measure* from the *Options/ Document* menu and select a dotted half note as the measure size. Click *OK*.

2. **Changing Key.** We also need to change to the key of G.

3. Press **Esc** and right-click (**Control-click** on Macintosh) in the pickup measure.

4. Select *Edit Key Signature* or simply click G major in Finale 2007 and 2008.

5. Set the key to G major and click *OK*.

6. **Text Inserts.** If you used the Finale 2008 *Setup Wizard,* you could have easily created the *Text Inserts* from the third page of the *Setup Wizard*. However, it is a good thing to learn how to change a text insert, so read on.

7. We will add the title, composer, and arranger. Generally, we would use the selection tool to change the text, but in the case of the title, we want this change throughout the piece where the title text is displayed on other pages. This is called a *text insert*.

   a. Select *File Info* from the *File* menu.

   b. Fill out the info as shown in the graphic on the following page. Click *OK* to return to the score.

The File Info dialog

8. In Finale 2007 and 2008, you may notice that there are a few default text boxes you do not want. Simply press **Esc** for the *Selection* tool, click on a text box and press **Delete**.

9. **Expression Editing.** Now we will change the tempo marking expression to Moderato with no metronome marking.

    a. Press **Esc** (when entering the *Selection* tool from *Simple Note Entry*, press the **Esc** key twice), then right-click (or **Control-click**) on the tempo marking and select *Edit Measure Text Expression Definition*.

    b. Click to the right of the text *108)* and backspace until only *Moderato* is showing. Click *OK*.

10. **Inserting Measures**. Finale will automatically add measures as notes are input, but for formatting reasons in this score, we will add thirty measures to the sixteen that are in the template.

    a. Press **Esc** (if the *Selection* tool is not already selected), then right-click (**Control-click**) in measure 3 and select *Insert Measures*. In Finale 2008, this is called *Insert Measure Stack*. You must double-click a measure to select a measure stack.

    b. Type **30** and click *OK*.

INPUTTING NOTES

1. Start with the bass clef of the Piano part. Select a quarter note from the *Simple Note Entry* palette.

2. Type **Ctrl/Command–Down Arrow** several times to reach the bass clef.

3. Input a quarter rest. (Select a quarter note [**5**], then type **0** on the numpad or numrow if working on a laptop). Typing **Tab** also inputs a rest.

VIDEO
CLIP 4:2
INPUTTING NOTES

Press and hold the 'Ctrl/Command key and type Down Arrow

4. Select half note (**6**) and type **D**.

5. **Adding Intervals.** Before going on, if using a full-sized keyboard, type **6** using the numrow, not the numpad. This adds an interval of a sixth above the D.

    a. This is **F6** if using the laptop map.

    b. **Macintosh Function Keys.** On Macintosh, the function keys may not work as function keys until you assign functions to them. In the Macintosh System Preferences/Hardware/Keyboard and Mouse page, you will see four tabs. Click on *Keyboard Shortcuts*. Here you can designate the function keys to act as traditional function keys.

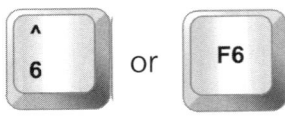

6. Now continue adding notes and intervals through measure 2.

7. In measure 3, type **Shift–Down Arrow** to move the cursor down an octave. Type the low **G**, then type **Shift–Up Arrow** to type the next note (D). Finish measure 3.

Press and hold the Shift key and then press Up Arrow

8. In measure 4, you may prefer to type the upper note first, then press and hold **Shift** and type the appropriate interval key to add the interval *below* the selected note. In measure 4, type **6**, then **G** for the half note G, then type **Shift–6** for a sixth below (**Shift–F6** on laptops).

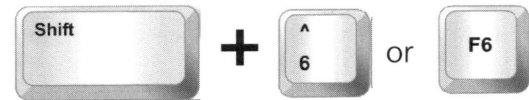

Press and hold the Shift key and then type 6 or F6

9. Finish the bass clef through measure 5.

10. If you prefer using a MIDI keyboard for input, you can simply play the correct chords without having to add intervals.

11. To start the treble clef Piano part, you could grab the mouse and click in the pickup measure, but here is a quick way to get there using the arrow keys.

   a. At this point, the note caret should be in measure 5 in the bass clef of the Piano part, since that is the last note you entered. Type **Ctrl/Command–Up Arrow** to select the treble clef staff in the Piano part, then press **Left Arrow** several times to go back to the pickup measure.

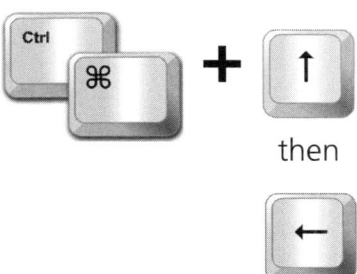

then

Press and hold the Ctrl/ Command key and then press the Up Arrow key, then press Left Arrow several times.

12. Select quarter note value (**5**) and enter the three notes in the pickup bar. In measures 1–5, input the notes with stems up only as shown in the finished example. Change duration as needed. **Note**: The half note chord in measure 2 is a stems-up chord. In measure 3, the dotted half note is the single B. Your music should look like the example below when you finish this step.

Layer 1 only in the Piano part treble clef staff

   a. **Note**: As you input the notes, do not be alarmed if the stems are not up as shown in the finished example. They will automatically flip when the contrapuntal notes in Layer 2 are added.

13. Always remember to save your work as you complete a section.

14. After finishing measure 5, **Ctrl/Option–click** on the first note in measure 1 (*not* the pickup measure).

15. **Contrapuntal Music.** In the bottom-left corner of the screen, select Layer 2 from the four number icons on Windows, or the dropdown menu on Macintosh.

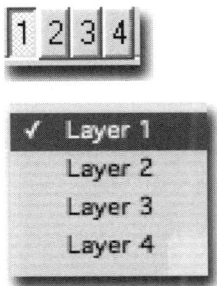

The Windows Layer buttons and Macintosh Layer dropdown menu

16. Change the note value to half note (**6**) and input notes that have stems pointing down. This is the way you input contrapuntal music when you need notes of different values on the same beat. Input the down-stemmed notes through measure 3.

17. **Mid-measure Layers.** In measure 4, the rest in Layer 2 starts on the third beat. There are two ways to start a layer mid-measure. One is to create a hidden rest, then input the notes. The other is to launch a new layer based on a beat in Layer 1. First we will discuss the hidden rest procedure.

a. **Hiding Rests.** With half note selected, type **0** (for rest). To hide the rest, type **H** (for hide).

b. Change to quarter note value (**5**) and type **0** (for rest).

c. Input the C quarter note.

18. Now try the mid-measure layer launch. Type **Ctrl/Command–Z** four times to undo steps a–c above.

a. **Mid-measure Launch.** Select Layer 1 from the bottom-left corner, or press **Esc** twice to access the *Selection* tool. Now simply double-click the notehead of the second half note chord in measure 4. This is the beat on which you want to start the rest and notes for the additional layer.

b. Select Layer 2 (from the bottom left corner, or type **Alt–Shift–2** on Windows or **Option–Command–2** on Macintosh). Again, the key logic is to *alter* the active layer by *shifting* to Layer 2.

c. Select the note value for quarter note (**5**).

d. Type **0** (for rest), then **C**.

19. **Moving Rests.** Before going on, we will move this rest. Use the **Left Arrow** key to select the quarter rest in measure 4 for editing.

a. Use the **Down Arrow** key to move the rest down. Initially, it may jump up to the default position for rests. Just keep pressing **Down Arrow** until the rest is in the proper position.

VIDEO
CLIP 4:3

FORMATTING AND
HIDING STAVES

FORMATTING AND HIDING STAVES

When inputting music, Finale automatically adjusts the number of measures on a system as you input notes. Since we only want the pickup bar through measure 5 on the top system, lock the system so that automatic music spacing will not put any more measures in this system. **Note**: You need to be in *Page View* to perform any page formatting commands. Make sure that *View* menu/*Page View* is selected.

1. **Locking Systems**. If the first system ends with measure 5, you simply need to lock the system. Select the *Mass Edit* tool. (In Finale 2008, press **Esc** to go to the *Selection* tool.) Now click on measure 5 and press **L** (for *lock*) on Windows, or type **Command–L** on Macintosh.

2. **Moving Measures**. If measure 5 is on the second system, or if measure 6 is on the first system, you can move the measure and lock the system in this way:

    a. To move measure 5 from the second to the first system, select the *Mass Edit* tool. (In Finale 2008, press **Esc** for the *Selection* tool.) Click on measure 5 and press **Up Arrow**. This pushes measure 5 to the first system and locks the system so that note spacing will not affect the number of measures in that system.

    b. To move measure 6 from the first system, select it and press **Down Arrow** to move and lock it to the second system.

Hiding Staves (Staff Optimization). Hide all of the empty staves in the first system. Click on the *Page Layout* tool.

The Page Layout tool

3. Right-click (**Control-click** on Macintosh) anywhere in the first system and select *Optimize Staff Systems*. Note that you could select a range of systems to optimize, but since we only have the Piano part for the first system done, just click *OK* to hide staves in the first system only.

4. Press **Page Up** or scroll up to the top of the score. The SATB staves disappear and Piano only will show in the top system.

THE STAFF NAMES CHANGE FOR CLOSED CHORAL SCORE

1. Starting with measure 6, we will input the Soprano and Alto parts on the Soprano staff and the Tenor and Bass on the Bass staff.

2. **Using Staff Styles**. To change the staff name from *S* to *SA*, press **Esc** (to choose the *Selection* tool) and double-click on the staff name *S*. (This selects the *Staff* tool).

3. Click to the left of the Soprano staff to select it.

4. Right-click (**Control-click**) on the highlighted staff to reveal the contextual menu for *Staff Styles*.

5. At the bottom of the list is a style named *22a Soprano/Alto staff*. Select this. This changes the abbreviated staff name from *S* to *SA*.

6. **Note**: This may result in a blue line above the staff. This is a reminder that appears only when the *Staff* tool is selected that this staff has a staff style assigned to it. If you wish to remove the blue line, click on the *Staff* menu and de-select *Show Staff Styles*.

7. Now select the Bass staff by clicking to the left of it.

8. Right-click (**Control-click**) and select the staff style named *22b Tenor/Bass staff*.

INPUTTING NOTES FOR THE CHORAL PARTS

If you do not have a MIDI device connected to your computer, you will need to continue inputting notes using letter names as you have learned. Input notes up to measure 35, including the Piano part. Then follow the instructions below starting with *Remove Blank Staves*. This will be great practice for you.

Keep in mind that measures 10–30 in the TB staff are rhythmically identical to the same measures in the SA staff. Copy the notes from the SA to the TB staff and re-pitch them. This will save quite a bit of time.

Also, make sure to use layers to create the contrapuntal parts for any notes that are contrapuntal or double-stemmed.

For those having access to a MIDI device, such as a MIDI keyboard, and have some keyboard skill, try the following exercise for inputting notes.

EXTRA CREDIT SECTION

VIDEO CLIP 4:4

REAL-TIME NOTE ENTRY

The HyperScribe tool

PLAYING NOTES AND RHYTHMS IN REAL TIME FROM A MIDI KEYBOARD

Please read through the next seven steps before trying this out.

1. Click the *Play* button to make sure that sound is working properly. Click the *Stop* button to stop playback. If you do not hear music playing, you may need to adjust volume or external sound equipment to hear notes play.

2. If you are not hearing any sound as you play the keyboard, select *MIDI* menu/*MIDI Thru* (In Finale 2008, *MIDI/Audio* menu/*MIDI Thru*). Make sure it is set to *Smart*. In the same menu, select *Play Through MIDI*.

3. Click on the *HyperScribe* tool. This enters Finale's recording mode.

4. Select *HyperScribe* menu/*HyperScribe Options*/*Tie Across Barlines*.

5. Click *OK*.

6. Make sure Layer 1 is selected in the lower left-hand corner popup menu.

7. Click on measure 6 in the SA staff. You will hear two intro measures of metronome click. Start playing the piece on beat 1 of the next measure.

    a. If you feel comfortable with your keyboard skills, play the music in time to the metronome as shown in the PDF example file.

    b. If you do not feel you have the skills to play this accurately, do not worry; we will try a different method later.

8. Try playing the next eight or ten measures. Click anywhere on the page to stop recording.

9. Type **Ctrl/Command–Page Up** to return to the first page.

Teacher, I Have a Problem

I can't hear the metronome! Finale defaults to the *SmartMusic SoftSynth Playback*. On Macintosh, you may need to select *MIDI* menu/*Internal Playback* (In Finale 2008, *MIDI/Audio* menu/*Internal Playback*.) If you choose to use the VST/AU sounds, such as Garritan Personal Orchestra or other VST/AU sounds, turn this off while recording. De-select *MIDI* menu/*Play Finale Through Native Instruments VST* (on Macintosh, *MIDI* menu/*Play Finale Through Native Instruments AU*). You can turn this back on when you are finished recording.

Teacher, I Have a Problem

All the notes I just recorded are red! You forgot to change back to Layer 1. You can easily change layers for any region. Select the region using the *Mass Edit* or *Selection* tool. Right-click (**Control-click**) in the highlighted area and select *Move/Copy Layers*. Set *Layer 2* to *Layer 1* and click *OK*.

CLEANING UP THE RECORDING

Quantization. Unless you are a very accurate player, you may notice several timing errors in the score. Finale has a function called *quantization*. This allows you to tell Finale the smallest note value to allow. This can be set before you begin playing, or you can change the setting after you play for any region of the score. This way, you could select eighth note as the smallest note value for a part of the score, and then in the few places you might need a smaller note value, you can change only those measures by selecting sixteenth note.

The default setting for quantization is sixteenth note, with tuplets allowed and the *Include Voice 2* option turned on. What does that mean? In Finale 2006, select *Options* menu/*Quantization Settings* (in Finale 2007 select *MIDI* menu/*Quantization Settings* and in Finale 2008, select *MIDI/Audio* menu/*Quantization Settings*) and we will go over this.

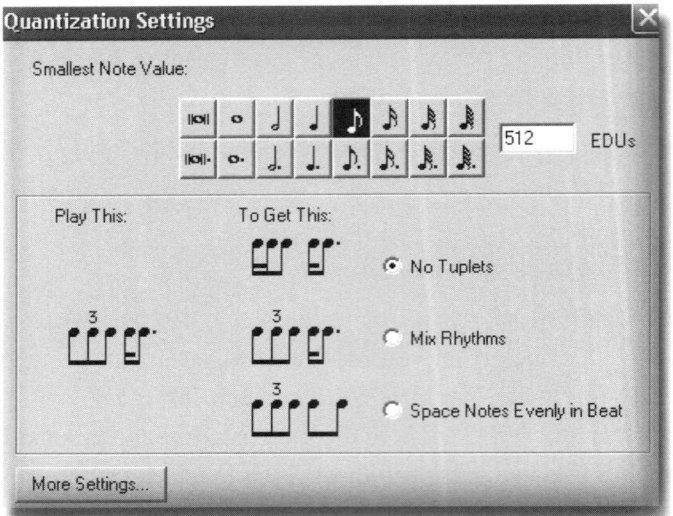

The Quantization Settings dialog

1. The top of this dialog shows several note values. This is where you specify the smallest note value you want Finale to transcribe. This piece uses eighth note as the smallest, so select that by clicking the eighth-note icon.

2. The middle section of this dialog asks if you want to allow tuplets. This score has no triplets, so select *No Tuplets*. **Note**: If the score did have eighth-note triplets, the smallest note value would have to be smaller than an eighth note for those measures since eighth-note triplets are smaller than an eighth note! This score has no triplets, so do not worry.

3. Click the *More Settings* button at the bottom-left of the dialog. Here you can change how Finale handles grace notes and other options, such as the *Include Voice 2* option. We have contrapuntal notes in several places in this score, as we did in the Piano part. We used layers to create these notes when in *Simple Note Entry* mode. When recording, we use a *second voice* command to transcribe contrapuntal notes. For right now, turn this function off and click *OK* to exit both dialogs.

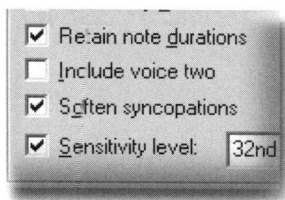

The More Settings dialog in Quantization Settings

4. Select the *Mass Edit* tool. (In Finale 2008, press **Esc** for the *Selection* tool.) Click to the left of the SA staff to select it. Right-click (**Control-click**) in the highlighted measures, then select *Re-transcribe*. Now see the results of these settings. (In Finale 2008, go to *MIDI/Audio* menu/*Re-transcribe*.)

Mass Edit and Selection tools

5. To view the results, type **Ctrl/Command–Page Up** and **Ctrl/Command–Page Down**.

6. **Deleting Notes.** If you need to delete any extra notes, press **Esc** and double-click on the note(s) to be deleted. Type **Ctrl/Option–Up Arrow** or **Ctrl/Option–Down Arrow** to select the note to delete, then press **Delete**.

Press and hold Ctrl/Option and then press the Up Arrow or Down Arrow key

7. **Changing Notes Enharmonically.** Remember: To change a note enharmonically, select the note, type **Alt/Option–E** (for *e*nharmonic). Some Macintosh versions of Finale do not use **Option–E** for enharmonic; use the backslash key (\) instead.

8. If you would like to change several notes enharmonically, you can select *Options/Edit* menu/*Enharmonic Spellings*.

   a. Change to *Favor Sharps*, *Favor Flats*, or *Use Spelling Table*. You can alter the spelling table as you like.

   b. Now select the area with the *Mass Edit* or *Selection* tool, then select *Mass Edit/Utilities* menu/*Respell Notes*. (In Finale 2008, this is *Utilities* menu/*Respell Notes*.)

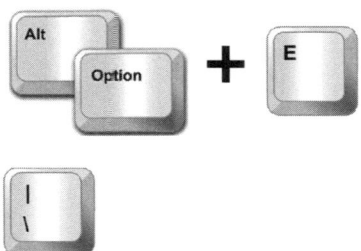

Press and hold Alt/Option and then Press the E key, or just press the backslash key

9. If there are more than a couple of mistakes, you may do better to try the *Playing Rhythm and Pitches Separately* exercise below.

Other Clean-up Functions. As a default, Finale generally doesn't tie notes over barlines in *HyperScribe* mode. That is why we changed this. You would want this on in the *a cappella* section of this piece. After measure 36 or in other pieces, you will probably do better by turning it off. Turn it off using the same procedure above in step four of *Playing Notes and Rhythms in Real-time from a MIDI Keyboard.*

MIDI In Latency. Another setting that controls the timing of a recording is the MIDI latency setting. Before you re-transcribed the music, you may have noticed that you were generally a sixteenth note ahead or behind. If you do not remember this, type **Ctrl/Command–Z** to undo the re-transcribe command. Study the result of the original recording and make note of whether you seemed to be ahead of or behind the beat. Once you have done this, you can type **Ctrl/Command–Y** to re-do the re-transcribe command. If you noticed a consistency in late or early timing, try this:

1. Select *MIDI* menu/*MIDI Setup*. (In Finale 2008, select *MIDI/Audio* menu/*MIDI Setup*.) On Windows, click the *Show Advanced* button. At the bottom of the dialog, notice the value box next to *MIDI In Latency.*

2. If you were ahead of the beat, enter a negative value, such as -30. If you were behind, select a positive value, such as 30. Click *OK* and try recording again.

SIMPLIFYING THE RHYTHM

One last clean-up function that works nicely is modifying rests. Experience shows that most people do not hold notes for the full duration. This can cause shorter note durations with rests after the notes. Quantization can remove this, but what if you do not want to change the quantization from sixteenth note to eighth note to remove rests? You may have sixteenth notes in a measure. For this, we turn to a powerful plug-in.

1. Select the area you would like to modify with the *Mass Edit* or *Selection* tool.

2. Select *Plug-ins* menu/*TG tools/Modify Rests.*

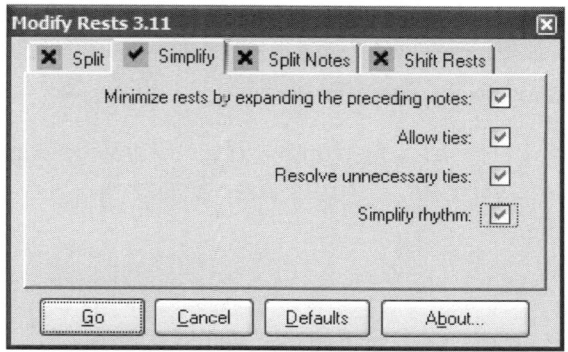

3. Click the *Simplify* tab. Check all four boxes.

4. Click *Go*, then *Close*.

Teacher, I Have a Problem

I can't play the music in time to the metronome! It's not easy to play music in time to the metronome and get all the pitches correct as well. Follow the next exercise to try a different method of real-time input.

PLAYING RHYTHMS AND PITCHES SEPARATELY

One of the main reasons you may want to try recording music in real-time is to avoid having to manually select the correct duration for notes and rests. So we will combine the speed of real-time rhythm input with the accuracy of step-time pitch input. Try this:

1. Select the *HyperScribe* tool and click on measure 6 in the SA staff. Wait for the two-measure count-in, then tap the rhythm of the music using a single key, such as middle C. Try your best to hold notes out to their full duration, especially when notes tie across barlines.

2. Record about ten measures and then click anywhere to stop.

3. If needed, clean up the rhythm as described above in *Cleaning Up the Score*. The *Modify Rests* plug-in described above should be helpful.

4. Click on the *Re-pitch* tool in the note palette.

5. Click on the first note in measure 6.

6. Now simply play the correct pitches. The Rhythms are already correct, so you do not have to select durations as you put in the notes. Make sure to re-pitch tied notes.

7. If you miss a note, simply select the note to correct by pressing **Left Arrow** or **Right Arrow** and then playing the correct pitch.

ANOTHER TWIST ON REAL-TIME RECORDING

If you are composing or arranging, you may not be comfortable enough with a section to play it correctly in time to a metronome. In this section we will discuss using *HyperScribe* mode with a flexible, user-controlled metronome. This is a great way to input a few measures at a time when you are composing or arranging music. This is done by using a device on your MIDI keyboard, generally a key or pedal, that you will tap to represent a beat in time. While you tap a key or pedal, you can play the notes you want recorded in the music. It takes some practice to coordinate tapping while playing. The pedal is a good choice, because many musicians are already familiar with the practice of tapping their foot while playing. Once you understand this function, it can be invaluable to you as a very handy way to input notes.

Start with measure 6 on the TB staff.

1. In Finale 2006, select *Options* menu/*Quantization Settings*; in Finale 2007, select *MIDI* menu/*Quantization Settings*; in Finale 2008, select *MIDI/Audio* menu/*Quantization Settings*.

2. Select eighth note as the smallest note value and *No Tuplets*.

3. Click the *More Settings* button. Under *Options*, check *Include Voice 2*. Click *OK* to exit the dialogs.

4. Select the *HyperScribe* tool.

5. Select *HyperScribe* menu/*Beat Source/Tap*.

6. Note that the default setting for *Tap Beat* is a quarter note. This is what you want for this score. For a time signature of 6/8, you may want a dotted quarter value, or even an eighth note value for more precise beat tempo control.

The HyperScribe tool

7. To set the item on the MIDI keyboard that you are going to tap, click the *Listen* button and then press a key on the MIDI keyboard, or tap once on the pedal that you are going to use. Click *OK*.

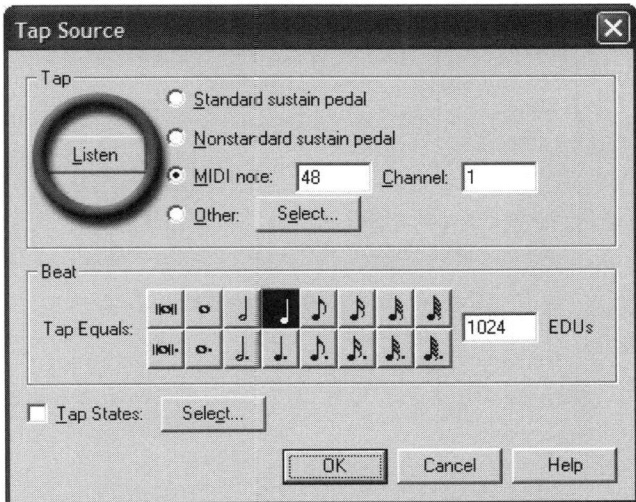

8. Click on measure 6 in the TB staff.

9. Tap the key or pedal to provide a metronome as you play the notes. You do not need to keep a steady tempo; you can slow down or speed up as much as you like. Note values are based on the timing of each tap you make.

10. When you are finished recording, click anywhere on the page to exit record mode.

11. To change back to the regular metronome, select *HyperScribe* menu/*Beat Source/Playback and/or Click*. Click *OK*.

RECORDING CONTRAPUNTAL MUSIC

If you are somewhat proficient on a keyboard, you may want to play both Layer 1 and Layer 2 notes all in one recording. When you record this way, Finale puts Layer 2 notes into a second voice within Layer 1. It is best to change Voice 2 notes into Layer 2 after recording, as we will discuss below. This makes for much easier editing.

1. First we need to turn the *Include Voice 2* function on. To do this, select the *HyperScribe* tool and then select *HyperScribe* menu/*HyperScribe Options*. Click the *Quant Settings* button.

2. In the *Quantization Settings* dialog click the *More Settings* button.

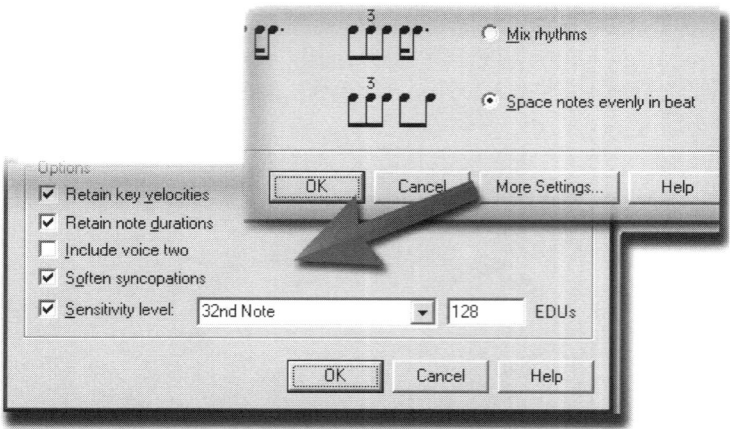

The More Quantization Settings dialog

3. In the *More Quantization Settings* dialog, under *Options*, check *Include Voice 2*. Click three successive *OK* buttons to exit the dialogs.

4. Click measure 9 on the TB staff. Either tap the beats while playing this part as described above, or just play in time to the metronome Finale provides.

5. Make sure to hold down the whole note D while you play the A and G underneath.

Changing Voice 2 to Layer 2. This type of contrapuntal notation is different than using layers. This is a second voice in the same layer. To remain consistent in editing, you may want to turn the second voice notes into a new layer. To do this:

The Mass Edit and Selection tools

1. Select the *Mass Edit* tool. (In Finale 2008, press **Esc** to go to the *Selection* tool.)

2. Select *Plug-ins* menu/*Note, Beam and Rest Editing*/*Voice 2 to Layer…* .

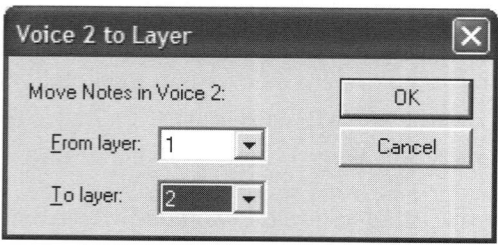

The Voice 2 to Layer dialog

3. Here you can change Voice 2 notes into Layer 2 notes. Click *OK*.

4. **Tied Notes.** Make sure that the G in measure 9 of the Bass part is tied to the G in measure 10. If not:

   a. Press **Esc** and double-click on the G in measure 9.

   b. Type **T** (for *tie*).

Teacher, I Have a Question

What if I feel proficient enough to play both staves of the Piano part simultaneously? You can play both treble and bass clef together by setting a split-point.

Input the notes up to measure 35. Use whichever note entry mode you choose. Keep in mind that the TB staff is rhythmically identical to the SA staff from measure 10 through 35. It may be quicker to copy these measures from the SA staff to the TB staff, then re-pitch them starting at measure 10.

BACK TO THE PROJECT

REMOVING BLANK STAVES

Before going on, make sure that all notes up to measure 36 are complete, including the Piano staff. Now, optimize or remove blank staves from systems two through five.

1. Select the *Page Layout* tool as before.

The Page Layout tool

2. Right-click (**Control-click**) in system two and select *Optimize Staff Systems*.

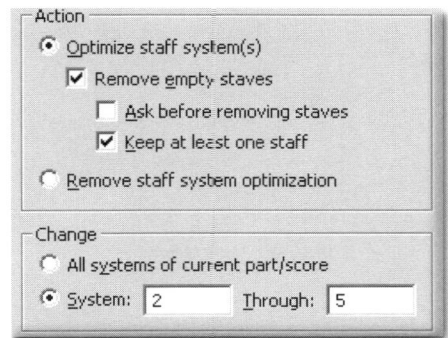

The Staff System Optimization dialog

3. This time, set a system range in the *Change* area. Select *System 2 Through 5*, typing in the numbers. **Note**: If you ever need to remove optimization from a system, you can also select *Remove Staff System Optimization* in the *Action* area. Click *OK*.

CHAPTER 5

REPEATS, LYRICS, FORMATTING, AND RECORDING FOR A CHORAL/PIANO SCORE

Concepts covered in this chapter:

- Repeats
- Optimization of Staves
- Changing Keys
- Input Dynamics Using the Expression Tool
- Inputting and Altering SmartShapes
- Copy and Paste Using Filters
- Interval Transposition
- Cross Staff Notation
- Expression Assignment Using Staff Lists
- Rehearsal Marks
- Lyrics
- Baseline Positioning
- Staff Spacing
- Page Layout and Formatting
- Separating Closed Score (Divisi) Voices
- Creating a Rehearsal CD
- Adjusting Playback

PROJECT FILE: BE STILL MY SOUL
(A CONTINUATION OF THE CHAPTER 4 PROJECT)

In the previous chapter we began creating the score "Be Still My Soul." Several various ways of inputting notes were presented. Now we will finish the score, adjust the page layout, and create a rehearsal CD of this score.

VIDEO
CLIP 5:1

SCORE OUTLINE

The Repeat tool

ADDING REPEATS

1. Click the *Repeat* tool. (In Finale 2008, you can use the *Selection* tool.)

2. Right-click (**Control-click**) measure 6.

3. Select *Create Forward Repeat Bar*. (In Finale 2008, select *Repeats*, then *Create Forward Repeat Bar*.)

Before adding the ending repeats, we will assign the repeat brackets to the staves on which we want them to appear.

1. From the *Repeat* menu (with the *Repeat* tool still selected), select *Repeat Options*. If the *Repeat* tool is no longer selected, you can also select it by double-clicking on the forward repeat sign you just entered. This will activate the *Repeat* tool and menu.

2. In the lower left-hand side of the repeat *Staff List* dialog, note that you can assign endings to the top staff, all staves, or a staff list. Staff lists allow us to assign expressions and other items like repeats to particular staves. Click on *Staff List* then *New Staff List*. **Note**: In Finale 2008, several of these *Staff Lists* are pre-created. You may simply need to select rather than create one.

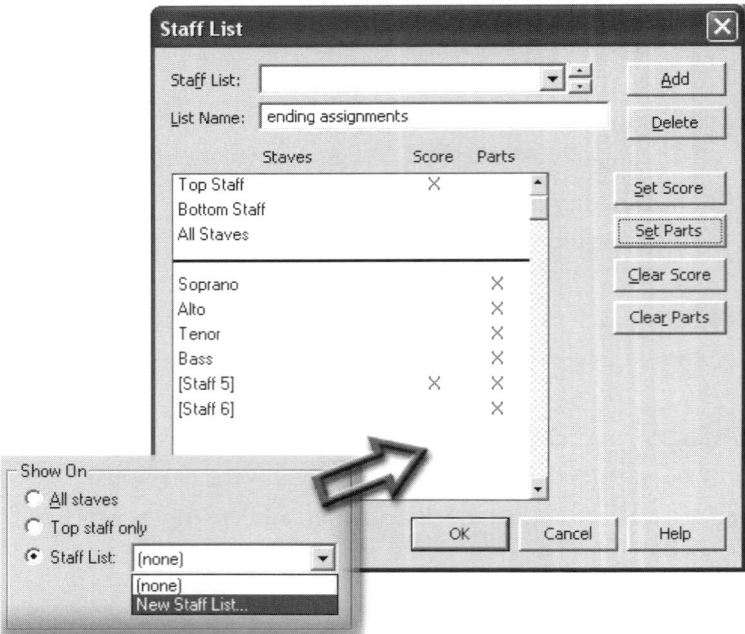

The Repeat Staff List

3. Enter an appropriate name for this list, such as *Ending Assignments.*

4. Click *Set Parts.*

5. Under the *Score* column, click to the right of *Top Staff* and *Staff 5* (this is the treble clef staff of the Piano grand staff).

6. Click *OK* twice to return to the score. Now you are ready to input the repeat endings. **Note**: If you input endings before you set the staff list, the brackets will appear on all staves by default.

7. Now go to measure 29.

8. When inputting a first and second ending, select the measure(s) in the first ending only. Right-click (**Control–click**) in measure 29 and select *Create First and Second Ending.* (Remember, in Finale 2008, select repeats from the contextual menu.)

9. If you like, start playback at the top of the score and note that Finale understands the repeat functions.

CHANGING BACK TO AN OPEN SCORE FORMAT

At measure 31, the score changes to open-score format, so we may want to change the abbreviated staff names back to S, A, T, and B rather than SA and TB. You will remember that we changed the staff names S and B to SA and TB respectively, using a staff style. Now we need to remove the staff style from measure 31 to the end of the score.

To do this in Finale 2006–2007:

1. Move to the top system on page 2. Press **Esc**, then double-click on the *SA* staff name. (Double-clicking on a staff name selects the *Staff* tool.)

2. Click on measure 31.

3. Type **Shift–Right Arrow**. This selects from this measure to the end of the score.

4. Right-click (**Control-click**) in measure 31 and select *Clear Staff Styles.*

5. Repeat steps 2–5 for the TB staff.

Press and hold the Shift key and then press the Right Arrow key

**Press and hold the Shift key
and then press
the End key**

To do this in Finale 2008:

1. Press **Esc** for the *Selection* tool. Double-click measure 31. This will select all staves, called a *stack* in Finale 2008.

2. Type **Shift–End** to select to the end of the score.

3. Right-click in the highlighted area and select *Staff Style/Clear Staff Style* from the contextual menu.

CHANGING THE KEY

1. Press **Esc** for the *Selection* tool.

2. Right-click (**Control-click**) in measure 36 and select *Edit Key Signature* from the menu. The key signature contextual menu appears.

3. Change the key to F major and click *OK*.

Alternate method:

1. If measure 36 is at the beginning of the system, it will display the key signature.

2. Press **Esc** for the *Selection* tool.

3. Right-click (**Control-click**) on the key signature (the F♯) and select *F major* as the new key.

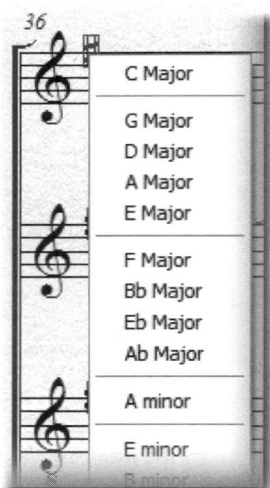

The key signature contextual menu

CHANGING THE BARLINE

1. Change the normal barline to a double barline at the end of measure 35.

2. Press **Esc** for the *Selection* tool.

3. Right-click (**Control-click**) in measure 35 and select *Double Barline*. (In Finale 2008, select *Barlines*, then *Double Barline*.)

4. Save your work.

ARTICULATIONS

This score has a few articulations on the first page. The *Metatool* (shortcut key) for breath mark is **B**.

1. Click the *Articulation* tool.

2. Press and hold **B** and click the first note in measure 10. Repeat this for all other notes that require breath marks.

CREATING EXPRESSIONS

Pre-created expressions have automatic placement parameters assigned to them to make input easy and fast. Most are assigned vertically to be either above or below the staff baseline. The baseline is an invisible line that lines up expressions. Baselines are also used to align lyrics, chords, and fretboards, as we will learn later. Because of pre-programmed automation such as this, it is faster to duplicate existing expressions and edit them rather than create from scratch new expressions to which you might need to assign placement parameters.

1. Press **Esc** and double-click on the quarter rest in measure 6 on the TB staff.

2. Type **X** (for expression), then press **Enter** or **Return** to go to the *Expression Selection* dialog.

3. The expression *a cappella* has not been created. We will select an existing expression that would be placed above the staff, such as *accel.*, and duplicate and edit it to become *a cappella*.

4. Scroll down (or press **Down Arrow**) to highlight *accel.* Click the *Duplicate* button on the right side of the dialog. Click on *Edit*. (**Note**: On Windows, the shortcut key for *Duplicate* is **P**; for Edit, it is **E**. There are no shortcut keys for these functions on Macintosh.)

VIDEO
CLIP 5:2

PERFORMANCE
MARKINGS

The Articulation tool

5. Now you can see the *Text Expression* designer. Select the text *accel.* if it is not already highlighted. Type *a cappella*, then click *OK* and then *Select*.

Note: Many times, pressing **Enter** or **Return** can select the OK button in dialogs. In the *Text Expression Designer* dialog, **Enter** does this, but **Return** adds a carriage return to the text expression. Be careful.

INPUTTING USING THE EXPRESSION TOOL

Expressions can be assigned as *Note Expressions* or *Measure Expressions*. Generally *Note Expressions* are used when inputting an expression in one staff only (as we did in *Creating Expressions* above). The advantage of *Note Expressions* is their collision intelligence. They avoid collisions with notes, stems and beams automatically.

Choose *Measure Expressions* to input an expression in several staves simultaneously. This option also allows you to set up a staff list (which allows you to pick and choose the staves on which the expression will appear).

1. Press **Esc** and double-click on the *a cappella* text expression you just entered. (You just accessed the *Expression* tool, so it is already selected.)

2. As you drag the cursor over the staff, you will notice the state of the cursor changes from an arrow with a small note next to it to an arrow without the small note.

3. To input a *Note Expression*:

   a. Drag the cursor over a note or rest until you see the *Note Expression* icon (see the example to the left).

   b. Double-click on note or rest.

   c. At the bottom of the dialog, make sure the *Note Expression* button is selected. You should only have to select it the first time. After this, Finale will understand note-attached expressions based on the state of the cursor.

   d. Select an expression.

   e. Click *OK*.

4. To input a *Measure Expression*:

   a. Drag the cursor over a measure (away from a note or rest) until you see the *Measure Expression* icon (see the example to the right).

   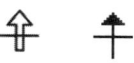

   b. Double-click near the measure.

   c. Make sure the *Measure Expression* button is selected.

   d. Select an expression.

   e. Click *OK*.

5. We need to input a *Measure-Attached* expression. Double-click to the left of the rest in measure 6 on the SA staff.

6. Select the first *p* dynamic (listed as *above the staff*). Click *Select* or press **Enter**.

7. From the assignment dialog, select *All Staves*. Click *OK*.

8. Finish inputting the dynamics up to measure 36.

9. If you would like, drag or use the arrow keys to nudge the expression more to the left of the measure.

Teacher, I Have a Problem

I clicked using the Note Expression *cursor and I still got a* Measure-Attached *expression!* If this is the case, Finale has not been set correctly to use the context sensitive assignment. First, input an expression using the expression tool by double-clicking in a measure. At the bottom of the dialog, select *Note Attached* and click *Select*, then *OK*. This tells Finale to select measure- or note-attached based on the state of the cursor.

POSITIONING EXPRESSION BASELINES

The expressions that are placed above the staff may be too high. In this case they are. Of course you could position each one of them one at a time with the selection tool, but here is a faster way to move them all at once. Above we talked about the baseline that Finale uses to line up expressions. By adjusting the baseline, you can adjust the position of many expressions all at once.

1. If there isn't a handle next to the expressions, press **Esc** and double-click on an expression to go to the *Expression* tool.

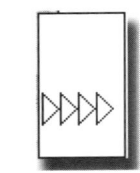

Positioning triangles

2. From the expression menu, select *Adjust Above Staff Baseline*.

3. To the far left are four positioning triangles. You will learn more about these when we get to the section on lyrics.

4. For now, click-and-drag the second triangle from the left down to position all of the above-the-staff expressions in the Soprano staff closer to the staff.

COPYING AND PASTING

1. Starting in measure 37 of the Soprano staff, input the quarter rest, type **X** for expressions and input the *f* labeled *below the staff*.

2. Finish inputting notes to measure 43.

3. **Note**: If you are using *HyperScribe*, turn off the option *Tie Across Barlines*. Go to the *HyperScribe* menu/*HyperScribe Options…* and make sure this option is unchecked; then click *OK* to return to inputting notes.

The Mass Edit and Selection tools

4. Select the *Mass Edit* tool. (In Finale 2008, press **Esc** to go to the *Selection* tool.)

5. Click on measure 37 in the Soprano staff, then type **Shift–Right Arrow**. (In Finale 2008, type **Shift–End**.)

6. Click and drag the highlighted area in measure 37 from the SA to the Tenor staff.

7. Release the mouse when the Tenor staff is selected. This copies the notes to the Tenor staff.

Press and hold the Shift key and then press the Right Arrow key

Teacher, I Have a Problem

I tried to copy the notes and nothing copied! If you performed the instructions above and nothing copied, you may have the copy filter set to *not* copy the notes. After selecting the area to copy, Right-click (**Control-click**) in the highlighted area and select *Items to Copy*. Make sure that all items are selected. (In Finale 2008, make sure that *Edit* menu/*Use Filter* is turned off.

TRANSPOSING THE NOTES

The notes in the Tenor staff are an octave too high; transpose them down an octave. Since this is a common function, we are going to set up a shortcut key to do this, known in Finale as a *Metatool*.

Note: If you are working in a school lab, you may want to check with the instructor before doing this. Assigning transposing *Metatools* is a global function. They may already be programmed or the instructor may not want them programmed. In Finale 2008, this is already pre-set as described below; however, you can change the settings if needed. See below for Finale 2008 instructions.

1. In the Tenor staff, select measures 37 to the end of the score using the *Mass Edit* or *Selection* tool (as we did above for the Soprano staff).

2. Type **8** on the numrow.

3. One of two things will happen: either the notes will transpose or you will see a dialog like the one below.

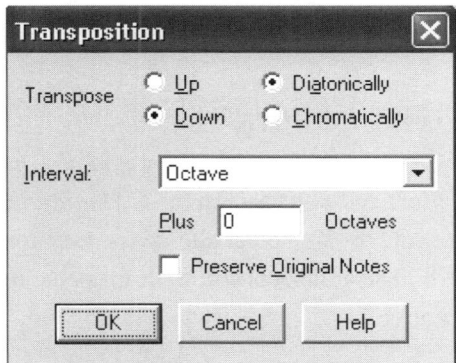

The Transposition dialog

   a. If the notes were transposed, then the *Metatool* key has already been assigned on the computer you are using. If the notes were transposed, but not by the correct amount (an octave), then see the *Teacher, I Have a Problem* section below.

   b. If the *Transposition* dialog appears, then the *Metatool* key has not been assigned. In the dialog, for *Transpose,* select *Down* and for *Interval*, select *Octave*, then press *OK*.

   c. From now on, anytime that you select an area of music using the *Mass Edit* or *Selection* tool and type **8**, the selection will be transposed down by an octave.

d.   If you prefer not to program a transposition *Metatool*, simply select the area, right-click (**Control click**) in the highlighted area, and select *Transpose* from the menu.

TRANSPOSITIONS IN FINALE 2008

1.   Keys **6–9** have been preprogrammed in Finale 2008. Using the *Selection* tool, select the area to transpose, then type:

   a.   **6** to transpose down a second

   b.   **7** to transpose up a second

   c.   **8** to transpose down an octave

   d.   **9** to transpose up an octave

2.   You can still alter the transposition setting for any of the four transposition *Metatool* keys. Type **Ctrl/Command–Shift–6** (or **7**, **8**, or **9**) to access the *Transposition* dialog to set the key to a new transposition setting.

Teacher, I Have a Problem

The transposition dialog didn't open and the music didn't transpose correctly! If you need to re-assign the **8** *Metatool* key (or any of the four transposition keys **6–9**), select the *Mass Edit* tool and type a number key, such as **8**. The transposition dialog opens and you can follow the instructions above.

VIDEO
CLIP 5:3

SHAPE INPUT

INPUTTING SLURS

Now input the slurs for the Soprano staff in measures 37–40 as you did in Chapter Three. Here is a quick review:

1.   Click on the *Shapes* tool, and then click on the *Slur* tool in the *Shapes* palette.

2.   In measure 37, double-click-and-hold on the first note.

3.   Drag to the right until the dotted quarter D in measure 38 is highlighted. (**Note**: Measure 38 may be on the next system down. Make sure measure 38 is visible before starting the slur. Then drag the slur from the first note down to the next system and release once the D is selected. It will look a bit strange until you release the mouse.)

4. Now release the mouse.

5. Repeat this for the next slur in the Soprano line.

Had we input these slurs *before* we copied the notes, they would have copied with the notes. Since we did not, this gives us an opportunity to practice using the copy filter as we did in Chapter Three to copy just the slurs. Generally you would not do this for only two slurs, as it is much faster just to input the slurs. But if you have many slurs, it is faster to copy them.

1. **Copying Slurs**. Select the *Mass Edit* tool. (In Finale 2008, press **Esc** to go to the *Selection* tool).

2. Click on measure 37 in the Soprano part. Type **Shift–Right Arrow**. (In Finale 2008, type **Shift–End**).

3. Right-click (**Control-click**) in the highlighted area. Select *Items to Copy*. (In Finale 2008, select *Edit Filter*.)

4. In the *Edit Filter* dialog, click on *None* in both areas. (In Finale 2008 there is only one *None* button.)

5. Click on *Smart Shapes Assigned to Notes* in *Entry Items*. Click *OK*. (In Finale 2008, this is in the *Markings* area).

6. Drag the selected area to copy the slurs to the Tenor staff. Remember, you can always type **Ctrl/Command–C** for copy and **Ctrl/Command–V** for paste. In Finale 2006–2007, you must select the entire area into which to paste. In Finale 2008, simply select the first measure of the area into which to paste. Finale will paste all measures previously selected when you typed **Ctrl/Command–C**.

   a. Also in Finale 2008: You can select the area to paste, then select *Edit* menu/*Paste Multiple*, then select the vertical number of staves into which you want to paste.

Other copy considerations. Since the lyrics are identical, you could type them in before you copy, or you can type them in later and copy the lyrics only. **Remember**: Copy filters stay set until you change them, so the next time you copy something, you will need to reset the filter to copy the items you want. In Finale 2008, simply uncheck *Edit* menu/*Use Filter*. Generally you would want to copy all items as a default.

The Mass Edit and Selection tools

FINISHING NOTE INPUT

Now finish inputting the rest of the notes in the score. Here is your chance to input notes, expressions, and slurs for the Alto part. Input the notes, expressions, and shapes for the Alto part to measure 44, then copy and paste all of this to the Bass staff and transpose.

Use copy and paste with transpose and re-pitch as much as possible. This will always speed up the work. If you are using *HyperScribe*, turn off the option *Tie Across Barlines*. Go to the *HyperScribe* menu/*HyperScribe Options…* and make sure this option is unchecked; then click *OK* to return to inputting notes.

CROSS-STAFF NOTATION

In the Piano part, bass clef staff, measure 53, note in the finished example that the last three notes display in the treble clef. This is called *Cross Staff* notation. This is very easy to do.

The Mass Edit and Selection tools

1. Select the *Mass Edit* tool. (In Finale 2008, press **Esc** to go to the *Selection* tool.)

2. Select *Edit* menu/*Select Partial Measures* (in Finale 2008 this is not required.)

3. Drag a box around the last three eighth notes in the Piano part, bass clef staff, measure 53.

Creating cross-staff notation

4. Type **Alt/Option–Up Arrow**.

5. **Flipping Stems**. Look at the quarter notes in the treble clef. Stem direction for these notes needs to change. To do this:

a. Press **Esc**.

b. Double-click on the quarter notes in the treble staff to select them in *Simple Entry* mode.

c. Type **L** for flip.

d. **Note**: You can also flip stems for a region using the *Mass Edit* or *Selection* tool.

   i. Select the region.

   ii. Right-click (**Control-click**) in the highlighted area and select *Utilities/Freeze Stems Up*. (In Finale 2008, this function can only be accessed from the *Utilities* menu. It is not available in the contextual menu.)

You could also select notes in the treble clef and then type **Alt/Option–Down Arrow** to cross staff notes to the staff below. **Alt/Option–Down Arrow** is a shortcut for a plug-in that is useful for other complex cross staff notation. It is found in *Plug-ins* menu/*TG tools/Cross Staff*. Here you can set alternating notes for cross staff notation.

PARTIAL MEASURE SELECT

Above, we changed the *Mass Edit* or *Selection* tool to select partial measures. Many advanced users prefer to use this setting all of the time. When *Partial Measure Select* is set, you can double-click any measure to select the entire contents or type **Shift–Left Arrow** or **Shift–Right Arrow** to select to the beginning and/or end of the measure. If you are in a lab, the instructor may prefer that you leave this setting off for others who are not as familiar with *Mass Edit* selecting.

SELECTING REGIONS IN FINALE 2008

In Finale 2008, there is no command for *Partial Measure Select*. To select a full measure, click it with the *Selection* tool. To select a partial measure, simply click-and-drag a box around the area you want to select. Do not click in the measure; click outside the staff, then drag around the desired area.

Once an area is selected, you can **Shift–click** to select to the end or beginning of a range of measures or partial measures. However, you can also add to the selection using these keys:

- **Shift–Right Arrow** selects the next note or rest to the right.

- **Shift–Left Arrow** selects the next note or rest to the left.

- **Ctrl–Right Arrow** (on Windows) or **Command–Shift–Right Arrow** (on Macintosh) selects the next measure to the right.

- **Ctrl–Left Arrow** (on Windows) or **Command–Shift–Left Arrow** (on Macintosh) selects the next measure to the left.

- **Shift–End** selects from the current point to the end of the score.

- **Shift–Home** selects from the current point to the beginning of the score.

- **Ctrl/Command–A** selects all.

Finale 2008 also has certain functions that can only be applied to a measure *stack*. This is a selection of all staves within the region. You can easily select a stack by double-clicking any measure. You can also select more or fewer staves by typing **Shift–Up Arrow** or **Shift–Down Arrow**.

INPUTTING AND ALIGNING HAIRPINS

In the previous chapter, we learned how to align hairpins horizontally. You can align hairpins (and other shapes) vertically in the same manner. When you align shapes vertically, shape length is adjusted to match the selected shape. In several places throughout the score, all four voices and Piano have hairpins that should be aligned vertically. It is also important to note hairpin staff assignment. Go to measure 44 to input these hairpins.

1. Input the crescendo hairpin for the Soprano part.

2. Before you double-click-and-drag, take note of the direction in which the cursor arrow is pointing. If it is pointing up, the hairpin will be attached to the staff above. If it is pointing down, the hairpin will be attached to the staff below. This is very important for alignment, playback, and part extraction.

3. Input all four hairpins. You do not need to worry about getting all four hairpins positioned exactly, but make sure that they

extend to the end of measure 45. **Note**: If measure 45 is on the next page, see the section below on *Dragging Shapes Over Page Breaks*.

4. Drag a box around all four hairpin handles.

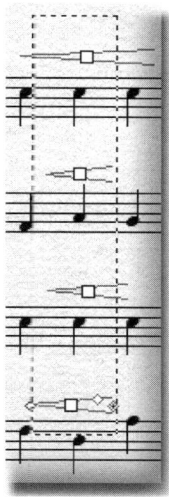

Selecting hairpins for vertical alignment

5. Right-click (**Control-click**) on the handle of the hairpin you want to use as the guide hairpin (the one that is the right length and properly placed).

6. From the contextual menu, select *Align Vertically*.

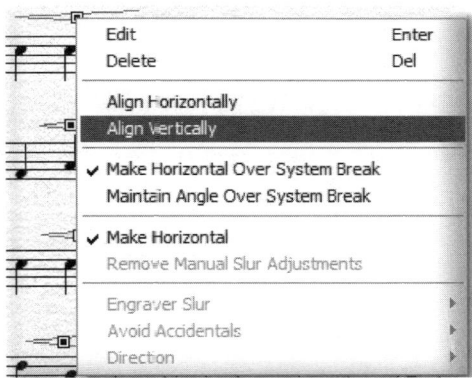

The Align Vertically command

7. Input the decrescendo hairpin for all four parts in measure 47. **Remember:** To input the decrescendo hairpin, you need only to drag backwards rather than select the *Decrescendo* tool if the *Crescendo* tool is already selected.

8. Now align these hairpins vertically as shown above.

9. Now select all eight handles for all of these hairpins in all four voices.

10. Right-click (**Control-click**) on the hairpin you want to use as the guide hairpin.

11. Select *Align Horizontally.*

12. With the handles still selected, press **Down Arrow** a few times to move the hairpins down to make room for lyrics.

13. Now repeat these steps to input and align hairpins for measures 52–55 as well as the hairpins on page 1.

14. Finish inputting and aligning all remaining hairpins in the score.

A Note on Finale 2008 Multiple Paste. As mentioned above, it is very fast in Finale 2008 to use the *Paste Multiple* function. Once you input any performance marking, like hairpins:

1. Select the area that has hairpins with the *Selection* tool.

2. Right-click (**Control-click**) and select *Edit Filter.*

   a. Click *None*, then select *Markings/Smart Shapes Assigned to Measures.* Click *OK.*

3. Type **Ctrl/Command–C** (for *c*opy).

4. Select the first measure to paste.

5. Right-click (**Control-click**) and select *Paste Multiple.*

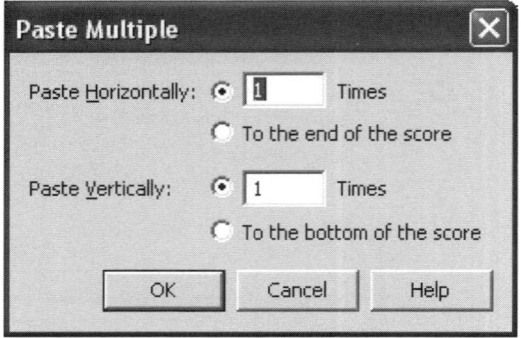

6. In the *Paste Vertically* field, enter the number of staves that you want to paste the hairpins into or simply click the *To the Bottom of the Score* button (the lowermost staff in the system).

7. Click *OK*. The hairpins are all uniform in size and position.

DRAGGING SHAPES OVER PAGE BREAKS

Finale has three different ways to view a score. We have been working in *Page View*; there is also *Scroll View* and *Studio View*. *Scroll View* and *Studio View* are quite similar. They display the music as a continuous stream of music without dividing the music into systems, as in *Page View*. Some people prefer using these modes, especially for larger scores.

If you need to drag a shape over a page break you can use either *Scroll View* or *Studio View* to do this. You can select the different views from the *View* menu or use the associated shortcut keys. **Ctrl/Command–E** toggles between *Page View* and *Scroll View*; **Ctrl/Command–Shift–E** selects *Studio View*.

Once you are in *Studio View* or *Scroll View*, you can type a measure number into the measure box at the bottom left of the screen. Press **Enter** and this will display that measure to the far left of the screen.

In this case, the hairpin extends over measures 44–45. If measure 45 is on the next page, follow these instructions:

1. Type **Ctrl/Command–E**.

2. In the measure text field type **44** and press **Enter**.

3. Input hairpins using the steps listed above.

4. When you are done, type **Ctrl/Command–E** to return to *Page View*.

EXTRA CREDIT SECTION

SHAPING SLURS

What? An S-shaped slur in measure 51! For extra credit, here is how to create it.

1. Press **Ctrl–+ (=)** on Windows or **Command–Shift–+ (=)** on Macintosh to zoom in on measure 51. If you want to zoom to a specific point, **Shift–Right-click** (**Command–Shift** on Macintosh) and click on the score where you want to zoom.

2. Input the slur, starting on the first note in the bass clef, then drag to highlight the last note in the treble clef.

3. You will now see several diamond-shaped handles, Three of them are labeled in the example on the next page.

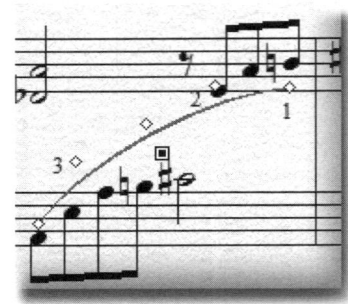

Diamond-shaped slur handles

4. By default, the slur will position over the top of the treble clef beam. Click-and-drag the handle labeled 1 in the example to the position shown.

5. Click-and-drag handle 2 down.

6. Click-and-drag handle 3 up and to the left.

Changing the shape of a slur is easy, because these handles are very flexible in letting you achieve the look you desire. You can use the **Tab** key to cycle through the selection of the handles, then use arrow keys to nudge the handles to the desired place.

BACK TO THE PROJECT

VIDEO CLIP 5:4
INPUTTING EXPRESSIONS

NOTES ON EXPRESSIONS

Input expressions using the *Note Attached* setting where there are expressions for individual parts, and using the *Measure Attached* setting where they are assigned to several staves. For example, in measure 46, use measure-attached expressions and assign them to *All Staves*.

Look at measure 48. Here the *pp* is assigned to Alto, Tenor, and Bass only. Input this as a measure-attached expression below the staff. But instead of assigning this to all staves, do this:

1. **Staff Lists**. Previously we created a staff list to assign repeat brackets to staves. We can also use staff lists to assign expressions.

2. When you input a measure-attached expression, clicking the *Select* button brings up the *Measure Expression Assignment* dialog. From here you can select a *Staff List*.

3. If an expression already exists in the score and you need to change the staff assignments, use the *Selection* tool to right-click (**Control-click**) on the expression and select *Edit Measure Expression Assignment* from the contextual menu.

4. Click the *Staff List* button.

5. From the dropdown menu next to *Staff List*, select *New Staff List*.

6. Type **ATB** (for Alto, Tenor, and Bass) in the *List Name* field.

7. Click on the staff names *Alto*, *Tenor*, and *Bass*, as shown in the example below.

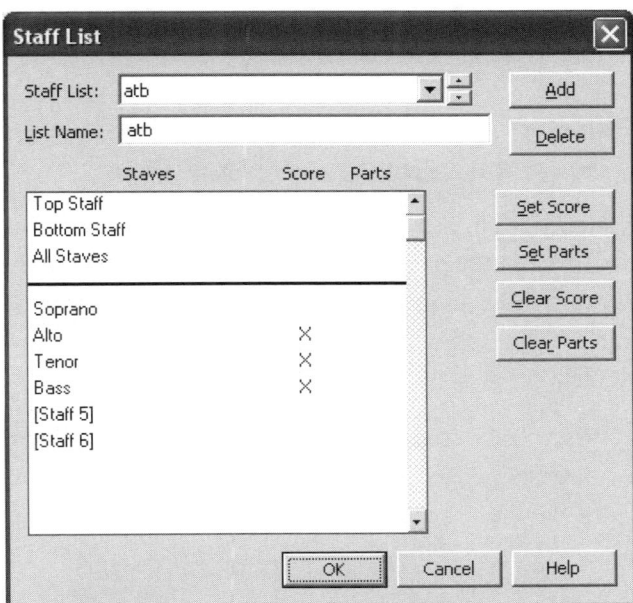

The Staff List dialog

8. Click *OK* to return to the *Measure Expression Assignment* dialog, then click *OK* again to return to the score.

In measure 56 input the expression *p* labeled below the staff and assign it to all staves. Note that the placement is correct for all staves, but the Piano part. This dynamic needs to be centered between the staves in the Piano part. You could try to move this expression below the staff with the *Selection* tool, but this will move the expression on all of the staves. To remove this link:

1. **Independent Expression Position**. Press **Esc** for the *Selection* tool.

2. Right-click (**Control-click**) on the *p* below the Piano treble staff.

    a. In Finale 2007–2008, select *Allow Individual Positioning* from the contextual menu.

b. In Finale 2006, select *Edit Measure Expression Assignment* and then select *Allow Individual Positioning* in the dialog.

3. **Note**: You could have selected this option when you input the dynamic and assigned it to *All Staves*, but editing it afterwards is a good exercise.

4. Click *OK* and then drag or use arrow keys to nudge the expression to the desired position.

TURNING OFF MEASURE EXPRESSIONS FOR THE PIANO BASS STAFF

In measures 45, 56, and 57 there are dynamics that need to be placed in each staff except the bass staff in the Piano part. In fact, there shouldn't be any expressions in the bass clef of the Piano at all. Depending on the template you started with, you may need to disable expressions in the bottom clef.

1. With the *Selection* tool (press **Esc**), double-click on the instrument name *Pno*. Now double-click in a measure in the bass staff of the Piano part. The *Staff Attributes* dialog opens.

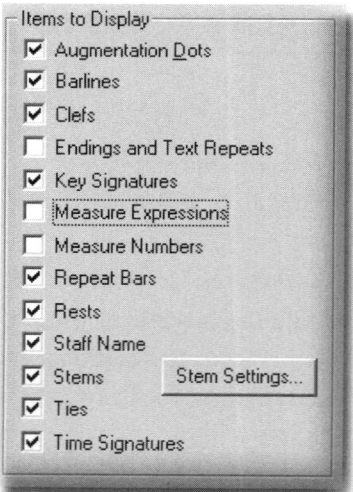

The Items to Display section of the Staff Attributes dialog

2. In the *Items to Display* area, clear the box next to *Measure Expressions*.

3. Before closing this dialog, note the other items that you can display or not display. Anything you change here will affect this staff throughout the entire score. Later you will learn how to apply these settings to a selected region.

4. Click *OK*.

Now you can input measure-attached expressions using the *All Staves* setting without them showing in the Piano bass clef.

REHEARSAL MARKS

Rehearsal marks are expressions. We will use the *Metatools* shortcut key method to input rehearsal marks.

1. Go to measure 6. If the *Expression* tool is not selected, press **Esc** and double-click on the dynamic *p* to go to the *Expression* tool.

2. Hold down the **A** key and click on the quarter rest in the SA staff. Make sure there is a little note in the cursor as you do so that this will be a *Note Expression*, because we only want this on the top staff.

3. Press **Left Arrow** to nudge the expression a bit to the left.

4. Go to the last note in measure 19 and input rehearsal mark B by holding down the **B** key and clicking on the note in the SA staff.

5. In measure 36, there is not a note or rest to which to attach rehearsal mark C. You could input a true whole rest in the Soprano staff or input this as a *Measure Expression*. If you choose *Measure Expression*, hold down the **C** key and click in measure 36 in the Soprano staff.

   a. Right-click (**Control-click**) on the handle of the C expression, select *Edit Measure Expression Assignment*, and then select *This Staff Only*.

The Measure Expression Assignment dialog

6. The rehearsal mark in measure 48 will also need to be measure-attached. Follow step 5 above to input the D rehearsal mark.

7. The default file has rehearsal marks A through D pre-created for you and has assigned these to *Metatool* (shortcut) keys **A** through **D**. But a rehearsal mark expression for letter E is not created.

VIDEO
CLIP 5:5

TYPING IN LYRICS

The Lyric tool

8. Double-click on the rest in measure 52 of the Soprano part.

9. Scroll down to select rehearsal mark D. Click Duplicate (**P**), then Edit (**E**). Note that these shortcuts are Windows only.

10. Type an uppercase **E** and click *OK*. Click *Select*.

LYRICS

There are several ways to input lyrics. You can type lyrics directly into a score or take existing lyrics from a text document (such as one created in Microsoft Word) and paste them into the score. First, we will learn how to type lyrics into the score.

1. Select Layer 1. You can attach lyrics to notes any layer, but in this score we will attach them all to Layer 1.

2. Click on the *Lyric* tool.

3. Click on the first note of the SA staff in measure 6 and type the first word.

4. Press **Spacebar** to move to the next note and type the next word, including the comma.

5. If you need to correct a word, press **Backspace/Delete** once to select the word to re-type. Pressing **Backspace/Delete** twice will erase the word. This is also accessible from the *Selection* tool. Click once on the lyric to select it then press **Backspace/Delete**. Double-click on the lyric to enter typing mode to re-type the lyric.

6. Continue until you reach the word *side*. Here you will need to press **Spacebar** three times to move the cursor to the correct note for the word *With*.

7. In the finished example, you will see a line to indicate the melisma (a syllable spanning more than one note). This line will be created automatically after you finish typing the lyrics.

8. In measure 10, note that the word patience is hyphenated. Type *pa*, then a hyphen to move to the next note, and then type *tience*.

9. Continue typing in the first verse, pressing **Spacebar** to skip notes that are part of a melisma.

10. Finish typing the lyrics through the first ending. Do not worry about lyrics colliding with notes, shapes, or expressions; we will fix that later. Click anywhere on the page to exit lyric entry mode.

11. Return to the first page (**Ctrl/Command–Page Up**) to enter verse two.

ADJUSTING STAVES FOR MORE LYRICS

Before proceeding to verse two, we will create some room between the staves for the second verse. Adjusting the space between staves to make room for more lyrics can be done manually or by using the new Finale 2007–2008 *Vertical Collision Remover* plug-in that automatically adjusts white space between staves, lyrics, and other elements. First, we will learn how to manually adjust the space between staves.

1. Zoom out to see more of the first page.

2. Press **Esc**, then double-click on the staff name *TB*.

3. Click on the handle (small box) on the bottom of the TB staff in measure 6 (circled in the example below).

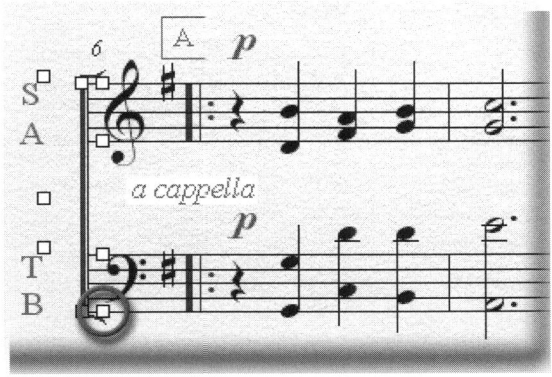

The lower staff handle

4. Press and hold **Shift** and click on the bottom handle in the next two systems.

5. Press **Down Arrow** to create more space between these systems.

6. Do not go too far. You may end up moving the bottom system of page one to page two. You do not want to do that.

7. We also need to adjust the system on the next page.

    a. Type **Ctrl/Command–Page Down** to see the next page.

b. You may want to press **Page Up** to see the top of this page.

8. Click on the bottom handle of the TB staff.

9. **Shift-click** on the bottom handles of both of the Piano staves (yes, we need to move them as well).

10. Press **Down Arrow** to make the space adjustment.

ADJUSTING STAVES FOR MORE VERSES

1. To input verse two, return to the first page (**Ctrl/Command–Page Up**).

2. Press **Esc**, then double-click on the first word (*Be*).

3. Press **Down Arrow** to select the next verse.

4. Type the lyrics to the end of the second ending for verse two.

5. Note that when you finish typing in the lyrics and exit lyric entry mode, Finale will place an unnecessary melisma line in the first ending for the second verse. We will deal with that later. Do not worry about it now.

VERTICAL COLLISION REMOVER

As discussed above, Finale 2007–2008 includes a new plug-in to quickly resolve collision problems between staves rather than manually adjusting the space between systems. Follow these steps if you have Finale 2007 or 2008.

The Mass Edit and Selection tools

1. Select the *Mass Edit* tool. (In Finale 2008, press **Esc** to go to the *Selection* tool.)

2. Highlight the area that needs to have spacing adjusted (in this case, the SA and TB staves for measure 6 through the second ending).

3. In Finale 2007, select *Plug-ins* menu/*New plug-ins for Finale 2007/Vertical Collision Remover*. In Finale 2008 select *Plug-ins* menu/*Scoring and Arranging/Vertical Collision Remover....*

4. There are many great settings to give you control over how you want Finale to adjust for collisions. For this example, next to *Overall Space between Systems*, move the slider to the left towards the *Tighter* position. Click *OK*.

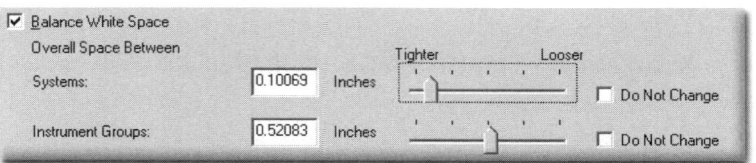

The Vertical Collision Remover dialog

COPYING LYRICS

Now we will move to measure 37 and enter the lyrics for the Soprano part. Remember the quick method for selecting the *Lyrics* tool.

1. Use the *Selection* tool to select any lyric verse. Press **Esc**, then double-click on a lyric in verse one (such as the word *end* in the first ending).

2. Click on the first note in measure 37 of the Soprano staff.

3. Press **Down Arrow** twice to access verse three of the lyrics. Now type the lyrics for measures 37 to the end of the score. **Note**: It isn't necessary to use verse three in most cases, but for the next exercise, click-assigning lyrics, it will work best if you use a different verse.

4. Select *Lyric* menu/*Clone Lyrics*. This is a fast way to set a copy filter for lyrics.

5. Click on measure 37 in the Soprano staff and type **Shift–Right Arrow** to select to the end of the score. In Finale 2008, type **Shift–End**.

6. Drag the highlighted measure to the Tenor part and release.

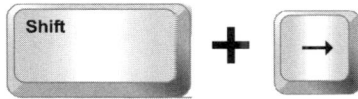

Press and hold the Shift key and then press the Right Arrow key

A Note on Copying and Cloning Lyrics. In Finale 2006–2007, there are two ways to copy lyrics: cloning (drag-copy) and the traditional copy/paste function. Using the drag-copy method with the *Clone Lyrics* command or with the *Mass Edit* copy filter creates a linked copy of the lyrics. Making a change to a word in the source lyrics will also change the copied lyrics.

If you need to copy lyrics but want an unlinked copy so you can edit them independently, follow these instructions.

1. Select the *Mass Edit* tool. (In Finale 2008, press **Esc** to go to the *Selection* tool.)

The Mass Edit and Selection tools

2. Select the measures from which you want to copy lyrics.

3. Right-click (**Control-click**) in the highlighted area and select *Items to Copy*.

4. Click on both buttons marked *None*. (In Finale 2008 there is only one *None* button.)

5. Check the box next to *Lyrics*. Click *OK*.

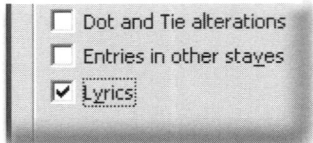

The Lyrics checkbox

6. Now use the standard **Ctrl/Command–C** to copy only the lyrics.

7. Select the destination region.

8. Use the standard **Ctrl/Command–V** to paste.

This function is simplified in Finale 2008. If you use the *Clone Lyrics* function after selecting the *Lyric* tool, a linked copy of the lyrics is created as in previous versions. If you use the *Selection* tool and select *Edit* menu/Edit *Filter* and select only *Lyrics*, this creates an unlinked copy of the lyrics regardless of the copy/paste procedure you choose. Drag copy, **Ctrl/Command–C** (copy) and **Ctrl/Command–V** (paste) all produce an unlinked copy.

CLICK-ASSIGNING LYRICS

VIDEO
CLIP 5:6

CLICKING IN LYRICS

In measures 36–43, the Soprano and Tenor basically echo the lyrics of the Alto and Bass. For a short section like this, it is faster to simply re-type the duplicate lyrics. You may want to continue typing the Alto lyrics, then copy them to the Bass part if you simply want to finish the score quickly.

However, you may want to learn an optional way to input lyrics. In other scores you may have large sections of repeated lyrics where the music is rhythmically different. Or you may have lyrics already typed in a word processing document and would like to copy the lyrics and input them into the score without retyping them. This exercise will teach you how to click-assign lyrics already typed into Finale, or another document created with a word processor such as Microsoft Word.

1. Return to page two of the score.

2. To insure the correct verse is selected, press **Esc** and double-click on the first word in the Soprano staff in measure 37.

3. Select *Lyric* menu/*Click Assignment*.

4. The *Click Assignment* dialog will display. In the scroll area along the bottom of this box, drag the scroll bar completely to the left so the word *Be* is the first word on the left side of the click assignment window.

The Click Assignment dialog

5. This dialog displays the lyrics in a continuous stream. As you click lyrics into the score, the word or syllable furthest to the left in the dialog is the active or next lyric to go into the score. (You may need to drag the dialog out of the way to see the score.)

6. Now click on the first note in the Alto part in measure 36. You will notice that the word *Be* is assigned to the Alto staff and the word *still* shifts to the left in the dialog. Now the word *still* is the next word to go into the score.

7. Continue clicking each note in the Alto part until you get to the word *Thy*.

8. Here the parts differ. The Soprano part repeats *Thy God*. So click on the scroll button to the bottom right (>) twice to skip the next two words. Now the dialog should show as in the lower example below.

Skipping lyrics in the Click Assignment dialog

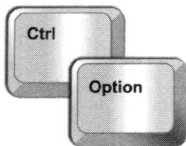

9. Press and hold **Ctrl/Option** and click on the next note (A). Note that this automatically assigned the remaining lyrics to each of the remaining notes in the Alto part. If you have a score that has a word or syllable for each note with few melismas, this command works well. Then you can shift the lyrics where you need to adjust the lyric assignment, as you will learn below.

10. To dismiss the *Click Assignment* dialog, click the close box, as you would with any regular dialog in most programs.

SHIFTING LYRICS

In step nine of the previous section, we assigned lyrics that were in the *Click Assignment* dialog. However, there are a few places where the lyrics do not match up note to lyrics. So we need to adjust a few lyric assignments by shifting the lyrics.

1. Go to measure 39 in the Alto staff.

2. Select *Lyrics* menu/*Shift Lyrics*.

3. The default for this dialog is *Shift Lyrics to the Right*, with the second option selected as shown in the example below. Make sure these options are correct, then click *OK*.

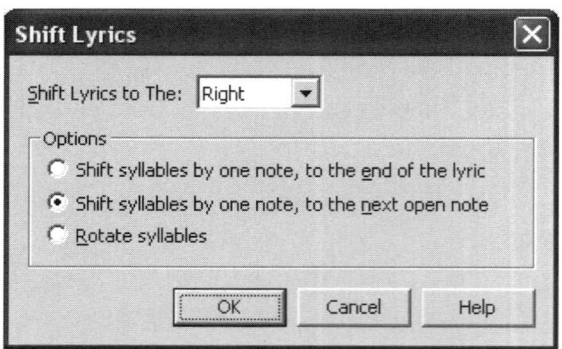

The Shift Lyrics dialog

4. In the Alto staff, click on the A with the word *To* underneath it.

5. This shifts all the lyrics over so that the word *To* is on the next note.

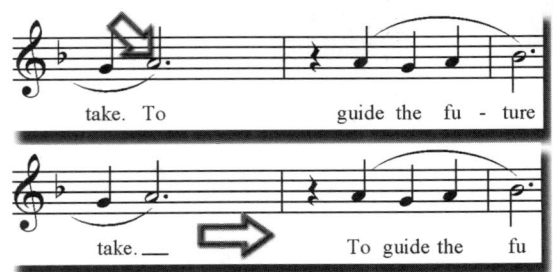

Shifted lyrics

6. In measure 42, the Alto has two extra words. Shift the words *the past* to the appropriate notes in measures 42–43 as shown in the example below.

   a. Press **Esc**. In the Alto staff, in measure 42, double-click on the word *as*.

   b. Press **Right Arrow** twice to move the cursor to the next note.

   c. Type the word *he*, then press **Spacebar** and type the word *has*.

   d. Click on white space on the page to exit typing mode.

CLEARING LYRICS

If you chose to use the click-assigning lyrics option above, you may notice, starting in measure 45 of the Alto part, that the lyrics are not assigned to the correct notes. You could continue shifting the lyrics as described above, or clear the remaining lyrics in the Alto staff and copy them from the Soprano staff.

The Mass Edit and Selection tools

1. Select the *Mass Edit* tool. (In Finale 2008, press **Esc** to go to the *Selection* tool.) Select measure 45 to the end of the score on the Alto staff. (Remember, type **Shift–Right Arrow** (in Finale 2008, type **Shift–End**) to select to the end of the score.

2. Right-click (**Control-click**) in the highlighted area and select *Clear Items*. Make sure that *Lyrics* is the only item selected. (In Finale 2006–2007, click both *None* buttons, then select *Lyrics*. In Finale 2008, click the single *None* button and choose *Lyrics* in the *Text* area.)

3. Click *OK*.

FINISHING THE LYRICS

1. In measures 36–44, either clone or copy the lyrics from the Alto part to the Bass part.

2. In measures 45 to the end, clone or copy the lyrics from the Soprano staff to the Alto and Bass staff.

3. Press **Esc**. In measure 47 of the Alto part, double-click on the word *shake*, then press **Right Arrow** twice to activate the lyric cursor on the first note in measure 48 of the Alto part. Type lyrics into the Alto staff for measures 48–51.

4. Now clone or copy the lyrics from the Alto staff to the Tenor and Bass staves for measures 48–51.

ADJUSTING THE VERTICAL POSITION OF LYRICS

Starting in measure 6, note that the lyrics are too close to the notes in the SA staff, and the second verse is too close to the first verse. We will move the second verse first to make room for the first verse, then we will move the first verse lower.

1. Press **Esc**, then double-click on the first lyric of verse two in measure 6.

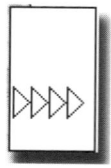

Positioning triangles

2. As you do this, you will notice four triangles to the left of the screen. As we learned from positioning expressions, these triangles also adjust the baseline positioning of lyrics. In the next chapter, you will see that we use this process to adjust positioning of chords and fretboard grids as well.

3. The first triangle from the left adjusts the lyrics for the entire score. The third triangle from the left adjusts lyrics for the current system only. We want to adjust *all* lyrics in the second verse to be lower.

4. Click on the first triangle from the left and drag it down to center this verse in the middle of the system.

5. You can lower the first verse for the entire score as well. A quick way to select verses is with the *Selection* tool. Press **Esc**, then double-click on the first word in verse one. Sometimes this will highlight the word in verse two. If so, simply press **Up Arrow** to select verse one. Note that the positioning triangles move to the verse one position.

6. Now use the leftmost arrow to adjust the first verse down a bit.

7. If needed, you can use the third triangle from the left to adjust lyrics for the current system only.

8. You may want to go to page two and use the *Selection* tool to double-click on the first word on the Soprano line in measure 37 and adjust lyric position with the leftmost triangle. Remember, this will adjust the lyrics in the other four voices.

9. If you want to adjust lyrics for only one staff, use the second triangle from the left. If you want to adjust the lyrics for one staff, and only the current system, use the third triangle from the left.

10. Since we used verse three for the lyrics in the open score section, we need to move those lyrics up closer to each of the parts.

    a. Press **Esc**, then double-click the first word in the Soprano part in measure 37. (This is the fastest way to insure that verse three is selected.)

    b. Drag the leftmost triangle up. You only need to do this for the Soprano staff, since using the first triangle adjusts the lyrics in the other staves as well.

ADJUSTING AND DELETING WORD EXTENSIONS

Remember the word extension at the end of the word *at* in the first ending? To delete this:

1. Press **Esc**, then double-click on the word extension.

2. Note that every word has a handle at the end of it. This allows you to manually adjust word extensions for any word. You can click and drag the box to edit the length of the word extension.

3. At the end of the word extension in the first ending, click in the box to select it, then press **Delete**.

4. **Note**: Once you are in this edit-word-extension mode with the *Lyric* tool, using the *Selection* tool to double-click a lyric will *not* enter lyric entry mode; edit-word-extension mode is still in effect until you select *Lyric* menu/*Type Into Score*.

EXTRA CREDIT
SECTION

OTHER LYRIC CONSIDERATIONS

Copying Lyrics from a Word Processing Document. If you want to copy lyrics from a word processing document for other projects in the future, here are some pointers.

1. Type the lyrics in the word processing document. Input all of the hyphens that you need in the lyrics. Select all of the verse one lyrics you have typed (click to the left of the first word in verse one, press and hold **Shift**, then click to the right of the last word [also known as a **Shift–click**] in verse one, then type **Ctrl/Command–C**).

2. Now return to your score in Finale.

3. Select *Lyrics* menu/*Edit Lyrics*. You could type the lyrics in the text field of this dialog, but you just copied them from the word processing document, so paste the lyrics you just copied into this dialog by clicking in the text field and typing **Ctrl/Command–V**. (V isn't intuitive; it is just what every program uses for paste, mainly because P is for Print and V is right next to C for copy.)

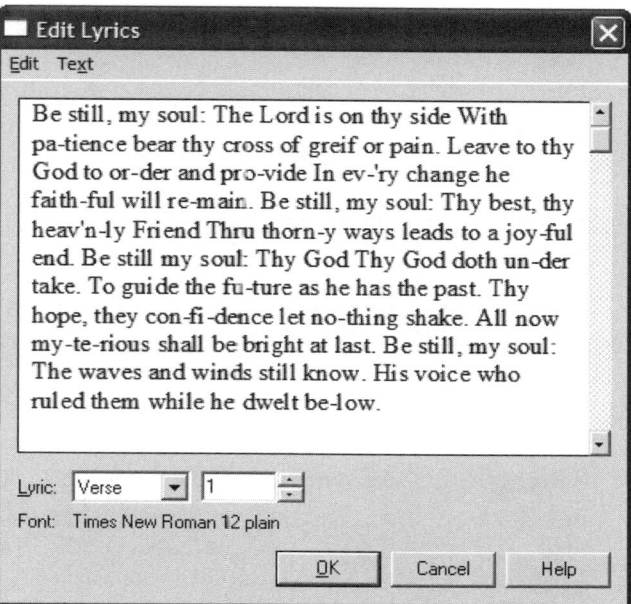

The Edit Lyrics dialog

4. If you have more than one verse of lyrics, as we do in this score, you need to paste those verses into a new verse text field.

    a. Return to your word processing document and copy the verse two lyrics using the procedure given above.

    b. Note that the verse number field at the bottom of this dialog.

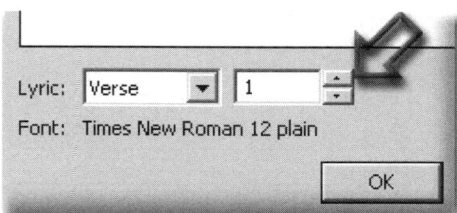

The verse number field

    c. Click the *Up Arrow* button (shown in the example above) to select a new verse (in this case, verse two), then type or paste the lyrics for verse two in the text field as you did with verse one.

    d. From the click assignment dialog, use the scroll bar on the right side of the box to select the verse.

5. In most scores, lyrics match up word- or syllable-to-note. Here and there you may have a few melismas requiring several notes for one word. If this is the case, it is faster to use **Ctrl/Option–click** to input the lyrics throughout the entire score as we did above.

6. Now use the *Shift Lyrics* command you learned above to adjust lyric note assignment as needed.

Changing Fonts. The *Lyric* menu/*Edit Lyric* dialog also allows you to select lyrics and change the font using the *Text* menu at the top of the screen.

1. Select lyrics by dragging the mouse over them, or click before the first word, then **Shift–click** the end of the last word as you would in a word processing program.

2. At the top of the screen, use the *Text* menu to change font size or other attributes.

Multiple Words on One Note. In some music (chant, for example), you may need to put more than one word on a note. Finale can do this in several ways. You could insert a blank character between words. This is done by typing **Alt–0160** (using the numpad, not the numrow) on Windows or by typing **Option/Spacebar** on Macintosh. You could use a text box with the lyrics and place that into the score. However, to insure that the music spacing remains consistent, it is best to use the blank notation method.

1. Consider the example below. The whole note has several words assigned to it.

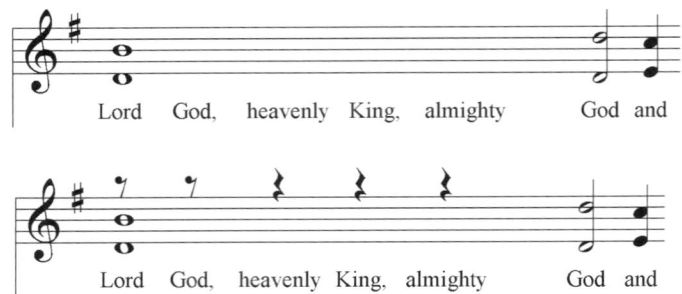

Using the blank notation method to enter more than one word on a single note

2. To create this, input rests in Layer 1 that would equal the number of words or syllables needed. (In this example, we used two eighths and three quarter notes.)

3. Type the lyrics into Layer 1.

4. Select Layer 3 from the numbers or dropdown menu in the lower left corner. Now input the whole note.

5. Press **Esc** for the *Selection* tool. Double-click the instrument name.

6. Select this measure, or drag a marquee around several measures to select them if needed.

7. Right-click (**Control-click**) to display the staff style list.

8. Select *Blank Notation: Layer 1*.

9. Lyrics are evenly spaced throughout the measure using spacing based on Layer 1 without displaying the rests in Layer 1.

Closed-Score Lyrics Above and Below the Staff. Above you learned about adjusting the vertical position of lyrics. It is common in choral scores to have lyrics specific to a certain voice either above the staff, (Soprano) or below the staff (Bass). It is best to use separate layers for these notes, and a separate verse for the lyrics, rather than use the base-line positioning arrows to move lyrics to the appropriate position.

1. Select the correct layer for the notes to which you are assigning lyrics.

2. Press **Down Arrow** to start a new verse.

3. Use the positioning arrows to move this verse to the desired place.

4. There is no need to remember what verse you used for a certain voice. Using the *Selection* tool (**Esc**), you can simply double-click on a lyric to return to that verse.

5. If you type lyrics in a new verse for a specific voice and the notes are not in a separate layer, you may get some unwanted word extensions (melisma lines).

   a. Press **Esc**, double-click on the melisma line, click on the handle, and press **Delete** as described above.

VIDEO
CLIP 5:7

FORMATTING AND
ADJUSTING COLLISIONS

**The Mass Edit
and Selection tools**

FORMATTING AND ADJUSTING COLLISIONS

Music Spacing. When you input notes and lyrics, music spacing is automatic. If this does not seem to be turned on, check in the *Edit* menu to see if *Automatic Update Layout* and *Automatic Music Spacing* are selected. In Finale 2008, select *Edit* menu/*Program Options* (on Windows) or *Finale 2008* menu/*Preferences/Program Options* (on Macintosh). Now and then you may want Finale to re-space an area of music. You may want to manually adjust the position of notes to accommodate lyrics and other collisions, or to just make it look the way you prefer.

Re-spacing the Music. If you notice notes colliding with other notes or lyrics, its always a good idea to perform a *Music Spacing* command. Re-spacing the music can alter the number of measures on a system. If you like the current number of measures on a system, you may want to lock the systems before performing a *Music Spacing* command.

1. Go to the last page of the score. You may notice that this page may only have one or two measures on it. Move these measures to the system above it (on the previous page) with the measure-moving command we covered previously.

    a. Select the *Mass Edit* tool. (In Finale 2008, press **Esc** to go to the *Selection* tool.)

    b. Press **Up Arrow**.

2. This not only moves the measures up, but it locks the system so re-spacing does not affect the number of measures on that system. You can move other measures if you like, locking those systems. If you like the placement of measures as they are, then lock the entire score with these steps:

    a. Select the *Mass Edit* tool. (In Finale 2008, press **Esc** to go to the *Selection* tool.)

    b. Type **Ctrl/Command–A** to select all measures.

    c. On Windows, type **L** (for lock) to lock the systems. On Macintosh, type **Command–L**.

3. Now press **4** on the numrow (above the **E** key). This will apply note spacing, which re-evaluates horizontal collision problems. You can also press **3** on the numrow (also above the **E** key), which will apply beat spacing (which spaces the music differently). In Finale 2008, press **5** for beat spacing.

a. You can also find these commands in the *Mass Edit* or *Selection* tool contextual menu. Right-click (**Control-click**) in the highlighted area, select *Music Spacing/ Apply Note Spacing* or *Music Spacing/Apply Beat Spacing*. (In Finale 2008, these commands are in the *Utilities* menu/*Music Spacing*.)

Things may be getting a bit crowded. We need more space between the staves. But first, we need to adjust the space between systems to allow us to do this. Otherwise, we will not be able to fit two systems per page as we have on pages two through five.

Keep in mind that much of the staff and system spacing can be accomplished automatically in Finale 2007–2008 using the new *Vertical Collision Remover* plug-in. You may want to run that plug-in again on the entire score. That could save you a lot of time.

Adjusting the Space between Systems. Using the *Page Layout* tool, you could simply drag a system to the desired place, but we want a more uniform look, and it is faster to do this to a region.

1. Click on the *Page Layout* tool.

2. Note that each system is now numbered on the left-hand side of the page.

3. Right-click (**Control-click**) on system two (measure 6).

4. Select *Edit Margins*.

The Page Layout tool

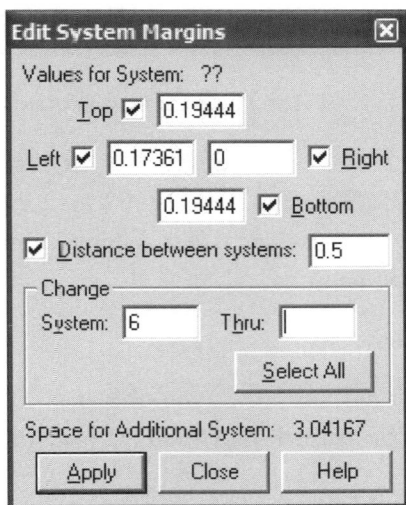

The Edit System Margins dialog

5. In the *Distance between systems* field, enter **0.4** (inches)

6. In the *Change* area, enter **2** in the *Systems* text field; leave the *Thru* text field empty. No number in the second field means "to the end of the score."

7. Click *Apply*, then *Close*.

8. Depending on the original spacing value, this could move all systems from system two through the end of the score up a little or down a bit.

Adjusting the Space between Staves. First we will apply a global adjustment to all staves.

1. Press **Esc** and double-click on any staff name. This will access the *Staff* tool.

2. Go to page 3 to see the results of this function.

3. From the *Staff* menu, select *Re-space Staves*.

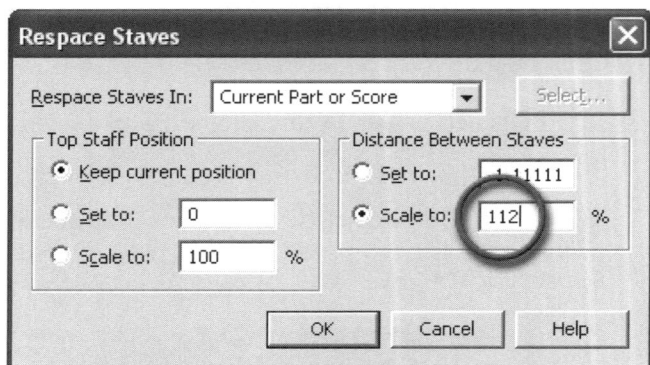

The Re-space Staves dialog

4. Under *Distance Between Staves*, click *Scale to* and set the value to **112**. (**Note**: In Finale 2007 and 2008, you can make this change to parts and score independently using the dropdown menu at the top.)

5. Click *OK*.

6. If this did not give you the desired results, simply press **Ctrl/Command–Z** to undo the last command.

7. Remember to save your work.

8. **Note**: If you are using Finale 2007–2008 and used the *Vertical Collision Remover* plug-in, staff optimization has been applied to all of the systems. Staff optimization overrides the *Re-space Staves* command. If you want, you can:

   a. Select a system using the *Page Layout* tool. Right-click (**Control-click**) in the system and select *Optimize Staff System*. Note that the box next to this option is checked to indicate that the system is optimized.

   b. In the *Staff System Optimization* dialog, check *Remove Staff System Optimization* and then select a range of systems which to apply this. Click *OK*.

The Staff System Optimization dialog

   c. Now you can follow the steps above for re-spacing staves, and it should work well.

Return to page one. Note that this global command had no effect on the staves in the closed score area. Remember that they have been optimized. That is good. These staves need different spacing. In fact, you already adjusted the spacing of these staves when we created more room for the second verse of lyrics.

If you need to re-adjust these staves, review the steps previously presented in the section *Adjusting Staves for More Lyrics*. Remember, you can also use the new *Vertical Collision Remover* plug-in for Finale 2007–2008.

Adjusting Repeat Ending Brackets. You may want to position all of the brackets, or just individual brackets for the endings.

1. **Adjusting the Brackets**. Press **Esc**, then double-click on the repeat sign or brackets.

2. Select the top handles in the SA staff by dragging a marquee around the handles.

3. Note that this action selects *all* of the handles for all of the brackets. You could press **Up Arrow** or **Down Arrow** to adjust all of them together, but we just want to adjust the SA staff.

4. Right-click (**Control-click**) any of the handles and select *Allow Individual Positioning*. (In Finale 2007–2008, this is *Allow Individual Edits per Staff*.)

Adjusting repeat ending brackets

5.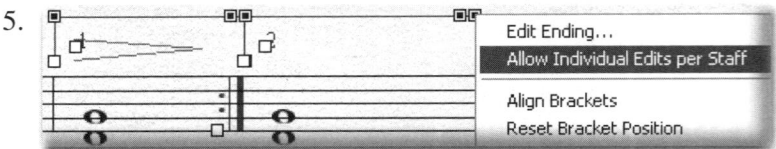

Now you can drag a marquee around the handles in the SA staff only.

6. Use **Up Arrow** or **Down Arrow** to adjust the brackets.

7. You can select any group of handles together to adjust bracket positions.

Moving Expressions and SmartShapes. Several of the expressions and *SmartShapes* need to be moved so they do not collide with music and lyrics. For individual items, simply press **Esc** and use the *Selection* tool to click on an item and either drag it, or press **Up Arrow** or **Down Arrow** to nudge the item to the desired position. Click on the expression *a cappella* in measure 6 and nudge it to the desired location.

Here are some other pointers.

1. **Moving Multiple Items**.

   a. Go to measure 44.

   b. Press **Esc**, then double-click on the any of the hairpins in measure 44. Note that all shapes on this page now have handles on them.

   c. Drag a marquee around all four handles of the hairpins in measure 44. If you like, you can zoom out. Press and hold **Shift** and select the handles for the hairpins in measures 45 and 47 as well.

   d. Now use **Down Arrow** to move these hairpins down.

e. Anytime you use the *Selection* tool to double-click an expression, shape or articulation, all items of that type will show handles that you can select to move or delete.

2. Changing Slur Direction.

a. Go to measure 47 in the Piano part. The slur collides with the hairpin.

b. Press **Esc** and double-click on the slur.

c. Type **Ctrl/Command–F** for *flip*.

d. Or press **Esc** and right-click (**Control–click**) on the slur and select *Direction/Flip*.

3. Changing Tie Direction.

a. The instructions for flipping a tie are very much like flipping a slur, except you need to highlight the note to which the tie is attached.

b. Go to measure 9. Use the *Selection* tool and double-click on the dotted-half noteheads. (This enters *Simple Note Entry* mode).

c. Type **Ctrl/Option–Down Arrow** to select just the G.

d. Now type **Ctrl/Command–F** to *flip* the tie.

4. Moving One Expression.

a. Remember, if an expression is measure-attached, moving it will adjust the position of this expression in all staves.

b. To move one expression, right-click (**Control–click**) on it, select *Edit Measure Expression Assignment* and *Allow Individual Positioning*. In Finale 2007–2008, the *Allow Individual Positioning* option is available in the contextual menu without having to go to a dialog.

Editing Text. At the beginning of the creation of this score, we input Jean Sibelius as the composer. I would like to see the arranger's name below his name. (It will make my mom proud.)

1. Press **Esc** and double-click on the text, *Jean Sibelius*.

2. Press **Right Arrow**. This places the cursor at the end of the existing text.

3. On Windows, press **Enter** (on Macintosh, press **Return**) to move the cursor down a line.

4. Type **Arranged by Tom Carruth**.

5. Since I am certainly not as important as Jean Sibelius, I would prefer that my name be smaller. (Mom will understand.)

6. Click and drag to highlight the text you just typed.

7. Now you could adjust font, size, and other text aspects from the *Text* menu. But we will learn a standard text shortcut that is used in many text-processing programs.

8. Press and hold **Ctrl/Command–Shift**, then press the **<** key (the comma key, next to the **M** key) a couple of times to make the text smaller.

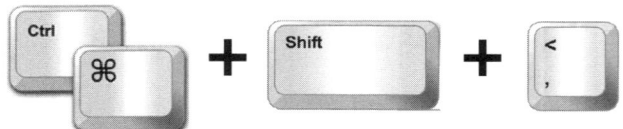

Press and Hold Ctrl/Command–Shift, then press the < key

9. To position your text block on the right side of the page (if needed), select *Text* menu/*Alignment* and set it to *Right*.

10. Press **Esc** to exit text-editing mode.

11. **Note**: In Finale 2008, the Arranger info can be created when using the *Setup Wizard*, *or* you can also set this by selecting *File* menu/*File Info*.

MORE ON LAYING OUT PAGES, SYSTEMS, AND MEASURES

Deleting Measures.

1. Go to the last page. (**Ctrl/Command Page Down** to get there).

2. Select the *Mass Edit* tool. (In Finale 2008, press **Esc** to go to the *Selection* tool.) Select measure 64 (it should be blank). (In Finale 2008, double-click measure 64 to select the measure stack.)

3. If there are measures past 64, type **Shift–Right Arrow**. (In Finale 2008, type **Shift–End**.)

The Mass Edit and Selection tools

4. Press **Delete**.

An Alternate Method for Adjusting Space between Systems. Return to page one and zoom out (**Ctrl/Command– –** [the minus key]). After adjusting the space between systems, you may notice that these systems are not distributed well. There could be quite a bit of blank space at the bottom of this page. Before, we used the *Edit Margins* command to adjust the space between systems. Now we will use a quick alternate method.

The Page Layout tool

1. Select the *Page Layout* tool.

2. Drag a marquee around the bottom-right handles of systems 1–3, but *not* system 4. (**Note**: If you wish to select all of the right bottom handles in your score, highlight one handle and then press **Ctrl/Command–A**.)

3. Press **Down Arrow** to create space between the systems. Adjust this until the systems look balanced on the page.

Manual Note Positioning. There is one last adjustment needed. In measure 58 of the Tenor staff, the eighth notes may be a bit too far apart. I would prefer that they were closer. You can move horizontal note positioning using the *Special* tools, but this is only recommended if you want to adjust unisons or seconds. Generally, when changing the position of a note, all other notes that are on that beat in other staves need to move with it. That is why we use the *Beat Positioning Chart*.

1. Zoom in on measure 58 to see this measure in more detail.

2. Press **Esc**, then right-click (**Control–click**) on measure 58 in the Tenor staff.

3. Select *Edit Beat Chart*. You will see a box above the top staff of the system.

The beat chart box

4. Within this box you will see two groups of handles. The top handles represent beats spaced evenly. You can drag the bottom handles to offset the notes horizontally.

    a. If a beat handle does not exist for the eighth note, double-click between the top set of boxes where you need another beat handle.

    b. You can also press and hold **Shift** and drag a beat, causing all beats to the right of the selected beat to move proportionately.

5. Drag the first bottom box to the left to give the eighth notes more room.

6. Drag the second bottom box to the left to space the eighth note better.

7. Press **Esc** to exit beat-chart-editing mode.

8. **Changing Lyric Alignment**. After changing the beat position, note that the word *while* in measure 58 of the Tenor staff is not aligned properly with the other voices.

    a. Press **Esc**.

    b. Right-click (**Control-click**) on the word *while* in the Tenor staff.

    c. Select *Align Center*.

9. If the word extension does not display, select *Edit* menu/*Update Smart Word Extensions and Hyphens*.

10. Once again, remember to save your work.

VIDEO CLIP 5:8

SEPARATING VOICES AND CONTROLLING TEMPO

CREATING A REHEARSAL CD

Separating the Closed Score Area to Individual Staves. In the *a cappella* section, the Soprano and Alto share a staff, as do the Tenor and Bass. Now we will separate them into four open-score staves.

In this score, we already have four staves. In other closed-score choral pieces, there may not be four vocal staves present in the score. It is very easy to copy all the music, go to the *Setup Wizard*, create an *SATB and Piano* score, and then insert the copied music into the new score for playback.

You can also add two staves into the original score using the *Staff* tool, but in Finale 2006–2007 it is more difficult to change the new staves to allow independent control over them in the mixer. In Finale 2008, this is done automatically for you as you create new staves using the *Staff* tool. First we will separate the Soprano/Alto and the Tenor/Bass.

1. Since we are going to alter this music, you may want to save this with a new filename first.

2. Select *View* menu/*Studio View*.

3. Type **Ctrl/Command– –** (the minus key) to zoom out.

4. Type **Ctrl/Command–Page Up** or **Ctrl/Command–Page Down** to scroll forward and backward in the score.

Press and hold Ctrl/Command and press the minus key

5. Select the *Mass Edit* tool. (In Finale 2008, press **Esc** to go to the *Selection* tool.) Select measures 6–30. Use the *Select Region* method.

   a. Click on measure 6 in the Soprano part.

   b. Select *Edit* menu/*Select Region*.

The Mass Edit and Selection tools

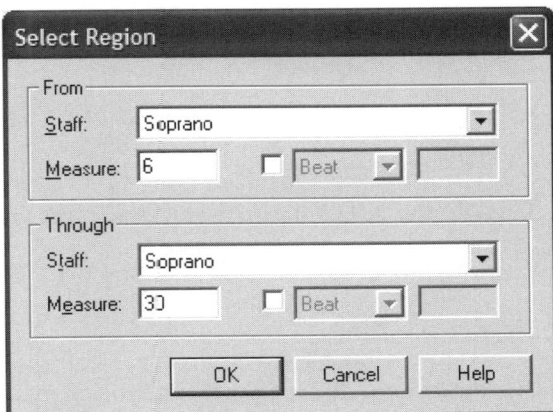

The Select Region dialog

   c. The *From* measure is already selected. In the *Through* area, set the measure to 30 and press *OK*.

6. Now drag the highlighted area to the Alto staff and release to copy it. (Remember, if it did not copy correctly, make sure the *Items to Copy* filter is set correctly. In Finale 2008, make sure *Edit* menu/*Use Filter* is turned off.)

7. Repeat these steps to copy the Bass staff to the Tenor staff.

8. Now select the Soprano staff again. You can simply click in the white space to the left of the clef in the Soprano staff. This will select the Soprano part for the entire score. This is fine for the function we are going to execute.

9. Select *Plug-ins* menu/*TG tools*/*Process Extracted Parts*.

10. Click on the *Standard* tab.

11. Set the settings as shown in the example below.

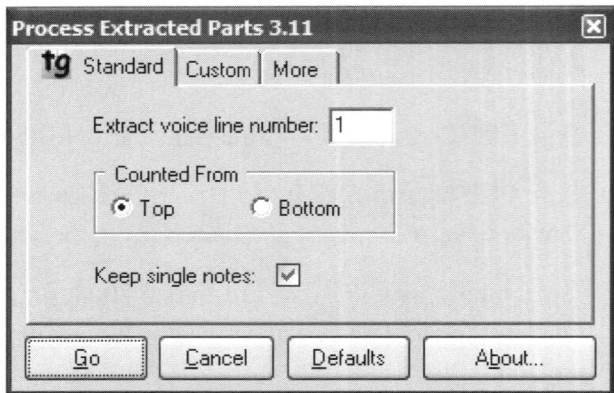

The Process Extracted Parts dialog

12. Click *Go. Do not* click *Close*.

13. Without closing the dialog, click to the left of the Tenor staff to select it. Click *Go* in the dialog.

14. Change the settings from *Counted from Top* to *Counted from Bottom*.

15. Click to the left of the Alto staff and click *Go*.

16. Click to the left of the Bass staff and click *Go*.

17. Now click *Close*.

18. Again, this would be a good time to save your work.

You may want to listen to this music. Click *Play* in the playback controls.

On Windows, in the playback control panel, click on the speaker icon (on Macintosh, the *Expand* arrow) to see the *Human Playback* settings. It is set to *Standard* for now. You may want to set this to *Romantic* or try a different setting of your choice (please do not use jazz or samba; mom wouldn't like that!)

Assigning Separate MIDI Channels. When you start a score using the *Setup Wizard*, Finale automatically assigns each staff to a different MIDI channel. However, the templates may not always be set this way. In this score, we started with the *SATB and Piano* template. Each of the four vocal staves may be set to the same MIDI channel number. This will make independent volume changes and instrument changes impossible. Since the next section deals with those items, we need to change each staff to have a separate MIDI channel now. To change a MIDI channel number, use the following steps to create an instrument to which you can assign a MIDI Channel and MIDI patch or program change (sound).

1. Select *Window* menu/*Instrument List*.

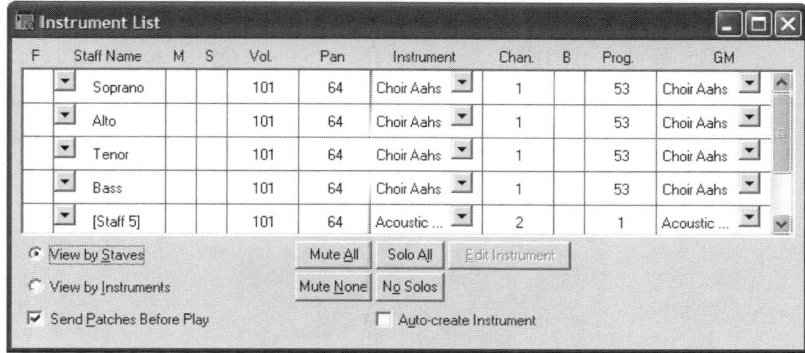

The Instrument List dialog

2. You will notice that each of the staves—Soprano, Alto, Tenor and Bass—have the same *Instrument* of *Choir Aahs* and *may* all be assigned to MIDI channel 1. (If you change settings for any one of these, it will affect all of them, since they are on the same channel number.)

3. If each choir staff already has a different MIDI channel number assigned, each voice part can be controlled independently and there is no need to continue with this exercise. However, if all of the choir staves are assigned to the same channel number, proceed to the following instructions.

4. We will leave Soprano on *Choir Aahs, Channel 1*, but we will change the other three voices to new channels.

5. On the Alto row in the *Instrument* column click on the arrow next to *Choir Aahs*.

6. Click on *New Instrument*.

7. Change the *Channel* number to *Channel 3* (*Channel 2* is used by the Piano).

8. Click *OK*.

9. Repeat this for the Tenor and Bass staves, setting them to channels 4 and 5.

10. Click the close box at the top of the dialog to return to the score.

Adjusting Volume, Panning, and Instruments. When preparing choir recordings, I prefer not to use the *Choir Aahs* sound because attacks and releases are too vague. I like to use different instruments for each of the four voices; it makes it easier to distinguish parts. On Windows, you can click on the instrument name (*Choir Aahs*) in the *Mixer* console and select a new sound from the instrument list. (**Note**: This list applies to General MIDI sounds only, and not to other VST/AU sound sets). In Finale 2006 on Macintosh, you will need to change this by selecting *Window* menu/*Instrument List*. Try setting the Soprano to *74 Flute*, the Alto to *72 Clarinet*, the Tenor to *71 Bassoon*, and the Bass to *59 Tuba*.

The Studio View Mixer

In addition to the *Studio View Mixer*, you can select a different *Mixer* from the *Window* menu (or, on Windows, type **Ctrl–Shift–M** [for Mixer]; on Macintosh, type **Option–Command–M**).

This *Mixer* has the same controls as the *Studio View Mixer,* with the addition of the reverb type and amount controls. Adjust them as you like.

Adjusting Tempo Changes. If you input a new tempo change with the expression tool, such as placing a *rit.* or *accel.* into the score, Human Playback will respond to those expressions. However, this music is to be performed very *rubato*. I want the rehearsal recording to have the same tempo expression that I would use when conducting the choir. So, let's conduct the computer!

1. If you are not in *Studio View*, select *View* menu/*Studio View* (**Ctrl/Command–Shift–E**). To toggle between *Scroll View* or *Page View*, type **Ctrl/Command–E**.

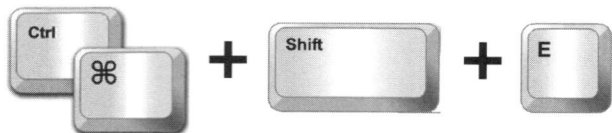

Press and hold Ctrl/Command and Shift, then press the E key

2. Here you will see all of the staves with a mixer to the left of each staff. You will also see a *TempoTap* staff at the top.

3. Zoom out to see all the staves (**Ctrl/Command– –** [the minus key]).

4. Click on the *HyperScribe* tool. In Finale 2008, click the *MIDI/Audio* menu and make sure *Play Through MIDI* is checked. You can set Finale back to *Play Through VST or AU* after recording the tempo.

The HyperScribe tool

5. Click on the first blue note in the *TempoTap* staff. A green cursor bar will appear.

6. Tap the space bar (or a note on your MIDI keyboard) in time to the tempo you want. You can slow down, speed up, pause, do whatever you would like to control the tempo the way you would direct this music.

7. You can stop recording the tempo any time you would like by clicking anywhere in the score.

8. When you stop recording, a dialog appears showing your last recorded tempo. Click *OK* to maintain this tempo until the next tempo change, or you can specify a different tempo.

9. **Tapping the Melody Rhythm**. For the a cappella part of this score, I would like to tap the rhythm of the melody line, not the quarter note beats. You can change the *TempoTap* beats with the *Simple Note Entry* tool, or copy and paste notes from any staff into the *TempoTap* staff. **Note**: Finale 2008 will only copy one measure at a time into the *TempoTap* staff.

The Mass Edit and Selection tools

    a. Select the *Mass Edit* tool. (In Finale 2008, press **Esc** to go to the *Selection* tool.) Click in the Soprano staff in measure 6.

    b. Use the *Select Region* method discussed previously, or try this method:

Press and hold Ctrl/Command and then press the Page Down key

        i. With measure 6 selected, type **Ctrl/Command–Page Down** several times till you come to the first ending. This is like selecting the next page in *Page View*.

        ii. Press and hold **Shift** and click in the Soprano staff in the first ending.

        iii. Type **Ctrl/Command–Page Up** to return to measure 6.

    c. Drag the highlighted area to the *TempoTap* staff and release.

    d. Note the tempo beats change to the rhythm of the Soprano part.

Tempo beats that match the rhythm of the melody

    e. Select the *HyperScribe* tool again.

    f. Click on the first note of measure 7 in the *TempoTap* staff and tap the new rhythm displayed in the *TempoTap* staff.

You can re-record the tempo track starting anywhere, as you would record in any staff with *HyperScribe*. You can also edit the tempo track.

1. Click the *Edit* button in the *TempoTap* console area.

2. This opens a graphic representation of the tempo.

3. You can drag-select any area, then from the MIDI tool menu, alter the tempo by a percentage, set it to an exact value, scale the value, or press **Backspace/Clear** to erase the tempo changes in the selected area.

4. Tempo can also be cleared with the *Mass Edit* or *Selection* tool using the *Clear Items* filter.

Saving the Music as an Audio File. You can adjust levels using volume sliders. For example, you may wish to create a rehearsal CD that has four recordings of this song, each recording with a predominant part. For example, the first track on the CD will be for Sopranos. You could set the mix so the Soprano part is louder, the other voices softer or silent. Set the Piano part to the desired level as well. Then do the same for the Alto recording, and so forth.

1. Set the volumes as you want for the Soprano recording.

2. Select *File* menu/*Save Special/Save as Audio File*. In this dialog, you could either save this as a *.wav* file on Windows or a *.aiff* on Macintosh; these are the file types commonly used to create a CD audio recording. You can also save this as a *.mp3* file. This format is a compressed audio format that is much smaller than a *.wav* or *.aiff* file. This is useful for email or posting to a website.

3. We will save it as a *.wav* on Windows or *.aiff* on Macintosh. Just enter a name for this recording and click *Save*. You may want to save this to your desktop or create a folder in a specific place on your hard drive.

4. When saving files using the *SmartMusic SoftSynth*, as we are now, the recording is created quickly without the computer having to play the music. If you are using the Garritan or other VST/AU sound sources on any Finale version other than 2008a, Finale *will* play the score as it records it. Also, when using VST/AU, there is not a *.mp3* option.

5. Now repeat this process for the Alto, Tenor, and Bass recordings. You may want to make a fifth recording that has all parts equally balanced for students to use once they have learned their part.

6. Once these audio files are created, put a blank, recordable CD into your writable CD drive, then follow the instructions for burning a CD provided with the software you use to do that, if you use third-party software. If you use the native Windows or Macintosh CD-burning facility, consult your operating system help files if you need information about how to do this.

CHAPTER 6

THE LEAD SHEET

Concepts covered in this chapter:

- Guitar and Tab notation
- Chords
- Suffix selection and creation
- Analysis
- Fretboards
- Libraries
- Advanced Tuplet creation and control

PROJECT FILE: LEAD SHEET

In this project we will start with a simple lead sheet. This will give you experience with the concepts involved. In the next chapter we will copy the lead sheet into a big band chart and use it to make a full score.

CREATING THE LEAD SHEET

1. Create the score as shown in the PDF example titled *Lead Sheet* using the *Setup Wizard*.

2. In the *Setup Wizard*, select the *SmartMusic SoftSynth* sounds from the dropdown menu on page two of the *Setup Wizard*. (Finale 2008 has all sounds available in VST mode. Select either mode.)

3. Create a score with *Guitar* and *Guitar (TAB)* staves.

VIDEO CLIP 6:1

CHORDS AND LEAD SHEET CREATION

Setting up a Guitar (TAB) staff in the Setup Wizard

4. Set the time to common time. Set the key to F major.

5. On page four of the *Setup Wizard*, select *Jazz* as the music font. (In Finale 2008, select the *Handwritten* document style from the first page of the *Setup Wizard*.)

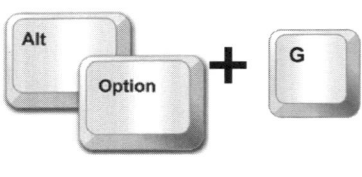

6. Input the notes using your preferred method. Here are some note input pointers.

    a. **Tie over Barlines.** In measure 7, you have a chord that will tie over the barline. Instead of entering an eighth note chord, entering ties, then moving to the next measure and entering another eighth note chord, use *Simple Note Entry* to input this chord as a quarter note. Finale will divide and tie the balance of the quarter note duration over into measure 8.

    b. **Grace Notes.** There are two ways to enter grace notes. One way is to input the C♯ eighth note as normal, then type **Alt/Option–G** to turn it into a grace note. Another way is to type **Ctrl/Command–G** to lock in grace note mode before you input the grace note. Type **Ctrl/Command–G** a second time or press the eighth note key twice to exit grace note mode. (The eighth note key is **4** on either the numpad or numrow.)

7. Copy measures 5–12 to measure 17. Use the insert method.

    a. Using the *Mass Edit* tool (or the *Selection* tool in Finale 2008), select measures 5–12. Type **Ctrl/Command–C** (for copy), then **Ctrl/Command–Page Down** to go to the next page.

    b. Select measure 17. Type **Ctrl/Command–I** (for *i*nsert).

    c. **Note**: An optional way to insert music in Finale 2008 is to press and hold **Alt/Command** and drag the highlighted source region to the desired insert point. You will see a red line showing the insertion point you are selecting as you drag.

8. **Lock in Triplets**. Measure 26 is a good place to lock in triplets.

    a. Before putting the first note into measure 26, type **Ctrl/Command–9** (the tuplet value).

    b. Press **4** (to set the duration value to eighth note) and then input the notes.

    c. At the beginning of measure 27, press the quarter note key (**5**) twice to exit tuplet mode.

Once the music is completed in the score, delete all the unused measures. As a refresher:

1. Select the first unused measure with the *Mass Edit* tool.

2. Type **Shift–Right Arrow**. (In Finale 2008, double-click the first blank measure to select a stack, then type **Shift–End**.)

3. Press **Delete**.

The Bend Shape. Input the bend from the *SmartShapes* tool. Bends, like slurs, are shapes attached to notes.

The SmartShapes tool

1. From the *SmartShapes* palette, select the *Bend* tool.

2. Zoom in on the grace note if you like.

3. In measure 9, double-click on the grace note to input the bend.

The Bend tool

4. Type **Ctrl/Command–F** to *f*lip the bend the other direction if desired.

5. Remember to duplicate this procedure in measure 21.

TABLATURE

Tablature notation is a type of notation used primarily for fretted instruments. Since it is possible to play the same pitch on different strings, tablature notation shows the string and fret position for each note. Staff lines represent strings on the instrument, the lowest staff line corresponding to the lowest string. In this case, the Guitar has six strings, so there are six staff lines. Numbers placed on the lines represent the fret number on that string.

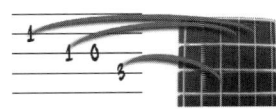

Tablature staff lines correspond to instrument strings

You can type or play notes directly into the Tab staff. If using a MIDI-equipped guitar, you can set each string to a different MIDI channel; then Finale can determine on which string you want a note to be placed. Otherwise, you can manually place the pitch numbers on the string yourself. However, Finale is very intelligent when copying music or playing music onto a Tab staff. It automatically calculates the best position for fret positions. We will look at the copy method. If you wish to type notes directly into the Tab staff, watch the Finale 2006 video *Create/Tablature* or the Finale 2007–2008 video *Measures and Staves/ Tablature*.

1. Using the *Mass Edit* tool (in Finale 2008, the *Selection* tool), click to the left of the Guitar staff to select it throughout the entire score.

2. **Note**: If you are using Finale 2006, the *Jazz Font Default* file is not correct! You will need to follow these instructions:

   a. Transpose the notes up by an octave with the transposition *Metatool*. In a previous chapter we suggested setting the **8** key as an octave down *Metatool* and the **9** key as one that transposes an octave up as it is in Finale 2008. If you did this, all you need to do is select the area and type **9**.

   b. Otherwise, select the area, right-click (**Control-click**) and select *Transpose* from the contextual menu.

3. Click and drag the first highlighted measure to the first measure of the Tab staff and release.

4. A question appears: "What would you like Finale to use as the lowest fret when placing notes in the tablature staff?" This allows you to copy certain regions and control what fret region you would like Finale to use when calculating the fret/pitch position.

5. For right now, leave the value at 0 and click *OK*.

6. In Finale 2006, make sure the Guitar staff is still highlighted and transpose it back down by an octave. (Use *Metatool* **8** as suggested in the previous chapter.)

7. **Editing Shapes**. I didn't like the length of the bend. To edit this:

   a. Press **Esc** and double-click on the bend in the score.

   b. Press **Tab** until the upper triangle (handle) is selected.

   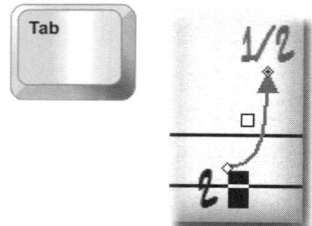

   c. Press **Down Arrow** and **Right Arrow** to shape the bend as you like.

Now Finale has copied the music and created the Tab notation for you. If you would like, you can easily change the number/pitch to a new string.

1. **Changing Tab String Assignments**. Press **Esc** and double-click on the *0*, the second eighth note in the third measure. This *0* is placed on the B string (second line from the top of the Tab staff).

Changing Tab string assignments

2. Press **Down Arrow** to move the pitch to the G string. Note that the number changes to a *4*. This is the correct fret for that pitch on this string.

Before going on, input the *Forward Repeat* in measure 17 and the endings in measures 28–29 as discussed in the previous chapter. Here is a quick reminder:

1. Click on the *Repeat* tool. Select *Repeat* menu/*Repeat Options*.

2. For *Show On*, select *Top Staff Only*. Click *OK*.

3. Right-click (**Control-click**) in measure 17 and select *Forward Repeat*.

4. Highlight the measure(s) you want in the first ending. In this case, highlight measure 28.

5. Right-click (**Control-click**) in measure 28 and select *Create First and Second Ending*. In Finale 2008, you can also input repeats by right-clicking (**Control-clicking**) with the *Selection* tool.

The Repeat tool

The Selection tool

SCORE FORMAT

We will do a quick format on this score before we go on. We need some space for chords and fretboards.

The Resize tool

1. Go to page one and select the *Resize* tool.

2. Zoom out using **Ctrl/Command– –** (the minus key) until you can see the full page.

3. Click in the top left corner of the page.

The Page Layout tool

4. Change the size percent to 80%. Click *OK*.

5. Select the *Page Layout* tool.

6. Click the handle in the lower right corner of the first system.

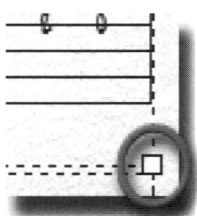

The lower-right system handle

7. Type **Ctrl/Command–A** to select all systems.

8. Press and hold **Down Arrow**. This will move the systems down, allowing more space between systems. Press and hold **Down Arrow** until there are only four systems on the first page and enough room between systems for chords and fretboards.

9. Click in the middle of the first system and drag it down a bit to make room for the chords and fretboards above the top staff. (Press and hold **Shift** before clicking to prevent moving the system from side to side.) Use the finished example as a guide. Do not worry about being too accurate. You can always adjust it later.

10. Go to page two and drag the top system down a bit.

11. Zoom back in using **Ctrl/Command–+** (the equal sign key). Zoom in to a level that makes it easy to click on and input items.

12. If you like, move measures up or down a system using the *Mass Edit* or *Selection* tool as you have already done several times.

CHORDS

Now we are ready to input chord symbols. Finale has several ways to input chords. You can type the chords into the score or play them from a MIDI device. As you play, Finale will analyze the notes played and display the closest matching chord symbol. Also, Finale can analyze chords individually or for a selected region. Chords can also be used for solfeggio and figured bass, as we will learn later on. For this project, we are going to input the chords by typing them.

1. Zoom in on the top system of the score.

2. Click on the *Chord* tool.

3. Make sure Layer 1 is selected and then click on the first note in the Guitar staff.

4. Type the chord name: an upper case **F**, followed by **6**.

5. Press **Spacebar** as you would if typing lyrics to move to the next note.

   a. Note that the look of the chord changes once you move to the next note. Many symbols that you type may not look correct until you finish typing the chord. As you move to the next note or click on the page to exit the typing mode, the chord will change to display the correct look.

6. Press **Spacebar** until you reach the first note of measure 2.

7. Type **G**, then a lower-case **b** for the flat.

8. Type a comma. Use a comma to separate an accidental assigned to the root note from an accidental assigned to the suffix. For example, this chord was a G chord with a flat nine suffix, so you would type **G,b9**.

9. Now type **6** and press **Spacebar** to move on.

10. Continue inputting chords until you input the F6 chord in measure 5. It may be faster at that point to simply click on the first note in measure 9 rather than pressing **Spacebar** for each note to get to measure 9. Continue entering chords to measure 15.

Measure 15 has a chord with a complex suffix (see the example to the right). If you tried typing this chord using the keystrokes listed above, you got a message saying that Finale cannot find this chord suffix and asks if you would like to add it to the Chord Suffix Library. This chord suffix *does* exist in the Finale default file. When you do not know the correct keys to type for a particular suffix, do this:

1. If you have already typed in **D7#9#11** and got the dialog asking to add this chord to the library, click *No*. Starting with the root letter only (D), type **:0** (colon and zero). Press **Enter**. This displays the suffixes that are available in the program.

The Chord tool

$D\,7^{\sharp 11}_{\sharp 9}$

2. Scroll to the correct suffix (in this case, suffix number 81). Double-click that suffix to assign it.

63 M9	64 ∅	65 Δ	66 7♭13
69 ♭13 ♯9	70 ♭13 ♭9	71 13	72 7♯11
75 9(♯5)	76 7 ♯9 ♯5	77 7sus(♭9)	78 13sus(♭9)
81 7 ♯11 ♯9	82 7 ♭13 ♯9	83 ♭9

The Chord Suffix Selection dialog

3. Now that you know the suffix number, the next time you need that particular suffix, type the root, colon and the suffix number. Then press **Enter** or **Spacebar** to move to the next note.

4. Memorizing suffix assignment numbers is not always an easy way to input complex chords. If you are going to use the same complex chord again in your document, Here is a tip:

   a. Go to the *Selection* tool (press **Esc**) and double-click on the selected chord symbol that you have already used once. (Finale will remember the correct series of keys needed to type this chord suffix).

   b. Click on a note where you want to type the chord. Type in root with complete suffix (in this example, **D7#9#11**). Finale finds the suffix you wanted.

5. Continue typing chords to measure 25.

In measure 25, we want to add a chord, but there is no note or rest to which to attach a chord. The whole rest that displays in measure 25 is not a real rest. You could easily input a whole rest in this measure and then add the chord. However, we may come across several places in a song where you might need real rests to which to attach chords (and other items). It is time-consuming to add all of the real whole note rests manually, so we will use a plug-in.

1. Select the *Mass Edit* tool, then type **Ctrl/Command–A** to select the entire score.

2. Select *Plug-ins* menu/*Note, Beam, and Rest Editing/Change to Real Whole Rests*.

Now you have real rests to which you can attach chords.

1. To get back to type-into-score mode, press **Esc** and double-click on a chord.

2. Click on the whole rest in measure 25 and input the chords.

3. Finish inputting all of the chords for this piece.

Teacher, I Have a Question

What if Finale doesn't list the chord suffix I am trying to create? Here you have two answers. First, to keep the default file size of Finale down, all of the pre-created suffixes have not been loaded into the default files. See below to see how to load more chord suffixes. Second, you can create your own chord suffixes as will be discussed below.

EXTRA CREDIT SECTION ✓

LOADING MORE CHORD SUFFIXES

Finale has many libraries for different chords, articulations, shapes and more. To load a library:

1. Select *File* menu/*Load Library*.

2. Here you will see several libraries and folders of libraries you can load.

3. To access more chord suffixes, open the chord suffixes folder.

4. Since we are using the *Jazz* font in this score, select *Chord Suffix Expanded (Jazz Text)* and click *Open*.

5. Now when inputting chords, if you type the root, then **:0** (colon and zero) and then press **Enter**, you will notice that more suffixes are available.

ALTERNATE BASS AND DIMINISHED SYMBOLS

This is how you can create a chord with an alternate bass like B♭ over C. There are three ways to display alternate bass in a chord.

A chord with alternate bass

1. Select the *Chord* tool and click on a note or rest to input a chord.

2. Type **Bb** then type **Shift–** (the backward slash key).

3. Now type **C** for the alternate bass and press **Spacebar** to move to the next note.

4. Other alternate bass options are to type **/** (the forward slash key) or **Shift– –** (the minus key). Type the chord and suffix, then type one of these keys, followed by the alternate bass. Note the variation on the form of the alternate bass each of these keys produce.

Two other forms of alternate bass

5. If you need a diminished sign, type **o** (lower case letter O). For a half-diminished sign type **Shift–5** (the % sign could be interpreted as reminiscent of the half-diminished symbol).

CREATING NEW CHORD SUFFIXES

When typing in chords as described above, Finale tells you when it can't find an exact match for the chord suffix. You are then asked if you want to create a new suffix (i.e., to add a suffix to the chord suffix library). If you click *No*, you will return to the type-in mode and you can try a different suffix, or select from the suffix dialog as we did above. If you click on *Yes*, you will see the *Chord Suffix Editor* dialog, where you can create and design your chord suffix.

VIDEO
CLIP 6:2

MORE ABOUT CHORDS
AND FRETBOARDS

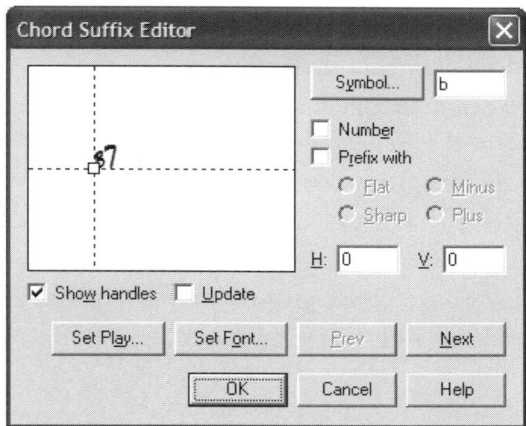

The Chord Suffix Editor dialog

1. In this example, let's assume that you typed the chord suffix **b7** for flat 7. Finale asks you if you want to add this to the document.

2. When you click *Yes*, Finale automatically puts the info you typed into the suffix designer area. You can leave this as is, just click *OK*, or you can edit it. I want this chord to display as in the example below.

3. I want to change the first character in this chord to be a flat, not a b. Click on *Set Font*.

4. Here you can change the font, size, etc. Generally, for a flat you would use either the *Maestro* or *Jazz* font. Right now the font is the Jazz *Text* font, which doesn't have musical symbols. So select the *Jazz* font, size 20, and click *OK*.

5. Since the letter b is the flat symbol in the jazz font, the symbol is correct.

    a. You can change the symbol from the symbol value.

    b. If you do not know what to type in the symbol value box for the symbol you want, click the *Symbol* button and select the symbol you want.

6. Now, all I want is the flat symbol to be raised slightly. Click the handle (little box) next to the flat sign and drag to the desired position.

7. If you wanted to change the font, size, or positioning of the 7, click *Next* to select the next element in the suffix.

CHORD ANALYSIS

Finale can analyze chords in several ways. You can play notes on your MIDI keyboard or Finale can analyze the notes in the score for a single chord, a region, or the entire score.

When Finale analyzes chords, it chooses the best match for the notes from the available chord suffixes. If it can't find a match, it will display a message telling you so. It will ask you if you want to create your own suffix or have Finale guess. Finale will guess the chord using basic chord analysis rules. You can then edit suffixes as discussed above.

You can also teach Finale chords. Select *Chord* menu/*Edit Learned Chords*. This is not covered in this book, but you can learn about it by selecting *Help* menu/*Owners Manual*.

There is also *Chord* menu/*Chord Style*. This allows you to select various chord styles including *Roman* for figured bass chords. Use this with the Figured Bass template in the Education Folder of templates on the CD-ROM.

Creating Solffegio. There is an easy way to have Finale automatically create solffegio using chord analysis.

1. Using the *Mass Edit* or *Selection* tool, select a single note melody line.

2. In Finale 2006, select *Plug-ins* menu/*New plug-ins for Finale 2006/Chord Analysis*. In Finale 2007–2008 select *Plug-ins* menu/*Scoring and Arranging/Chord Analysis*.

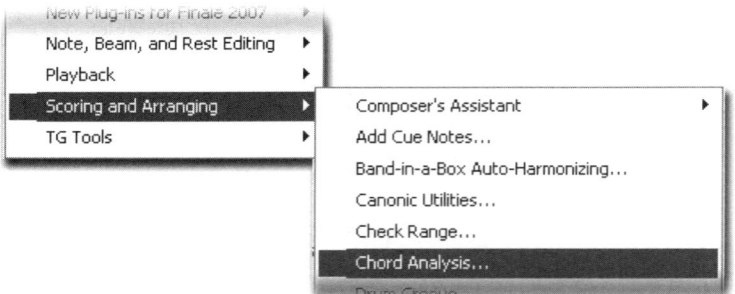

The Chord Analysis plug-in

3. Setup the *Chord Analysis* dialog as shown in the example on the following page. Click *OK*.

4. Initially this names each note. Now select the *Chord* tool or use the *Selection* tool and double-click on a chord.

5. Select *Chord* menu/*Chord Style/Solfeggio*.

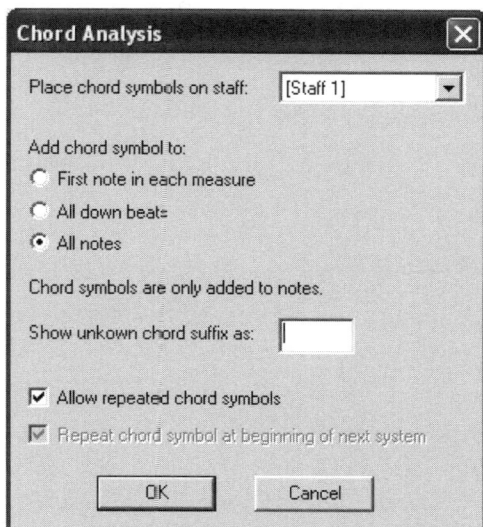

The Chord Analysis dialog

Note that you can also deselect *Chord* menu/*Enable Chord Playback.*

Changing Chords for a Region. Another powerful feature of Finale is the ability to change chord attributes for a region. For example, you may want to not show the root for figured bass chords. Or you may want to show fretboards for one area and not another.

1. Using the *Mass Edit* or *Selection* tool, select the area you want to alter.

2. Right-click (**Control-click**) and select *Change/Chords.* (In Finale 2008, select *Utilities* menu/*Change/Chords.*)

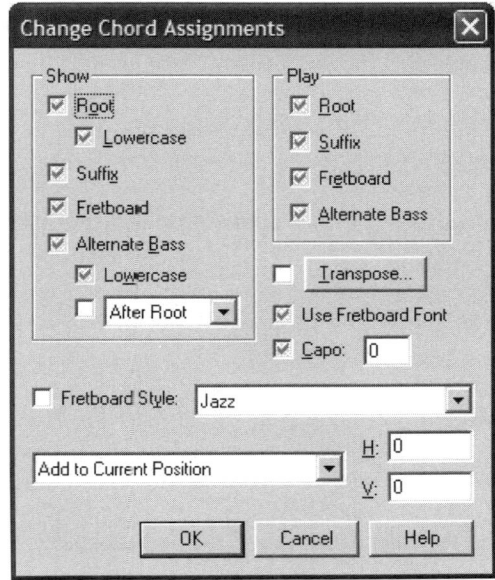

The Change Chord Assignments dialog

3. Here you can turn off and on different items to display or play. You can capo fretboards, transpose chords, and more.

4. Select the alterations you like and click *OK*.

BACK TO THE PROJECT

FRETBOARDS

Finale can automatically assign guitar fretboards to chords.

1. Select *Chord* menu/*Show Fretboards*.

2. In our example, the fretboards are smaller. Select *Chord* menu/*Resize Fretboard* and set the size to 75%.

EXTRA CREDIT SECTION

CREATING OR SELECTING ALTERNATIVE FRETBOARDS

You can create your own fretboards and your own fretboard instruments. For example, you may want a fretboard for Ukulele or Mandolin.

Note in the PDF example of this project that the first chord shows the F6 chord with a different fretboard than the default. You can either select a new fretboard graphic from a list, or create your own. First we will select from a list.

1. Press **Esc** and Right-click (**Control-click**) on the fretboard you want to change. In this case, the first one in the score.

2. In the contextual menu, select *Edit Chord Definition*. Here you can change all kinds of information about this chord.

3. In the *Fretboard* area, click *Select* and choose a new fretboard position. Click *OK* twice to return to the score.

Creating or Modifying Fretboards. You can also create or modify your own fretboard.

1. Press **Esc** and Right-click (**Control-click**) on the fretboard you want to modify.

2. From the contextual menu, select *Edit Fretboard*.

3. Here you can modify the fretboard as you like.

   a. From the *Instrument* dropdown list, you can select a new instrument, or click *Edit Instrument* to create your own instrument.

b. Once you create or modify a fretboard, you may want this fretboard associated with this suffix for all roots. To do this, click *Show Group*, then *Generate*, and this fretboard will be created for all chords regardless of the root.

c. More information on this is available by selecting *Help* menu/*Owners Manual*.

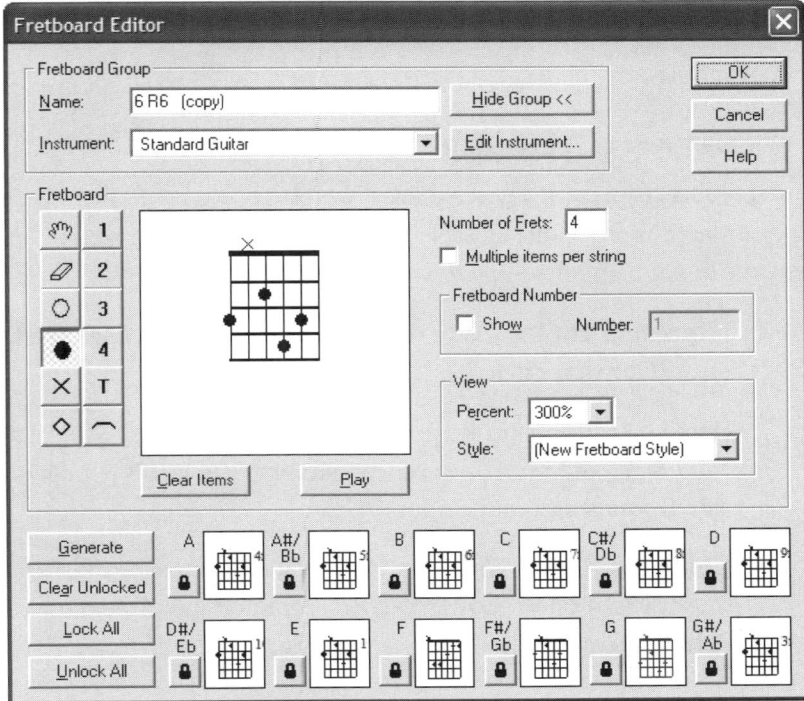

The Fretboard Editor dialog

BACK TO THE
PROJECT

POSITIONING CHORDS AND FRETBOARDS

You can change the position of chords and fretboards as you would lyrics using baseline controls.

1. Press **Esc** and double-click on a fretboard or chord symbol.

2. To the left of the screen, you will see four baseline positioning triangles. These arrows function like lyric baseline controls.

3. **Note**: Go to the *Selection* tool (press **Esc**) and double-click a fretboard to position fretboards, or double-click a chord symbol to adjust those elements.

4. Of course, you can change the position of a single chord or fretboard simply by dragging it with the *Selection* tool.

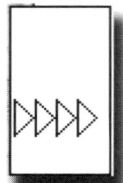

Baseline control triangles

EXTRA CREDIT
SECTION

IMPORTANT TUPLET INFORMATION

This score has triplets in several places, which gives us a perfect opportunity to learn more about tuplets and editing them. Of course, you can alter any tuplet using the *Selection* tool.

1. **Flipping a Tuplet.** Go to the *Selection* tool (press **Esc**). Right-click (**Control-click**) on a triplet number.

2. Here you can change the placement to *Above*, *Below*, *Stem Side*, *Note Side*, and more, or you can simply *Flip* it to the opposite side from its current position.

3. **Changing Tuplet Brackets.** You can also change the triplet shape. Right-click (**Control-click**) again on the triplet number. Select *Shape Type* and choose *Nothing*, *Slur*, or *Bracket*.

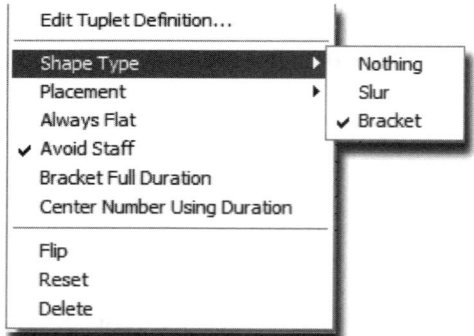

The tuplet context menu

   a. If you select *Bracket* or *Slur* and see no change, it may be that the auto-bracket feature is turned on.

   b. This means that, if the tuplet (a triplet in this case) is comprised of only beamed notes, Finale will not display a bracket or slur. If there is only a partial beam or none at all, then Finale will display a bracket or slur.

4. You can force Finale to display tuplet brackets or slurs. Right-click (**Control-click**) and select *Edit Tuplet Definition*.

    a. Here you can change many attributes about this tuplet. In the *Appearance* area, click *Always Use Specific Shape*.

    b. You may want to experiment with other *Appearance* controls.

    c. **Note**: This information can be set as the default. Select *Options* menu/ *Document Options/Tuplets* or *Document* menu/ *Document Options/Tuplets* and change these settings *before* inputting tuplets.

    d. If you have already input tuplets and want to change the settings of the tuplets for any region, you can do so with the *Mass Edit* or *Selection* tool.

        i. Select an area and right-click (**Control-click**) and select *Change/Tuplets*. In Finale 2008, select *Utilities* menu/*Change/Tuplets*.

5. **Detailed Tuplet Positioning Control.** Finale tuplets are very intelligent, in that they avoid collisions with notes and more. If you have a need to change the position and shape of a tuplet, follow these instructions:

    a. Press **Esc** and double-click on a tuplet.

    b. You may want to zoom in so you can edit more easily.

    c. You will see several handles that will allow you to control the position, hook lengths, direction, and number position independently.

Tuplet handles

        i. Drag a handle to adjust it, or click on a handle and use the arrow keys to nudge for more precise control.

d. If all you want to do is move the tuplet, simply drag the tuplet to the desired position with the *Selection* tool. (**Esc** key).

6. **Nested Tuplets.** Sometimes you may have a need for nested tuplets. Imagine five eighth notes in the space of four, with one of the eighth notes replaced by a sixteenth-note triplet.

Nested tuplets

a. Input the first two notes *without* making them a tuplet.

    i. **Note**: To input more notes than will fit in the measure, you may need to select the *Simple Note Entry* tool and then select *Simple menu/Simple Entry Options* and clear the box next to *Check for Extra Notes*.

b. Enter the sixteenth-note triplet as normal. Type the first sixteenth-note, type **9** for tuplet, then finish the other two sixteenth-notes.

c. Enter the last two eighth notes as regular eighth notes.

d. Press **Esc**, then double-click on the triplet number. Type **Ctrl/Command–F** to *f*lip the tuplet to the other side.

e. Now click on the first eighth note (the E in this case) and set the dialog to **5** (eighths) in the space of **4** (eighths).

f. Click *OK* to return to the score.

7. **Ratio Tuplets**. Sometimes you may want a tuplet to display as a ratio.

a. Press **Esc** and right-click (**Control-click**) on the tuplet.

b. In the *Appearance* area, select *Edit Tuplet Definition*
    and click on the dropdown menu next to *Number:* to
    select one of the available options.

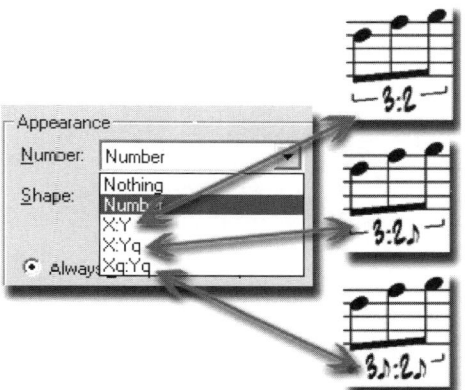

CHAPTER 7

CREATING THE JAZZ SCORE

Concepts covered in this chapter:

- Copying Music between Documents
- SmartFind and Paint
- Auto Harmonization
- MIBAC Rhythm Section Generator
- Piano Split Points
- Tremolo
- Slash Notation and Other Staff Styles
- Percussion Notation
- Exploding Music
- Grace Notes
- Cue Notes
- Metatools (shortcuts)
- Instrument Doubling (Changing Instruments Mid-score)
- Expression Staff Lists
- Play Second Time Only
- SmartShapes
- Alignment and Custom Shapes
- Part Extract and Printing
- Using FinaleScripts
- Libraries and Default files

PROJECT FILES: H. S. JAZZ BAND, H. S. JAZZ BAND BRASS

In the previous chapter, we created a simple leadsheet song for Guitar. Now we will use the melody and chords as the basis for a jazz ensemble score.

Open the file created in the previous chapter entitled "Lead Sheet" if it is not already open.

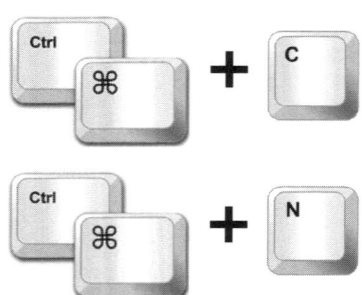

COPYING MUSIC FROM ONE DOCUMENT TO ANOTHER

1. Select the *Mass Edit* or *Selection* tool and click to the left of the first measure of the Guitar staff to select the entire staff throughout the score.

2. Now type **Ctrl/Command–C** to copy. (Make sure that the *Items to Copy* filter is set to *All* in both sections of the dialog. In Finale 2008, make sure *Edit* menu/Use *Filter* is unchecked.)

3. Now start a new document by typing **Ctrl/Command–N** for new document. This will launch the *Setup Wizard*.

4. In Finale 2008, select *Jazz Band Ensemble*. Then in *Document Styles,* select *Band Styles/Band (Jazz Font)*. Make sure the page orientation is set to *Landscape* for the score and *Portrait* for parts. Click *Next*.

Selecting an ensemble in the Setup Wizard

5. In Finale 2006–2007: In the *Setup Wizard* type in the name of the score, (**H. S. Jazz Band**), the composer (**Tom Carruth**) and copyright info. *Make sure* to set *Page Size* to *Landscape*.

    a. In Finale 2007, set the score to *Landscape* but leave the parts set to *Portrait*.

6. Click *Next*. On the second page, set *Instrument Set* to *SmartMusic SoftSynth*. If you have purchased the Garritan Big Band and Jazz set, then you may want to select instruments for that set.

7. **Using the Ensemble List in the Finale 2006–2007 Setup Wizard.** On the second page of the *Setup Wizard,* click the dropdown menu and select *Jazz Band* from the *Select an Ensemble* list.

    a. **Note:** Do not use the *Ensemble* list if you prefer using the VST/AU sounds, such as the Garritan Jazz and Big Band library of sounds.

    i. Select *Garritan Jazz* from the dropdown menu at the top of the *Setup Wizard*.

    ii. Select each sound as you normally would, *including* a Flute sound. (Trust me, you will need it later.)

8. The *Ensemble* list will populate the score staff list with the appropriate instrumentation. However, we need to make one change. This jazz band does not have a guitar player. (It may sound impossible, but it does happen).

    a. Scroll down the list on the right and select *Guitar*, then click *Remove*.

9. Click *Next*. You can save changes to this ensemble list or create a new list for future scores. For now, click *No*.

    a. Finish creating the score with the *Setup Wizard*.

        i. In Finale 2008, use the third page to enter the song title and composer.

        ii. Input time and key signatures (common time and concert F).

        iii. In Finale 2006–2007, *make sure* to select *Jazz Font* on the fourth page of the *Setup Wizard*.

    b. Click *Finish* to complete the *Setup Wizard*.

10. **Deleting Staves**. If you selected a Flute staff in the *Setup Wizard* because you were using the VST or AU sounds (such as the Garritan sounds), then you should delete the extra staff that was created for the Flute. We do not need a separate staff for Flute, so:

    a. Press **Esc** and double-click the staff name *Flute*.

    b. Click the first measure of the Flute staff and press **Delete**. (Trust me, you will find out later why we did this.) In Finale 2008, make sure the small handle is selected.

11. **Inserting Music**. Select the *Mass Edit* or *Selection* tool. Click in the first measure of the Alto 1 staff. On Windows, type **Ctrl–I** for *insert*. This shortcut doesn't work on Macintosh unless you have Finale 2008, so Macintosh users will need to select *Edit menu/Insert*. (You can always execute these commands from the *Mass Edit* or *Selection* tool contextual menu.)

12. **Transposing**. You may need to transpose the music up an octave, depending on what version of Finale you are using. If needed, use the *Mass Edit* or *Selection* tool and click to the left of the Alto Sax 1 staff to select, then press the correct *Metatool* (**8** for octave up as suggested above).

13. **Deleting Extra Measures**. After inserting the music, you will want to delete the extra measures at the end of the score. You have done this several times already.

    a. Type **Ctrl/Command–Page Down** to go to the next page. Do this until you see the end of the score. (You will see a key change with blank measures after it in this score).

    b. Select the *Mass Edit* or *Selection* tool and click in the first blank measure (where the key change is). In Finale 2008, double-click to select a stack. Type **Shift–Right Arrow** to select from this measure to the end of the score. (In Finale 2008, type **Shift–End**.)

    c. Press **Delete** to delete the extra measures. Type **Ctrl/Command–Page Up** to return to the first page.

    d. Make sure to save your work.

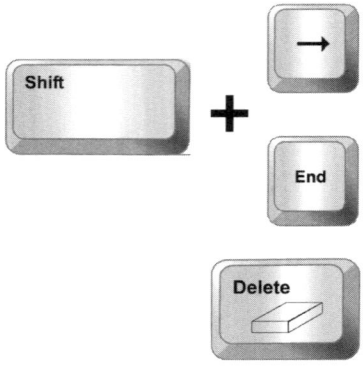

14. **Changing Measure Number Assignments**. The Finale default is to show measure numbers only at the beginning of each system. We may want them more often so we can find measures quickly.

    a. Select the *Measure* tool.

    b. Select *Measure* menu/*Measure Numbers/Edit Regions*. (In Finale 2008, select *Measure* menu/*Edit Measure Number Region*.)

    c. In the *Measure Numbers* dialog, under *Positioning and Display*, change the values as shown in the example below.

The Measure tool

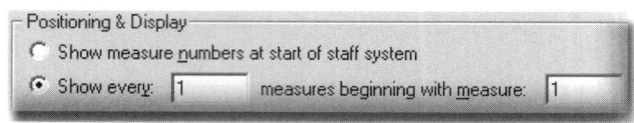

The Measure Numbers dialog

    d. If you prefer, you can move the default position of the measure numbers. I like them above the staff for this score.

e.   Click *Position* at the bottom right side of the dialog. Drag the measure number placeholder (the zero) to set the default position for all measure numbers relative to the staff.

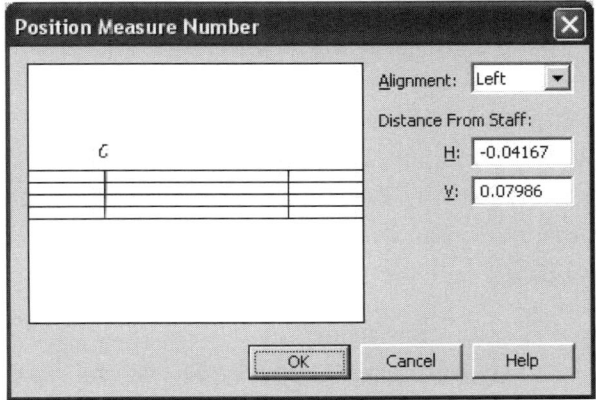

The Position Measure Number dialog

f.   Click *OK* to return to the score.

15. **Extracting the Melody Line**. Finally, we will remove all of the extra notes in the Sax part. We only want the top notes.

a.   Select the *Mass Edit* or *Selection* tool and select the entire Sax 1 staff (click to the left of the staff).

b.   Select *Plug-ins* menu/*TG tools/Process Extracted Parts*.

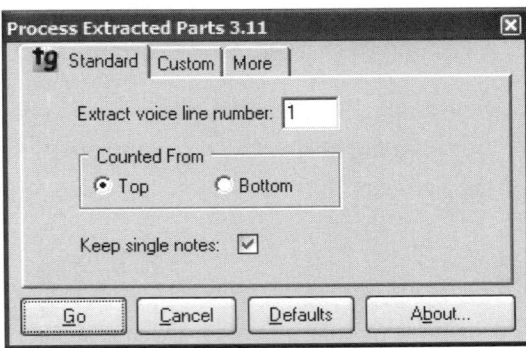

The Process Extracted Parts dialog

c.   Select *Counted From Top*, click *Go*, then *Close*.

SCROLL VIEW AND PAGE VIEW

Finale allows you to work in three different views: *Page View, Scroll View*, and *Studio View*. *Studio View* is useful when adjusting volume and other mixer functions, as well as using the *TempoTap* feature discussed

VIDEO
CLIP 7:1

STAFF SETS,
SMARTFIND AND PAINT,
ARTICULATION EDITING

in the previous choral project. *Page View* is the view in which we generally work. However, many Finale users like using *Scroll View* when working on large scores. *Scroll View* is displayed as music running in a continuous line without system breaks as in *Page View*. *Scroll View* will not always show the correct placement of items as *Page View* does. However, when working on large scores, *Scroll View* has a nice feature called *Staff Sets*. Using *Staff Sets,* you can view only the staves you want to work on with out having to concern yourself with other staves. For example, in the next section, you may want to try *Scroll View* as an optional way of working. Listed below are the instructions on how to access *Scroll View* and how to create a *Staff Set* for viewing only the Sax parts.

1. Select *View* menu/*Scroll View*. Note that you can also toggle between *Scroll View* and *Page View* using **Ctrl/Command–E**.

2. Once in *Scroll View*, you can scroll through the score using scroll bar at the bottom of the page or type **Ctrl/Command– Page Up** or **Ctrl/Command–Page Down** to scroll forward or backwards in the score. Press **Page Up** or **Page Down** without **Ctrl/ Command** to view staves higher or lower in the score.

CREATING A STAFF SET

The Staff tool

1. To view the Sax staves only, you can create a staff set of the Sax staves.

2. Click the *Staff* tool.

3. Select all of the handles you wish to include in the staff set. In this case you could simply drag a box around all five staff handles of the Sax part.

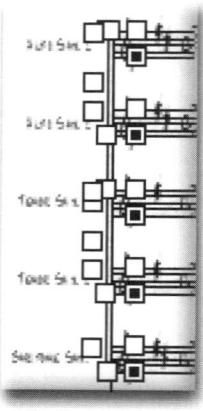

Selecting staff handles

4. Press and hold **Ctrl/Command,** then select *View* menu/ *Program Staff Sets/Set 1*. Make *sure* to press and hold **Ctrl/ Command** while selecting these menu items; otherwise, this will not work.

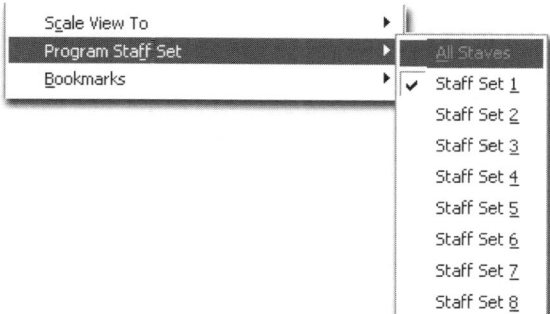

Selecting View menu/Program Staff Set/Staff Set 1

5. Now you should see only the Sax staves. You could program another set for the Trumpet section, the brass section, or the rhythm section. To choose the set you wish, select *View* menu/*Select Staff Set*. Note that if you do not press and hold **Ctrl/Command** while doing this, the menu item changes from *Program Staff Set* to *Select Staff Set*.

USING SMARTFIND AND PAINT

Before creating the other Sax parts, it would be smart to input the articulations and phrase markings into the Alto 1 part so they will transfer automatically when we create the other three Sax parts.

1. Zoom in (**Ctrl/Command–+** [the equal sign key]) and input the articulations and slurs into the Alto 1 staff. Stop when you get to the end of measure 6. Zoom out (**Ctrl/Command– –** [the minus key]).

2. Select the *Mass Edit* or *Selection* tool and select measures 5–6. The rhythm pattern here is repeated several times throughout the score, so you only need to input these performance markings once.

3. Right-click (**Control-click**) in the highlighted area and select *Set SmartFind Source*. In Finale 2008, select *Edit* menu/ *SmartFind and Paint/Set SmartFind Source Region*. (Note in the menu that you could have done this by typing **Ctrl/ Command–F** for *find*). This sets the rhythmic phrase for which Finale will look. Graphically, this action will place a box around each measure that is set as the source rhythmic area.

4. Type **Ctrl/Command–A** to select *all*.

5. Right-click (**Control-click**) in any measure in the Alto Sax 1 staff and select *Apply SmartFind and Paint*. In Finale 2008 select *Edit* menu/*SmartFind and Paint/Apply SmartFind Source Region*.

    a. Note that you could have typed **Ctrl/Command–Shift–F** to accomplish this.

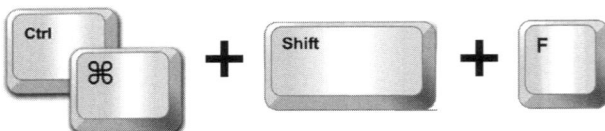

6. You will see the *SmartFind and Paint* dialog. The default is to copy all performance markings. You can select just the ones you want to copy and paint. For now, leave the default settings.

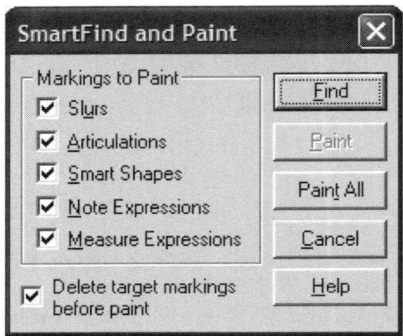

The SmartFind and Paint dialog

7. Click *Find*. Finale will highlight the next group of notes that are identical to the rhythmic content of the *SmartFind Source Region*. Click *Paint*. Finale paints the articulations and slurs onto this group. Then the selection moves to the next group of notes that are rhythmically identical to the source measures that we selected.

8. To quickly finish, click *Paint All*. Finale will paint articulations on all the remaining rhythmically identical phrases, then display how many times it did this.

9. To de-select the source measures, type **Ctrl/Command–F** again or right-click (**Control-click**) in a measure and select *Deselect SmartFind Source*. In Finale 2008 select *Edit* menu/*SmartFind and Paint/Deselect SmartFind Source Region*.

10. Input the markings for measures 7–8, set them as the source measures, and paint the markings to the other measures with like rhythmic content.

11. Do this also with measures 9–10.

12. Finish the performance markings (slurs and articulations) in the Alto 1 staff.

13. Imagine how much time this would save if you did have all of the Sax parts notated without the articulations and slurs!

14. **Adjusting Articulation Parameters**. **Note**: In this score, I prefer the accents to be inside the slurs.

    a. Press **Esc** and right-click (**Control–click**) on an accent.

    b. Select *Edit Articulation Definition*.

    c. In the bottom-left side of the dialog, select *Inside Slurs*.

    d. Take a minute to look at some of the other items available for articulation editing, including playback commands. Click *OK*.

15. Since the Sax will not be doing any Guitar bends, Press **Esc**, click the bend shape in measure 9 and press **Delete**. Do this for the bend in measure 21 as well.

AUTO HARMONIZING

VIDEO
CLIP 7:2

AUTO HARMONIZING AND
RHYTHM GENERATOR

Finale can do some auto-arranging for you. First we will use the *Band-in-a-Box* harmonizing function to harmonize the Saxophones.

1. Select the *Mass Edit* or *Selection* tool and click to the left of the Alto 1 staff to select it.

2. Select *Plug-ins* menu/*Scoring and Arranging/Band-in-a-Box Auto–Harmonizing*.

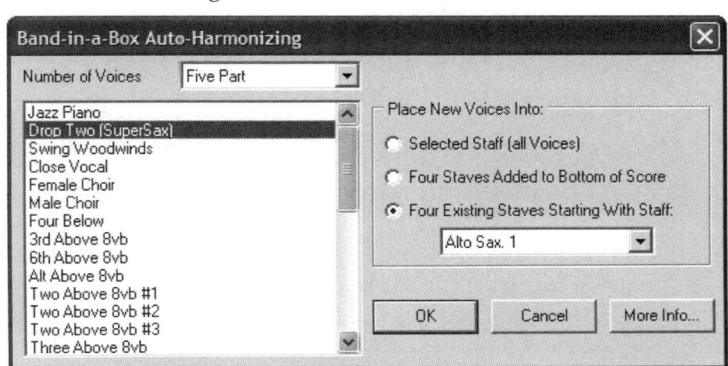

The Band-in-a-Box Auto-Harmonizing dialog

3. In the *Number of Voices* dropdown menu select *Five Part*.

4. In the *Style* pane to the left, select *Drop Two (SuperSax)*.

5. Under *Place New Voices Into,* click *Four Existing Staves, Starting With Staff* and select *Alto Sax 1* from the dropdown menu. Click *OK*.

6. This creates a five-part harmony in the Sax section. If you like it, great; if you don't, change it.

7. **Clearing Measures of Notes**. First, I like to have the Bari Sax follow the Trombone part. So clear the notes in the Bari Sax part. Later you can copy and re-pitch the notes from the Trombone part.

a. Select the *Mass Edit* or *Selection* tool and click to left of the Bari Sax staff. On Windows, press **Backspace**; on Macintosh, press **Clear**. (**Note**: Certain Macintosh laptops do not have a **Clear** key. In Finale 2006–2007, select *Mass Edit* menu/Clear Entries and SmartShapes; in Finale 2008, select *Edit* menu/*Clear All Items*.

8. Clear the notes in the Alto 2 and Tenor 2 parts, measures 1–3. (They are rhythmically different.) Input notes for measures 1–3 in the Alto 2 and Tenor 2 staves as shown in the finished example.

9. **Courtesy Accidentals**. Remember that, in the Alto 2 staff, the second measure starts with a C♯. To force a courtesy accidental, select the note using the *Simple Entry* or *Selection* tool and press **P** for *p*arenthesize accidental.

10. **Re-pitch the Notes**. This step is optional. If you want the notes in the Sax parts to be correct as shown in the PDF example, re-pitch them using the *Re-pitch* tool. Since you have already done this a few times, just move on to the next step for now.

a. Click the first note of measure 3 on the Alto 2 staff and re-pitch the notes either by typing note names or playing the correct notes on a MIDI keyboard as shown in the finished example.

b. **Note**: Grace notes do not re-pitch. Use **Up Arrow** and **Down Arrow** to re-pitch them.

c. Watch out. In measure 25 the Altos rest, but the Tenors do not. Put those notes in separately.

11. Re-pitch the two Tenor Sax parts.

AUTO RHYTHM SECTION

The *Auto Rhythm Section* plug-in can be useful for many projects. When I created this song originally, I created my own rhythm section, but to speed the project along, we will let the *MIBAC Rhythm Section Generator* plug-in create these parts for us. Of course, keep in mind that you can change any area you like.

Note: In the Macintosh Universal Binary version of Finale 2007–2008, this plug-in is not available. You can, however, use the *Drum Grove* plug-in for the percussion. You may need to input the Piano and Bass manually.

1. Select *Mass Edit* or *Selection* tool and select the top staff (Alto 1) again. Click measure 5, type **Shift–Right Arrow**. (In Finale 2008, type **Shift–End**.) This selects from measure 5 to the end of the score on that staff.

2. Select *Plug-ins* menu/*Scoring and Arranging/MIBAC Jazz Rhythm Section Generator*.

The MIBAC Jazz Rhythm Section Generator dialog

3. In the *Style* dropdown menu, select *Swing*.

4. Under *Generate*, for *Piano* select *Notation w/Chord Symbols*; for *Bass*, *Notation*; and for *Drum Set*, *Notation w/Percussion Map*.

5. Under *Place Music Into*, select *Existing Staves as Specified*.

   a. For *Piano,* select *Staff 14* (or *Staff 15* if you started with Garritan Jazz). This is the Piano treble clef staff in this score.

   b. For *Bass,* select *Bass*.

   c. For *Drum Set,* select *Drum Set*.

6. Click *OK*.

7. You will see notes in the Piano, Bass, and Drum staves.

8. **Using the Clear Items Filter**. Now we need to clear the chords on the Alto Sax 1 staff.

   a. Select the *Mass Edit* or *Selection* tool and click to the left of the Alto Sax 1 staff.

   b. Right-click (**Control-click**) in the highlighted area.

   c. Select *Clear Items*. (In Finale 2008, select *Edit Filter*.)

   d. Click both of the *None* buttons. (In Finale 2008, there is only one *None* button.)

   e. Click *Chords*. (In Finale 2008, click *Chords and Fretboards*.)

   f. Click *OK*.

9. The *Rhythm Section Generator* selected a different clef for the Drum Set staff than is in the Jazz Font Default file. To make this the same as the clef in measure 1:

   a. **Deleting or Changing a Clef**. (**Note**: In Finale 2008, this may not be necessary.) Press **Esc** and double-click the clef sign in the Drum Set staff at the end of measure 4.

   b. Select the clef that matches the clef in measure 1.

   c. Click *OK*. This deletes the clef, since there is no clef change.

10. The Piano part is all in the treble clef. It will be easier to read if it is divided between treble and bass.

    a. **Splitting Notes on a Grand Staff**. Using the *Mass Edit* tool, click to the left of the treble Piano staff, then press and hold **Shift** and click to the left of the bass Piano staff. This selects both staves.

    b. Select *Plug-ins* menu/*TG tools*/*Smart Split Point*. Note the options for keyboard staff-splitting. For now, click *Go*, then click *Close to* return to the score.

11. The *Smart Split Point* plug-in does not always split notes tied over bar lines correctly. Note this in measures 5–6 as well as others. If the plug-in is applied to measure 6 separately, the plug-in will split this correctly.

   a. Select both staves of the grand staff for measure 6.

   b. Select *Plug-ins* menu/*TG tools/Smart Split Point*.

   c. Click *Go*, but *do not* click *Close*.

   d. Select the grand staff for other measures you want to correct and then click *Go*. Continue this throughout the score where you need to fix the split-point for tied notes. Then click *Close* to exit the plug-in.

12. The *Auto Rhythm Section* plug-in sometimes turns off the Human Playback function since it already has its own playback style programmed into the notation. For this score, this is not what we want, because it will cause the other instruments to not swing, nor will any of the performance markings work correctly. There is a way to have *both* the MIDI information created by the plug-in *and* Human Playback work together.

   a. **Turning on Human Playback**. In the playback controls, click the speaker icon on Windows, or the dropdown expand button on Macintosh to reveal the playback options.

   b. Click *HP Preferences*.

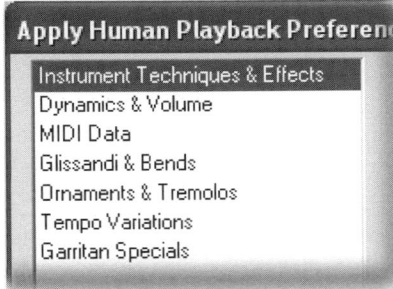

The Human Playback Preferences dialog

   c. In Finale 2007–2008, also select *MIDI Data* from the left-hand column of the dialog.

   d. **Human Playback Settings**. Under User MIDI Data, set all four popup menus to *HP (Incorporate Data)*. This way Finale will use both MIDI data and the playback interpretation that Human Playback provides.

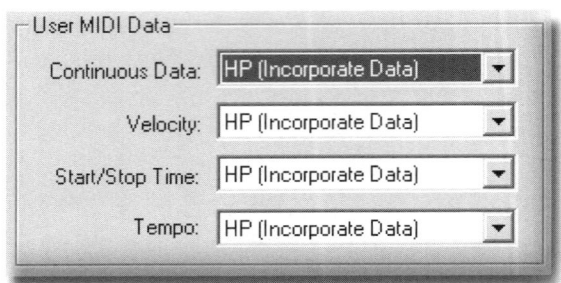

The User MIDI Data dialog

e. Click *Save & Close*. In Finale 2007–2008, check the box next to *Attach to Active File* in the lower-left corner, then click *Save & Close*.

f. From the *Human Playback Style* dropdown menu, select *Jazz*. Then return to the score.

13. Input the notes for the Piano and Bass staves as shown in the finished example for the first four measures.

VIDEO
CLIP 7:3

TREMELOS,
STAFF STYLES,
AND EXPLODE MUSIC

CREATING A TREMOLO

In the Piano part, measures 34–35 have tremolo chords. This is easy to create in Finale.

1. Since these are whole notes, first input notes that are of half that value. Input the notes into these measures as shown in the example below.

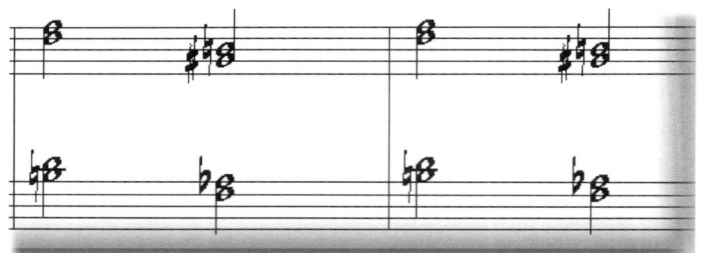

Creating a tremolo

2. Select the *Mass Edit* or *Selection* tool and select both measures in both staves.

3. Select *Plug-ins* menu/*TG tools*/*Easy Tremolo*.

4. Click *Go* and then *Close*.

EXTRA CREDIT
SECTION

TREMOLO STYLES

The plug-in you just used to create the tremolo notation has two styles. If using whole note notation, the tremolo beams are inside the whole notes. If you were to use any other beamed tremolo notation, such as half note notation, the plug-in creates the connected-beam tremolo style shown in example A below. You may prefer other styles of tremolo with beams that are disconnected from the stem like example B below.

Example A
Connected-beam tremolo style

Example B
Disconnected-beam tremolo style

You can purchase the full set of TGtools plug-ins that will automatically create the disconnected-beam tremolo style from *www.tgtools.com*. But if you are short of cash or do not use this function much, you can alter the tremolo style created by the plug-in that comes with Finale.

Try this: Find an empty measure for a temporary experiment. Input two quarter notes, then apply the tremolo plug-in as described above.

After running the plug-in as described above:

1. Click the *Special Tools* icon. On Windows select *Window* menu/ *Advanced Tool Palette*.

2. From the palette that displays when you select *Special* Tools, click the *Beam Extension* tool.

3. Click the measure that you want to edit. You will see handles for the beams.

4. Double-click the first handle. You will see the dialog in the example below.

The Special Tools icon

The Beam Extension tool

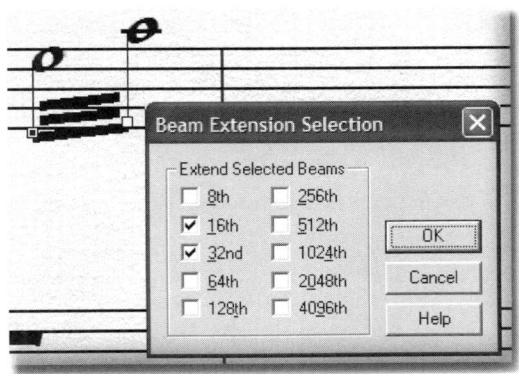

The Beam Extension Selection dialog

5. Select the beams you want to separate from the stems. In this example, that would be the sixteenth and thirty-second-note beams. Click *OK*.

6. Click the handle and drag or press **Left Arrow** and **Right Arrow** to adjust the distance of separation between stems and beams.

BACK TO THE PROJECT

CREATING SLASH NOTATION

Starting with measure 5 in the Percussion stave, we want to change the notation to slash notation. This is done easily with a staff style.

1. **Using Staff Styles**. Press **Esc**, then double-click the staff name *Drum Set*.

2. Click measure 5 of the Drum staff. Type **Shift–Right Arrow**. (In Finale 2008, type **Shift–End**.) (Remember, this selects from the selected measure to the end of the score.)

3. Right-click (**Control-click**) in the highlighted area and select *Slash Notation*. **Note**: In Finale 2007, there are two choices for *Slash Notation*. Use the first or top choice in the contextual menu.

4. When you do this, you may see a blue line above the Drum Set staff. This is to remind you that there is a staff style applied to this area. If you wish not to see the blue line, Select *Staff* menu/*Show Staff Styles* to uncheck this option.

5. **Altering a Staff Style**. This will work great for the Drum part, with one exception: There are a few places in the Drum staff where we need cue notes for specific hits. These notes are not in Layer 1. The *Slash Notation* staff style hides all layers by default, so we would not see the cue notes.

    a. In Finale 2007, you will not need to make this alteration if you selected the first *Slash Notation* option. However, you may want to follow the next instructions just to become familiar with staff-style editing.

    b. With the *Staff* tool still selected (this tool was selected when you double-clicked the staff name *Drum Set*), select any measure in the Drum Set staff.

c. Right-click (**Control-click**) in the highlighted area.

d. Select *Define Staff Style*.

e. Make sure *01. Slash Notation* is listed at the top.

f. In the *Define Staff Style* dialog click *Select* next to *Alternate Notation*.

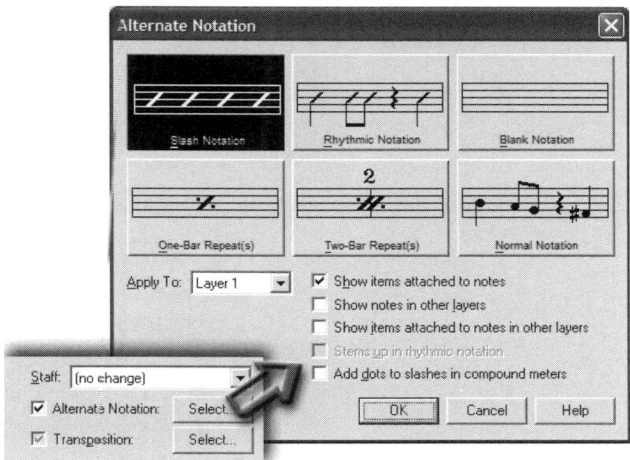

The Alternate Notation dialog

g. Check the box next to *Show Notes in Other Layers*.

h. Click *OK* to return to the score.

Teacher, I Have a Question

What if I am trying to input chords over slash notation where there are no notes to which to attach chords to? This is a common request. You do need an entry (note or rest) to which to attach chords. In 4/4 time, you could input four quarter rests into the first measure, copy them over thirty times for thirty measures (use paste multiple in Finale 2008), then attach the chords to them and apply the *Slash Notation* staff style over those measures.

EXTRA CREDIT
SECTION

EDITING KEYBOARD SPLIT POINTS

The *Smart Split Point* plug-in does a nice overall split-point adjustment, but it is not perfect (sorry, it cannot read your mind). If you like, you can try this plug-in again with different settings. There is also a plug-in that allows you to set a fixed note from which to split the staves, but you will generally find there will be one or two places you where want to manually split notes. If editing keyboard notation is something you may need to do in the future, then you will want to learn this procedure.

The Note Mover tool

1. On Windows, select *Windows* menu/*Advanced Tool Palette*. (The *Advanced* tools are already in the main tool palette on Macintosh.)

2. Click the *Note Mover* tool.

3. In the *Note Mover* menu, make sure that *Delete after Merge* is selected.

4. Zoom in. Click in the staff of the measure you want to change.

5. Drag a box around the handles of the notes you want to move.

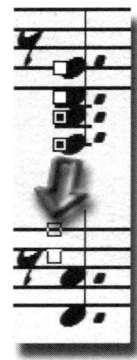

Moving notes with the Note Mover tool

6. Click and drag any of the selected notes into the desired staff and release. No need to place them in the correct position on the staff; anywhere in that staff will do. Finale knows what notes they are.

BACK TO THE PROJECT

Before going on, copy measures 1–4 in the Bass staff to the Drum Set staff. The notes will show in the Drum Set staff on ledger lines two octaves below the staff. This will be explained in the next section on Percussion Mapping.

PERCUSSION

We will cover Percussion Mapping in more detail in another assignment later in this book. For now, we need to understand how the percussion map works, then learn how to edit the percussion map later.

In notation software, a map has to be used to translate on-staff pitches into MIDI note assignments. For example, in a General MIDI system such as the *SmartMusic SoftSynth* used in Finale, the Bass Drum is mapped to the low C two octaves below middle C on a MIDI keyboard. But on the staff, it is placed in the F space of the treble clef staff. (This is the default, which can be changed, as we will learn later.) When you copied the notes from the bass clef to the drum clef, Finale placed the notes many ledger lines below the staff. That is because these pitches have not been mapped for the Drum Set.

If you have a MIDI keyboard, this is easy to fix. We want to have the Bass Drum, Snare Drum, and Crash Cymbal play on each of these quarter note hits.

The Re-pitch tool

1. Click the *Re-pitch* tool in the *Simple Note Entry* palette. Click in the staff lines of the Drum Set staff above the first note.

2. The MIDI note for Bass drum is C, two octaves below middle C (number 36 in MIDI). The MIDI note for snare drum is D, one full step above the Bass drum note (MIDI note 38). The crash cymbal note that we want to use is C♯ (MIDI note 49), a major seventh above the snare drum note.

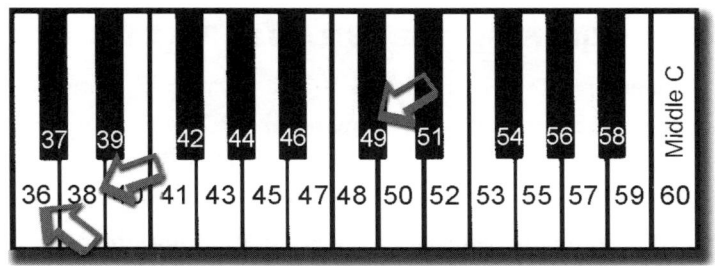

MIDI keyboard note assignments for percussion sounds

3. Press all three of these keys together to input the notes for these sounds on all of the pitches in the first four measures of the Drum Set staff.

4. If you are not using a MIDI keyboard, this can be a bit time-consuming, but not too difficult.

5. Click the *Re-pitch* tool as described above.

6. Click next to the stem of the first note *in* the Drum Set staff. (Click above the note head in the staff area.)

7. Type **F**. This inputs the Bass Drum. Type **5** on the numrow to add a fifth above that (on laptops, type **F5**). Then press **+** (the equal sign key) once (explanation follows).

8. Now type **6** (on laptops, type **F6**) to add a sixth to above the C. You should have these notes in the first measure of the drum part. Repeat this for the fourth beat.

9. Now repeat this for measures 2–3, or just highlight measure 1 with the *Mass Edit* or *Selection* tool, drag it to measures 2 and 3, and then change measure 4.

Teacher, I Have a Question

When I input a note on the C space for Snare Drum, why do I get a side stick sound instead? This is a very common question. The default sound for the C space is a side stick sound. If you input this note, then type **+** (the equal sign key), it will choose the next available sound for that space, which is Snare Drum. There is a way to turn off the side stick so Snare Drum *will* be the default sound for the C space. See Percussion Mapping in the next chapter.

EXPLODING THE BRASS PARTS

Open and print the PDF file "H. S. Brass Parts." Starting on measure 16, input all the Trumpet notes shown in the PDF example into the Trumpet 1 staff and all of the Trombone notes into the Trombone 1 staff. Use the note input method most comfortable to you. Once you have done this, use the following steps to separate the notes into the correct parts.

1. Using the *Mass Edit* or *Selection* tool, click to the left of the Trumpet 1 staff.

2. Right-click (**Control-click**) on the highlighted area and select *Utilities/Explode*. In Finale 2008, select *Utilities* menu/*Explode Music*. If you find yourself using this function often, you may want to remember that the shortcut key for this menu is 2. Select the area and type **2** on the numrow.

3. Set the dialog as shown in the example on the following page. Set the *Split Into* field to four staves. At the bottom in the *Place Music Into* area, select *Existing staves starting with staff* and select *Trumpet in* (the first Trumpet staff below the Bari Sax staff).

4. Click *OK*.

5. Now repeat this for the Trombone parts, selecting Trombone 1 as the value for the *Existing staves starting with staff* dropdown menu.

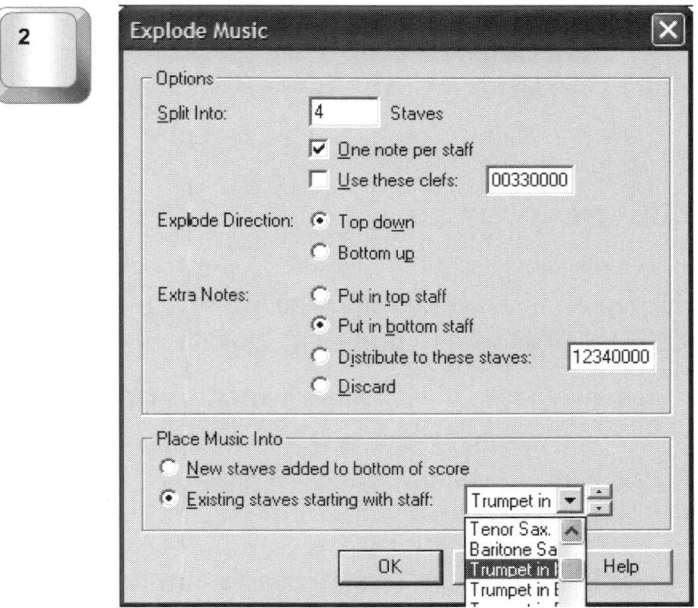

The Explode Music dialog and shortcut key

6. The explode feature works well when there are enough notes in the chord to divide between the number of splits or staves you select. If you split into four staves but some of the chords only have three notes, as in measure 17 of the Trumpet part, Finale will distribute them into the first three staves selected and leave the bottom staff with rests for those chords. It is easy to copy the notes you want from one staff to another to fix this.

   a. Select *Edit* menu/*Partial Measure Select*. (In Finale 2008, this is not necessary. To select a partial measure, simply drag-select the part of the measure you want to select).

   b. Select the last quarter note in measure 16 of the Trumpet 3 staff and drag-copy to the last quarter beat in measure 16 of the Trumpet 4 staff.

   c. Repeat this procedure for any other notes that need to be copied or doubled, such as the eighth notes in measure 22 of the Trombone part.

   d. **Note**: You can also explode parts by copying all notes to all parts, then use the *Process Extracted Parts* plug-in as we did in the last project. This can automatically double single notes.

7. Finish the brass parts in measures 1–4. Use copy and paste as much as possible. Copy the Trombone 4 part to the Bari Sax staff and re-pitch the Bari Sax part.

VIDEO
CLIP 7:4

GRACE NOTES
AND CUE NOTES

GRACE NOTES

Since measure 17 is a full measure, you will not be able to input notes and turn them into grace notes. You will need to lock in the grace notes and use the mouse-click method to input these.

1. In the *Simple Note Entry* palette, click the *Grace Note* icon. If you like the idea of using the *Selection* tool, press **Esc**, double-click a note in measure 17, then type **Ctrl/Command–G** to lock in grace notes.

2. Zoom in on the Trumpet parts at measure 17.

3. Press **4** for eighth notes and click in the desired grace notes.

   a. If you miss the correct pitch, just press **Up Arrow** and **Down Arrow** to correct your mistakes.

4. In this case, there are two grace notes right at the beginning of the measure. Input the second grace note first. This makes it easier to place the first note before it.

   a. **Note**: Sometimes this can look strange, as grace notes may overlap other grace notes. Press **Up Arrow** and **Down Arrow** to change the pitch and the spacing will correct itself.

5. Exit grace note lock-in mode the way you entered this mode: Click the grace note icon to de-select it, or just press a note duration key twice.

CREATING CUE NOTES

There are several places in the score where we have cue notes. Basic cue notes are very easy to create using the *Cue Notes* plug-in.

1. Using the *Mass Edit* or *Selection* tool, select measure 23 in the Alto 1 staff.

2. Select *Plug-ins* menu/*Scoring and Arranging/Add Cue Notes*.

3. In the *Add Cue Notes* dialog select the Trumpet 1–4 staves. Click Trumpet 1 in the *Add cue notes to the following staves* list, press and hold **Shift**, and click Trumpet 4.

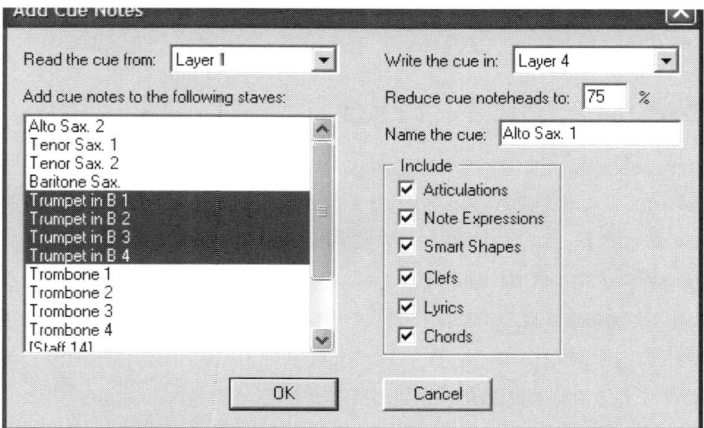

The Add Cue Notes dialog

4. Note that these cue notes will be in Layer 4.

5. Click *OK*.

6. These cue notes will sound during playback, which you probably do not want. You can turn off Layer 4 in each of the Trumpet staves in the *Instrument List*, but since we do not want Layer 4 to play in any staff, we can turn this off globally (for the entire score).

    a. Select *Options* menu/*Document Options* or *Document* menu/ *Document Options*.

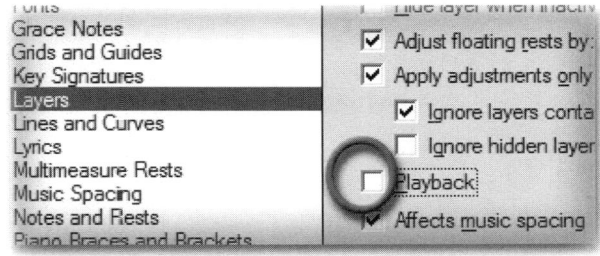

The Layers pane in the Document Options dialog

    b. Click *Layers*.

    c. Select *Layer 4* from the dropdown menu.

    d. Clear the checkbox next to *Playback*.

    e. Press *OK*.

DRUM CUE NOTES

Now we are going to create cue notes for the hits in the Drum Set. Ultimately, as you can see in the finished example, the drum part will be primarily slash notation with the shots in cue notes. These cue notes are above the staff and have no ledger lines. Also, they are single-pitch notes and do not sound; they are just for visual rhythmic representation. This is quite common in jazz charts. You could input notes directly into Layer 3 in the percussion staff, but you can also create them from other staves that have the correct rhythm—whichever method is most efficient for you. Here you will learn to copy notes from the Trombone 4 staff, since they are rhythmically correct for the cue notes.

1. Using the *Mass Edit* tool, select from measure 17 to the end in the Trombone 4 staff. (Type **Shift–Right Arrow**. In Finale 2008, type **Shift–End**).

2. Right-click (**Control-click**) and select *Move/Copy Layers*.

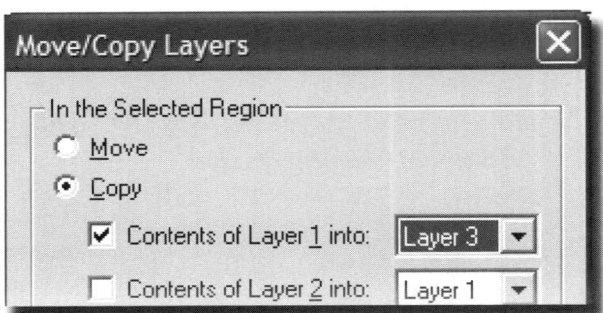

The Move/Copy Layers dialog

3. Click *Copy* and in the *Contents of Layer 1 into* dropdown menu, select *Layer 3*.

4. Click *OK*.

5. Select *Options* menu/*Show Active Layer Only* or *Document* menu/*Show Active Layer Only*. (I use this function quite often, so I have memorized the key command. It is to the right of the menu command. On Windows, select *Window* menu/*View Menu Toolbar* to get an icon to click. Either of these methods is faster than selecting from the menu.)

The Active Layer icon

6. Select *Layer 3* in the *Layers* popup menu at the bottom-left of the screen. Do not be alarmed, your music wasn't erased; you are just working on Layer 3 only right now.

7. Drag the highlighted measures to the Drum Set staff to copy them.

8. With the measures still selected in the Trombone 4 staff, press **Backspace** or **Clear** to clear these notes from the Trombone 4 staff. (Macintosh laptops do not have a **Clear** key. Use the *Mass Edit* menu instead.)

9. Click to the left of the Drum Set staff to select it.

10. Select *Plug-ins* menu/*Note, Beam, and Rest Editing/Single Pitch*. Set the pitch to C6 (because this pitch will display correctly on the percussion staff) and click *OK*.

11. With the Drum Set staff still selected, Select *Plug-ins* menu/*Note, Beam, and Rest Editing/Ledger Lines (Hide)*.

12. With the Drum Set staff *still* selected, right-click (**Control-click**) in the highlighted area and select *Change/Note Size*. Set the size to 75%. (In Finale 2008, select *Utilities* menu/*Change/Note Size*.)

13. Select *Options* menu/*Document Options* or *Document* menu/*Document Options*. Click *Layers*. In the *Settings For* dropdown menu, select *Layer 3*. Here you can change the behavior of Layer 3 for the entire document. Set this dialog as shown in the example below. We want stems up always; we also want the rests moved up six lines and spaces so they will display in the same area that the notes will show. And we want to disable playback. Press *OK*.

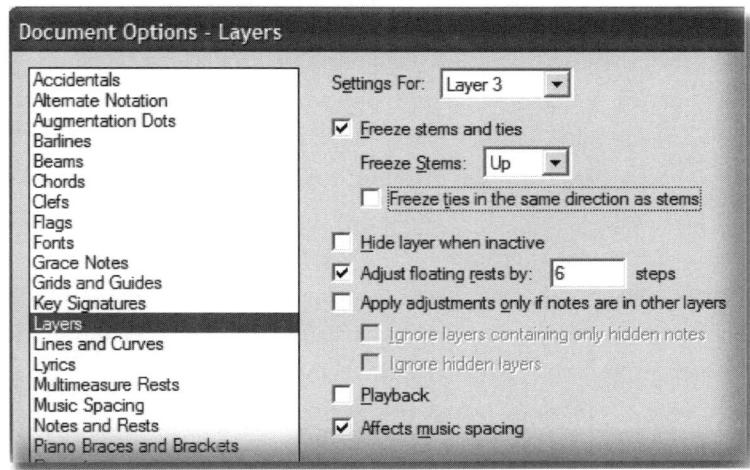

The Layers pane of the Document Options dialog

14. In the Drum Set staff, clear the measures in which you do not want cue notes. Use the *Mass Edit* or *Selection* tool and clear measures 20–22, 25, and 34 to the end in the Drum Set staff. (Do not worry; this will only clear Layer 3, not the notes in Layer 1).

15. Hide any rests you do not want to see. For example, in measure 19, we want to hide the final rest.

   a. Press the **Esc** key and double-click the dotted-half rest.

   b. Press H for *h*ide.

16. Select *Options* menu/*Show Active Layer Only* or *Document* menu/*Show Active Layer Only* to turn off this feature and see the final results.

17. This may change the music spacing in other staves.

   a. Select the *Mass Edit* or *Selection* tool.

   b. Type **Ctrl/Command–A** to select *all*.

   c. Type numrow **4** to re-space the music.

18. Return to Layer 1 using the numbers in the lower left corner or the dropdown menu in the lower left corner.

BACK TO THE **PROJECT**

VIDEO CLIP 7:5

BRASS ARTICULATIONS AND INSTRUMENT DOUBLING

The Articulation tool

INPUTTING THE BRASS ARTICULATIONS (PROGRAMMING SHORTCUTS)

Some people like to input all articulations, then all expressions, then all SmartShapes. I find this to be more work. I like to input the performance markings for a page, or whatever I can see on the screen. Use the *Selection* tool to access the different tools; it is faster to switch between tools and helps to keep your focus on the score, not on tools and menus.

As you input articulations for the brass part, note that the fall-off symbol is an articulation. (You can also use a SmartShape for this, but the shape is more consistent if you use an articulation. Human Playback will recognize both.) Since we have this symbol in several places, we will create a *Metatool* shortcut key for it. *Metatools* always speed up your work in Finale.

1. Press **Esc** and double-click any articulation, or click the *Articulation* tool, whichever you find faster.

2. Go to measure 17 and click the first note in the Trumpet 1 staff. In the *Articulation Selection* dialog, we are going to use articulation number 65. Note that there is no *Metatool* key assignment for this articulation. A letter or number in parentheses in the top right-hand corner of the box indicates that there is a Metatool key assignment (and what it is).

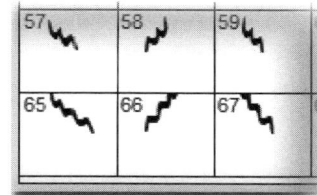

The Articulation Selection dialog

3. Take a quick look at the keys that are already assigned to other symbols. Perhaps you would like to use F for *fall-off*, but notice that F is already assigned to the fermata symbol. Since there are no fermatas in this score, we will use F.

4. Click *Cancel* to return to the score.

5. Type **Shift–F**. The *Articulation Selection* dialog opens again.

6. Double-click articulation number 65 (the fall-off symbol).

7. Now you can use this Metatool key assignment to input the fall-off for measure 17. Zoom out (**Ctrl/Command– –** [the minus key]) and scroll down a bit so you can see all the brass parts.

8. Press and hold **F** and drag a marquee around the first note in measure 17 in all the brass parts, then release. **Note**: Dragging from the bottom (Trombone 4) to the top makes it easier to select because the Trumpet note is too close to the Bari Sax note.

9. This will input the fall-off symbol, but it might not be positioned correctly. Drag a box around all the handles of the fall-off symbols to select them.

10. Now use arrow keys to position them as shown in the final example.

11. It is best to input accents *after* the fall-offs. Accents do not need manual positioning, so they will not need to be selected. This makes it much easier to drag a marquee to select the fall-offs.

12. Now press and hold **A** for *accent* and drag a marquee around the first note in all of the brass parts again.

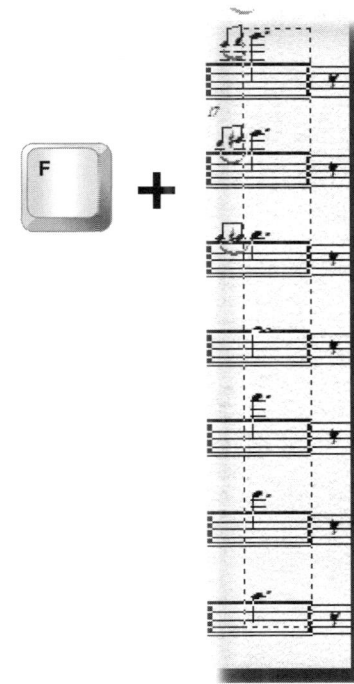

Selecting the brass parts to apply an articulation with a Metatool shortcut

13. **Note**: Had we input the articulations before we exploded the brass parts, the articulations would have been done for all parts, but this is good practice using *Metatool* input.

14. In measure 22, the Trombones have a fall-off as well. Dragging a marquee around all four notes using the fall-off *Metatool* will not work, because the note is tied from the previous measure. You will need to press and hold **F** and click each note individually. Generally, an articulation is only applied to the first note of the tied figure. In this case we need it to be on the second note.

INSTRUMENT DOUBLING

In jazz and musical theater scores, it is common for the woodwinds to double on instruments. In the Alto 1 part, measures 17–20 are played on Flute. Of course, in a real score, we would find a place that has rests before and after the instrument change to give the performer time to change instruments, but in this project file, we do not have that luxury. This involves two steps. First we will do the transposition from the key of E♭ to C. This is easily done using a staff style. Then we will create some expressions to switch from the Sax to the Flute and back.

The Staff tool

1. Press **Esc**, then double-click the staff name Alto Sax 1 (A Sax 1) or click the *Staff* tool.

2. Select measures 17–20.

3. Right-click (**Control–click**) in the highlighted area and select *Flute Transposition*.

4. This part needs to be transposed up an octave. With the measures still selected, click the *Mass Edit* or *Selection* tool.

5. If you have programmed key **9** to transpose up an octave as we did in the previous project, type **9** and you are done!

   a. Right-click (**Control–click**) in the highlighted region and select *Transposition*.

   b. From the dialog, select *Up* and *Octave* for the interval.

   c. You may want to review the chapter about assigning keys **6–9** for transposition.

6. Now we will change the sound to a Flute at measure 17 and back to Sax at measure 21. This can be done two ways:

   a. Press **Esc**. Double-click the first note in measure 17 of the Alto 1 staff (temporarily the Flute staff now).

   b. Type **X** for expression, then press **Enter**.

   c. We need to create an expression, but remember, it is easier to duplicate, then edit, rather than create from scratch.

   d. Click the expression *Rock*, then click *Duplicate* (**P**). Now click *Edit* (**E**). (The shortcuts are for Windows only.)

   e. Change the text from *Rock* to *To Flute*.

7. If you are using a General MIDI device, such as the SmartMusic SoftSynth from the *Setup Wizard*, follow these instructions; if not, go on to step 8.

   a. Click the *Playback* tab at the top.

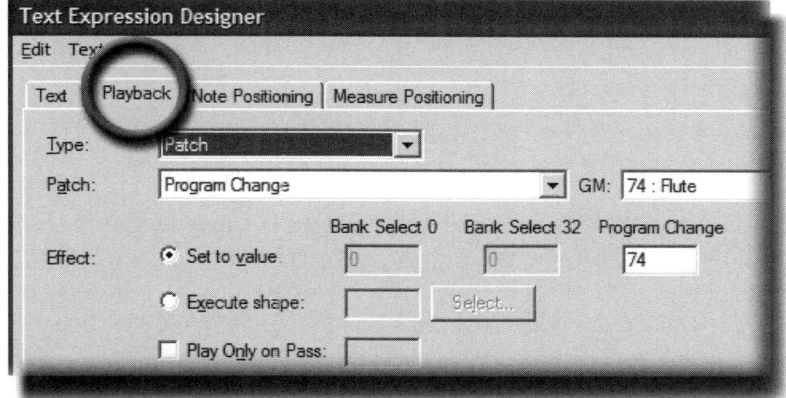

   The Playback tab in the Text Expression Designer dialog

   b. Set the *Type* dropdown menu to *Patch*.

   c. Set the *GM* dropdown menu to *74: Flute*.

8. Click *OK* then *Select* to return to the score.

9. Press and hold **Ctrl/Option** and click the first note (not the grace note) in measure 21 of the Alto 1 staff. Press **X**, then **Enter**.

10. Duplicate the expression *To Flute*, then click *Edit* and change the text to *Back to Alto Sax*.

    a. Again, if using General MIDI, click the *Playback* tab and change the GM dropdown menu to *66: Alto Sax*.

    b. Click *OK* then *Select* or press **Enter**.

11. See below for a way to change sounds using layers. This is best way to do this if you are using VST/AU sounds like the Garritan Jazz and Big Band set of sounds or the new Garritan Sounds for Finale in Finale 2008.

EXTRA CREDIT SECTION

ANOTHER METHOD FOR CHANGING SOUNDS IN A STAFF

The method described above using program changes works great if you are using General MIDI instruments, like the SmartMusic SoftSynth in Finale. But if you are using the Garritan Jazz and Big Band set of sounds or other VST/AU sounds, this system of program changes will not work. Also, if you are creating a percussion staff that has pitched and non-pitched percussion in the same staff, the program-change method will not work.

In these cases, it is best to put the notes for the new instrument on a different layer. Try this exercise:

1. Using the *Mass Edit* or *Selection* tool, select measures 17–20 in the Alto 1 staff (the Flute section).

2. Right-click (**Control-click**) and select *Move/Copy Layers*. We used this function before when creating cue notes for the percussion staff, but this time we are going to move notes from one layer to another, rather than copying as we did before.

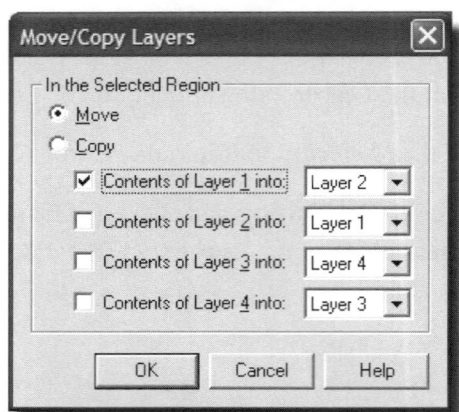

The Move/Copy Layers dialog

3. In the *Move/Copy Layers* dialog, click *Move*, then check the box next to *Contents of Layer 1 into*. In the dropdown menu on this line, select *Layer 2* then Click *OK*.

4. Now we need to assign the Flute sound to Layer 2 in the Alto 1 staff. Select *Window* menu/*Instrument List*.

R	Staff Name	M	S	Vol.	Pan	Instrument	Chan.
▲				93	40	Alto Sax ▼	1
	Layer 1			93	40	Alto Sax ▼	1
	Layer 2			93	40	Alto Sax ▼	1

The Instrument List dialog

5. In the previous project, we created some new instruments with new channels. Since we started this score with the Setup Wizard and included a Flute sound, the instrument is already created.

6. Click the expand button to the left of Alto Sax 1. This opens up all layers for that staff. Now you can set instruments for each layer independently.

7. In the Instrument column, click the dropdown list next to Alto Sax on the Layer 2 row. Select Flute from this list. This is why we created a Flute staff at the beginning of this project. Otherwise, we would have had to create a Flute instrument at this point.

8. Close this dialog to return to the score.

BACK TO THE PROJECT ↰

EXPRESSION STAFF LISTS

In large ensemble scores in which you want the same expression for several instruments, it is more efficient to use a Staff List rather than assign each expression individually to a staff. We used this method in the choral score before.

In measures 13–15 of the Sax parts and several places throughout the score, the expressions are measure-attached. Remember, for a measure-attached expression, double-click in the measure using the cursor that *does not* have the small note attached to it.

The Expression tool

1. Click the *Expression* tool, or press **Esc** and double-click an existing expression (like the text, *Back to Alto Sax*, that we just created).

2. Double-click before the first note in measure 13 to input a measure expression (remember, there should be no small note on the cursor).

3. Select the expression *ff*. You can either double-click the expression in the list, or single-click it, then click *Select*.

4. In the *Measure Expression Assignment* dialog, click *Staff List* and select *New Staff List* from the dropdown menu. The *Staff List* dialog appears. In Finale 2008, if you selected the *Band (Jazz Font)* document style as instructed at the beginning of this project, you do *not* need to create this staff list. Finale 2008 creates staff lists automatically based on instrument groupings. The Sax section (WW list) and Brass section staff lists are selectable from this dropdown menu. If you need to create a staff list or alter one, follow these instructions:

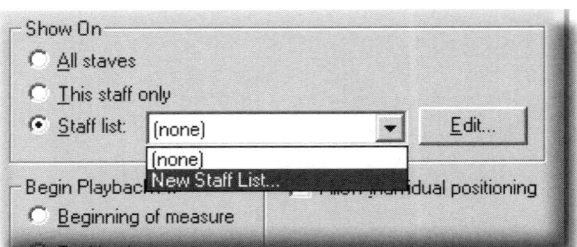

Creating a new staff list in the Measure Expression Assignment dialog

5. In the *List Name* text field, type **Sax Section**. Once this list has been created, you will be able to use it for other expressions that you want to assign only to the Sax section. Next time this Staff List will be available from the dropdown menu in the *Measure Expression Assignment* dialog, where you selected *New Staff List*.

6. In the *Staff List* dialog, click the name of each instrument to which you want to assign this expression. This places an X in both the *Score* and *Parts* columns.

   a. Suppose you want to see Sax expressions in the score only on the Alto 1 part, but want to see them in each extracted part. Click the X in the *Score* column that is next to the parts on which you do not want to see expressions in the score; this removes the X. Leave the X in the *Parts* column.

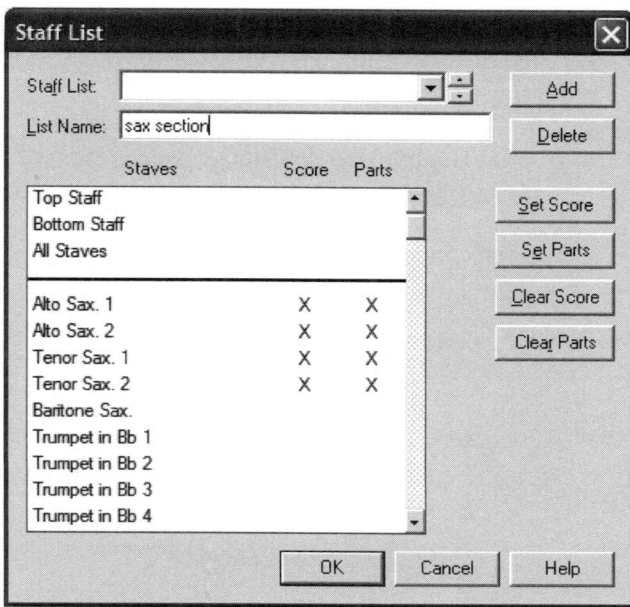

The Staff List dialog

b. Here is a quick way to create a rehearsal mark or tempo expression. Click to the right of *Top Staff* under the score column, then next to *All Staves*, click under the *Parts* column. Now you will see the marking only on the top staff for the score, but each extracted part will display the marking.

c. Also, if you want to assign an expression to most of the instruments with the exception of one or two staves, it is faster to click the *Set Score* and *Set Parts* buttons. This will set staves for the entire score; then you can quickly de-select the instruments you do not want included in the staff list.

7. Click *OK* twice to return to the score.

8. Input the other text expressions as shown in the sample PDF.

9. **Creating an Expression Using the Jazz Text Font**. In the Drum Set staff in measure 23, there is the expression, *Fill*, and in measure 34 there is the expression, *Solo*. Both have the Jazz font bracket over the top. In Finale 2008, these may already be created for you. However, this is a good concept to learn. To create this:

    a. Select the *Expression* tool and double-click in measure 23 of the Drum Set staff to input an expression.

b. Click the expression cup, then click *Duplicate* (or type **P**), then click *Edit* (or type **E**). (These shortcuts are for Windows only.)

c. Press **Right Arrow** to move the cursor to the end of the text *cup*.

d. **Backspace** to delete the letters *c-u-p* but *not* the bracket itself.

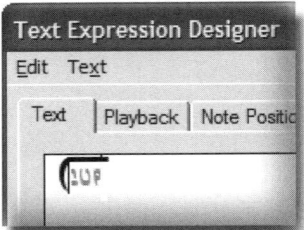

Changing the text in the Text Expression Designer

e. Type **Fill**.

f. Assign this expression as you normally would. Repeat steps 9–a through 9–e for the *Solo* expression in measure 34.

10. Save your work.

USING METATOOLS TO INPUT EXPRESSIONS

We discussed above using *Metatools* (shortcut keys) to input articulations. You can also assign *Metatools* to expressions and SmartShapes. Most expressions and SmartShapes already have *Metatools* assigned to them. Select *Help* menu/*User Manual/Keyboard Shortcuts* to see a full listing of default *Metatools*.

You can setup *Metatool* key assignments for expressions using the same procedure you learned for articulations, the only difference being that the *Expression* tool is selected instead of the *Articulation* tool. In the previous chapter we used *Metatools* to input rehearsal marks. We will do that here.

The Expression tool

1. Select the *Expression* tool by clicking the *Expression* tool icon in the main tool palette or pressing **Esc** to select the *Selection* tool and double-clicking any expression already in the score.

2. When using *Metatools* for expressions, the cursor may be positioned for either a note-attached or measure-attached expression. Remember that a small note appears next to the cursor when you hover over a note, indicating that you are about to create a note-attached expression. If there is no note on the cursor, you are about to create a measure-attached expression. These rehearsal marks should be measure-attached expressions.

3. Press and hold **A,** then click to the left of the first note in the seventh measure of the Alto Sax 1 staff.

   a. Right-click (**Control–click**) the expression's handle.

   b. Select *Edit Measure Expression Assignment.*

   c. Create a *Staff List* for rehearsal marks as shown in the example below. (In Finale 2008, a rehearsal marks staff list is pre-created. It is named *Top Staff* in the *Staff List* dropdown menu.)

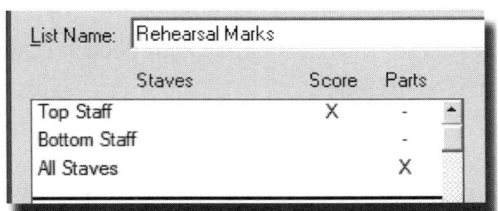

   Creating a rehearsal marks staff list

   i. Select *New Staff List* as before.

   ii. Name this list *Rehearsal Marks* or whatever you choose.

   iii. Click *Top Staff* in the *Score* column; click *All Staves* in the *Parts* column.

   d. Click *OK* twice to return to the score.

4. Press **Esc,** then right-click (**Control–click**) on the rehearsal expression you just entered.

5. Select *Edit Font* and change the font size to 24-point. (I like rehearsal marks larger.)

6. Set the font size to 24-point for rehearsal marks B–D.

7. If you do not know the *Metatool*, double-click to input the expression. In the *Expression Selection* dialog, notice the number or letter to the right of the expression. That is the currently-assigned *Metatool* for that expression.

8. A new feature in Finale 2007–2008 is called *Quick Change Expressions*. For example, suppose you meant to input an *ff* but input an *f* instead. Or you input a new rehearsal mark and wanted to change all the other rehearsal marks throughout the rest of the score.

    a. Select an expression by double-clicking using the *Selection* tool. If you are already in *Expression* tool mode, simply select the handle.

    b. Make sure the handle is selected. Now press the correct *Metatool* key for the expression you want. For example, you have rehearsal mark B and want to change it to C. Select the handle for B and press the C key twice.

Teacher, I Have a Problem

I clicked using the note-attached cursor and I still got a measure-attached expression! If this is the case, Finale has not been set correctly to use the context sensitive assignment. First, input an expression using the *Expression* tool by double-clicking in a measure. At the bottom of the dialog, select *Note Attached*. Then select *Expressions* menu and check to make sure that *Metatool: Context Sensitive* is selected.

VIDEO
CLIP 7:6

PLAY 2ND TIME ONLY
AND CUSTOM SHAPES

PLAY SECOND TIME ONLY

The Trumpets are only going to play once in the repeated section. This is accomplished by two expressions. One will set the key velocity to 0 the first time the section is played. The second expression will set the key velocity to a *basic value* of 100 on the second time the section is played. (*Human Playback* alters the value slightly as needed throughout the score.)

Key velocity is a MIDI value that specifies how hard (actually, how fast) a key on a MIDI keyboard is played. This generally controls both volume and timbre.

In the example shown in the finished score, the expression *Play 2nd Time Only* is actually two expressions. The first one is *Play* and the second is *2nd Time Only*.

The Expression tool

1. Press **Esc** and either double-click an existing expression in the score (like the text, *Back to Sax* that we just created) or click the *Expression* tool.

2. In measure 18, double-click the Trumpet 1 staff to input a measure-attached expression (the cursor will *not* have a small note
next to it).

3. In the *Text Expression Selection* box, click *Blues*, click
Duplicate (or type **P**), then *Edit* (or type **E**). (The shortcuts are
for Windows only.)

4. Replace the text *Blues* with **Play**.

5. Click the *Playback* tab.

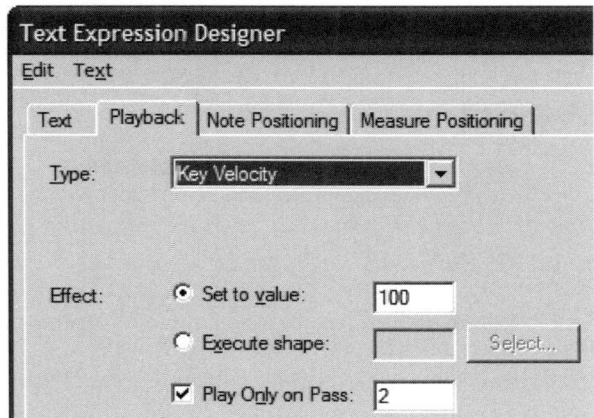

The Playback tab in the Text Expression Designer dialog

6. In the *Type* dropdown menu, select *Key Velocity*; In the *Effect*
section, click the *Set to Value* button and type **100** in the text
field. Check the box by *Play Only on Pass* and set the value to
2. This tells Finale to change the key velocity to 100, but only
on the second pass (the repeat).

7. Click *Select*. Now select *Staff List* and create a staff list (see
above) for the Trumpet section. Assign the *Play* expression to
the Trumpet section staff list once it is created.

8. Click *OK* twice to return to the score.

9. Double-click again in measure 18 in the Trumpet 1 staff to input
another measure-attached expression. Select the *Play* expression you just created, click *Duplicate* (or type **P**), then *Edit* (or
type **E**). (The shortcuts are for Windows only.)

10. Replace the word *Play* with **2nd Time Only**.

    a. **Font Size and Superscript**. If you like, you can
highlight the "nd" of the word *2nd*, then select *Text
menu/Size/9* to change the size to 9-point.

b. Now select *Text* menu/*Superscript* and input **0.09** (inches) in the *Amount* text field. Click *OK*.

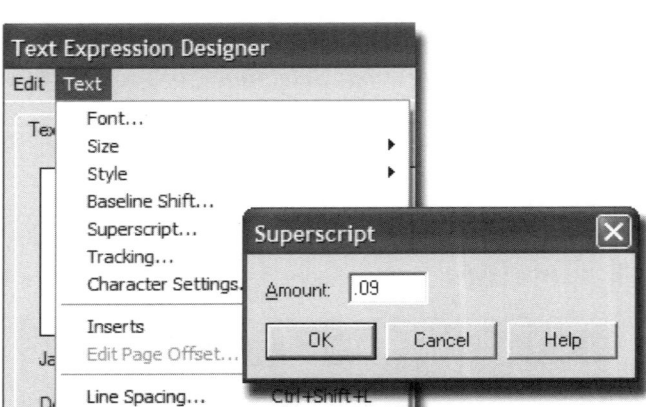

The Superscript dialog in the Text menu

11. Click the *Playback* tab. Change the *Set to Value* text field to **0** and set the *Play Only on Pass* text field to **1**.

12. Click *OK* and assign this expression to the Trumpet staff list.

13. This expression should still be selected. Press **Right Arrow** to move it to the right of the expression *Play*.

Generally you would be finished with this, but there is one more thing to consider. The Trumpet part actually starts playing in the first ending and we just turned playing off using the *second Time Only* expression. So we need to turn on the key velocity in the first ending.

1. Double-click the Trumpet 1 staff in the first ending, to input a measure expression.

2. Select the expression *Play*. Click *Duplicate* (**P**), then *Edit* (**E**). (The shortcuts are for Windows only.)

3. You are going to use this expression to turn on the velocity, but it will happen on the first pass. To remind you what this expression does, in the Description text field, type **turns on vel. for pass 1**. This description will show only in the *Expression Selection* dialog next to this expression. It will help you remember which *Play* expression this is if you need to use it again.

4. Click the *Playback* tab. Set the *Play Only on Pass* text field to **1**.

5. Click *OK* and assign this expression to the Trumpet staff list.

INPUTTING AND ALIGNING SMARTSHAPES

Input the slurs and hairpins throughout the score. Align the hairpins as discussed in the previous project. Here are some more hints on aligning hairpins (and other smart shapes assigned to measures).

1. In the finished example, in measures 20–21 of the Trombone staves, you will see a decrescendo followed by a crescendo.

2. Input the shapes as you want them to show in the Trombone 1 part. Remember, to input the decrescendo, you can select the crescendo icon and drag from right to left.

3. **Note**: You could copy the hairpins to the other Trombone staves using the copy filter. In Finale 2008, this is quickly done by selecting *Edit* menu/*Paste Multiple* and entering a value in the *Paste Vertically* text field. In Finale 2008, you may want to try this method:

   a. After putting in some hairpins and aligning them horizontally for one staff, select the area using the *Selection* tool.

   b. Right-click (**Control-click**) and select *Edit Filter*. Click *None*, then check the box next to *Smart Shapes (Assigned to Measures)*. Click *OK*.

   c. Copy the hairpins using **Ctrl/Command–C**.

   d. Select the top staff into which you want to paste the hairpins.

   e. Right-click (**Control-click**) in the highlighted area and select *Paste Multiple*.

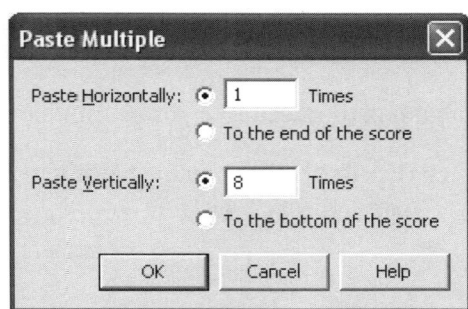

The Paste Multiple dialog

   f. In the *Paste Vertically* text field, enter the number of staves into which you want to paste the hairpins. Note that you could select *To the bottom of the score*.

4. This is one way to input multiple hairpins. Here is yet another method that may be faster.

5. After inputting the first Trombone hairpins, input the other hairpins into Trombone parts 2–4. Do not worry about them looking perfect; just get them into the staff. *But* make sure that the cursor arrow is pointing to the correct staff, and that the hairpin extends through both measures to which it will be assigned.

6. Drag a box around all of the decrescendos to select their handles.

7. Right-click (**Control–click**) on the handle of the top hairpin in the Trombone 1 staff and select *Align Vertically*. All of the other staves will resize and align to the hairpin in the top staff.

Aligning hairpins with the contextual menu

8. Now repeat this for the crescendo in measure 21. Align these four hairpins vertically.

9. Now drag a box to select all eight hairpin handles.

10. Right-click (**Control–click**) on the hairpin in measure 21 of the Trumpet 1 staff and select *Align Horizontally*.

Teacher, I Have a Problem

When I tried to align the hairpins, they moved to different staves! If this happened, then you did not watch which staff the cursor arrow was pointing to. If the arrow was pointing down to Trumpet 3 and you meant for it to be assigned to Trumpet 2, when you align the hairpins, they will jump to the staff to which they were assigned. For ease of alignment and for correct playback, delete the hairpin and input it again.

AVOIDING COLLISIONS OF SHAPES

As you input some of the hairpins, you may notice in measures 25–26 that the triplet numbers get in the way. You can either flip the triplet number to the other side, or flip the note stems and beams the other direction.

1. **Flipping Stem and Beam Direction**. To flip the note stems and beams, press **Esc** and double-click a note within a triplet group.

2. Type **L** for F*l*ip. (Remember, F is a pitch in simple entry, so we use the second letter of the word f*l*ip.)

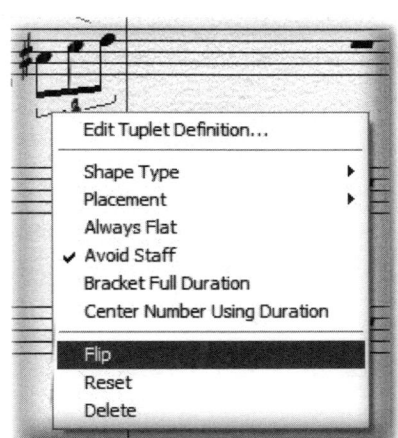

3. **Flipping Triplets**. To flip triplet numbers and brackets, press **Esc** and right-click (**Control-click**) on a triplet number. Select *Flip* from the contextual menu or change the placement to above or below as you prefer.

The contextual menu for the Tuplet tool

You may also need to flip some of the ties in measures 34–35.

1. Press **Esc** and double-click the whole note in the Bari Sax staff.

2. **Flipping Ties**. Type **Ctrl/Command–F** for f*l*ip.

3. Type **Ctrl/Command–Down Arrow** to move to the next staff down (Trumpet 1) and flip the tie in this staff.

4. You could also select an area with the *Mass Edit* tool, right-click (**Control-click**) in the highlighted area, and select *Change/Ties*. Here you can change other attributes of ties for a select region.

Teacher, I Have a Question

Since SmartShapes *are assigned to* Metatools, *can* Metatools *also be assigned to custom* SmartShapes? Yes, they can. Click on the *Custom Shape* icon. Hold down a QWERTY key or number (not a numpad number). Double-click the shape you want to assign to that key, then click *Yes* to save the *Metatool*.

VIDEO
CLIP 7:6

PLAY 2ND TIME ONLY
AND CUSTOM SHAPES

CUSTOM SMARTSHAPES

Toward the end of the score, note that we use a different style of crescendo than the traditional hairpin. Here we use a dotted line starting with the abbreviation *cresc*. This *SmartShape* is not in the default file. You will need to create it.

1. Click the *SmartShape* icon in the main tool palette or press **Esc** to select the *Selection* tool and then double-click a *SmartShape*.

Press and hold Ctrl/Option and click the Question Mark icon

2. Press and hold **Ctrl/Option** and click the last shape in the shape palette. (the *Question Mark* icon). The *Smart Line Selection* dialog opens.

3. Here you will see additional *SmartShapes* that have been pre-created for you. But the *cresc*. shape has not. However, there is one that is very close. Scroll down and select *rit*. Click *Duplicate* (**P**) then *Edit* (**E**). (The shortcuts are for Windows only.)

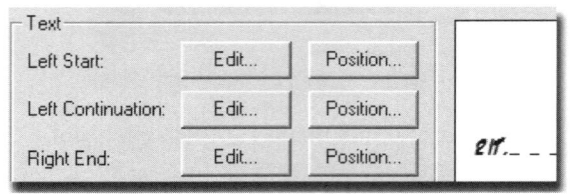

The Smart Line Designer dialog

4. At the bottom of the dialog, click *Edit* next to *Left Start*.

5. Select the text *rit*. Type **cresc.** to replace it.

6. If you like, you can select the text *cresc.* and change the font to the *Jazz Text* font.

7. Click *OK* to return to the score. This newly-created shape is active as long as the *Custom Shape* icon is selected. Input and align this shape as you would any other measure-attached *SmartShape*.

SCORE FORMAT AND COLLISION CONTROL

As you may recall in the choral score that we created, we learned many useful functions for formatting the score and editing the position of different items to avoid collisions. Now we will review those and learn a few new procedures.

1. The first thing I like to do is to have Finale perform a note spacing command. This could change the number of measures on a system, so if you do not want to change the number of measures on a system:

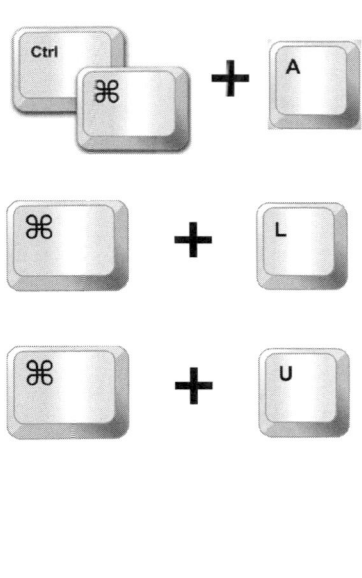

a. **Locking Systems**. Select the entire score with the *Mass Edit* or *Selection* tool (**Ctrl/Command–A** for select *a*ll).

b. On Windows, type **L** for *l*ock; on Macintosh, type **Command–L**.

c. **Unlocking Systems**. We are going to make the score larger, so locking the systems is not recommended. With the score still selected, on Windows, type **U** for *u*nlock; on Macintosh, type **Command–U**.

d. **Note Spacing**. With the score still selected, now we can have Finale adjust the note spacing by pressing one of the note spacing *Metatool* keys. There are two, and they adjust the spacing a bit differently from each other.

i. **3** is for beat spacing (In Finale 2008, the Metatool is **5**). This is generally a wider spacing that is based on time signature beats rather than measure content. In this spacing, an eighth note would get roughly half the space of a quarter note.

ii. **4** is for note spacing. This is generally a tighter spacing that is based more on the number of notes in the measure, less on the duration of notes.

2. I want this score to be just a bit bigger (I am getting old and have a difficult time reading those small little notes).

   a. Zoom out to see the entire page (**Ctrl/Command– –** [the hyphen key]). Return to Page 1.

   b. **Resizing the Score**. Click the *Resize* tool.

   c. Click the top left corner of the score (in a blank area, not on notes or a staff).

   d. In the *Resize Page* dialog, set the *Resize Page to* text fields to **140** and then click *OK*. (In Finale 2008, the document style is already close to what we want, so you may only want to increase this to 110% rather than 140%).

   e. Type **Ctrl/Command–U** to *u*pdate the layout.

3. I can read this better, but now the music is extending off the page. This can be fixed by moving the staves closer together.

   a. **Respacing the Staves**. Press **Esc** and double-click a staff name (such as A Sax 1).

   b. Go to page 2 and zoom out to see the entire page.

   c. Select *Staff* menu/*Respace Staves*.

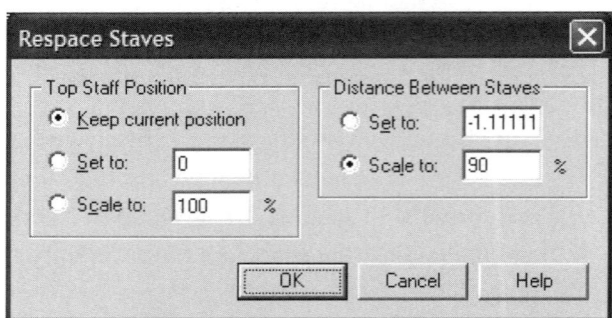

The **Respace Staves** dialog

   d. Under *Distance Between Staves* click the button next to *Scale to* and set the value to **90**.

   e. Click *OK*.

The Resize tool

4. **Moving the First System Up**. Everything but the first page looks good. The staves on the first page still extend below the edge of the page.

    a. Use the *Selection* tool (**Esc**) to move the title and composer text up. It is also a good idea in this score to change the font size.

        i. Select the *Selection* tool and double-click the title.

        ii. Drag-select the title text.

        iii. Use the font size key commands we discussed before (**Ctrl/Shift–<** or **Shift/Command–<** to decrease the font size; **Ctrl/Shift–>** or **Shift/Command–>** to increase it) or select *Text* menu/*Size*.

        iv. Press **Esc** and drag the title and composer text up a bit.

    b. Click the *Page Layout* tool.

    c. Click the top left handle of the system margin.

The Page Layout tool

The top left system margin handle

    d. Drag it down until it is slightly above the rehearsal mark.

    e. Now click in the middle of the selected system and drag it up.

    f. In Finale 2008, you may want to delete the dedication text and other text boxes you do not need.

5. This looks better, but we still need room for the copyright information. We need to adjust the space between the staves for this page only to fix this problem.

    a. **Setting Individual Staff Spacing**. With the *Page Layout* tool still selected, right-click (**Control-click**) in the system and select *Allow Individual Staff Spacing*.

b. Press **Esc** and double-click any of the staff names, such as Alto Sax 1.

c. Note the handles on the top and bottom lines of each system. The top handle adjusts the spacing throughout the entire score; the bottom one adjusts spacing for this system only. You may remember this from the choral project in a previous chapter.

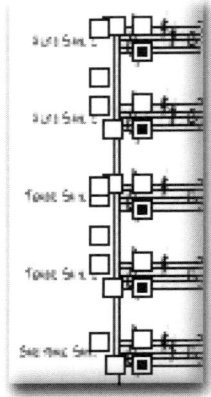

Staff spacing handles

d. Zoom out to see the all staves on this page (**Ctrl/Command– –** [the minus key]).

e. Starting just above the bottom handle of the top staff, drag a marquee around all of the bottom handles to select them.

f. Select *Staff* menu/*Respace Staves*.

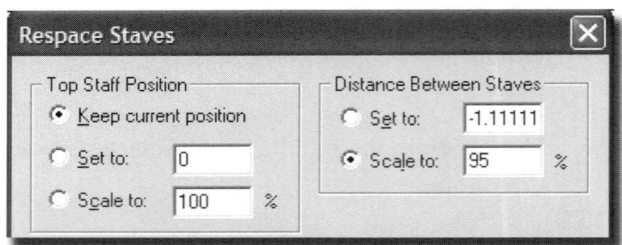

The Respace Staves dialog

g. In the *Respace Staves* dialog, under *Distance Between Staves,* click the button next to *Scale to* and enter a number between **90** and **95** in the text field.

6. Click *OK*. If you have problems with other systems on other pages extending below the page, you may want to repeat steps 5a–g for those pages.

7. **Vertical Collision Remover**. Finale 2007–2008 features a new *Vertical Collision Remover* that can solve many staff spacing problems automatically.

   a. Select an area with the *Mass Edit* or *Selection* tool that has items between staves that are colliding vertically, such as shapes or expressions.

   b. Select *Plug-ins* menu/*New Plug-ins for Finale 2007/Vertical Collision Remover* or, in Finale 2008, *Plug-ins* menu/*Scoring and Arranging/Vertical Collision Remover*.

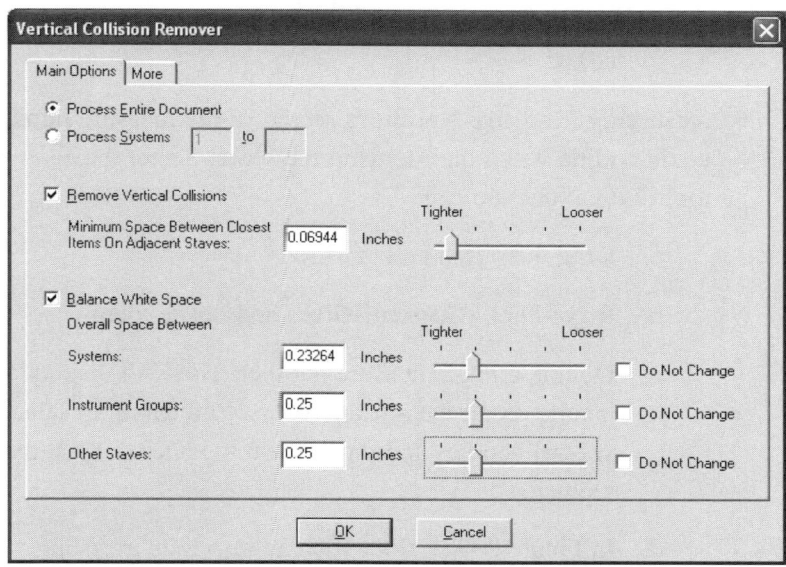

The Vertical Collision Remover dialog

   c. Note the sliders available for loose or tight spacing. Try sliding them closer to the tight spacing position.

   d. In Windows, click the *More* tab and note the available settings, including the *Keep Number of Systems* option. On Macintosh, all of the settings are in one dialog. Set as desired, then click *OK*.

8. If you are not using the *Vertical Collision Remover* in Finale 2007–2008, you will notice we have a problem on page 4. The notes in Trumpet 1 and Bari Sax are too close together, so *SmartShapes* are colliding. We need to adjust staff spacing here.

   a. Select the *Page Layout* tool.

   b. Right-click (**Control-click**) in the center of the system and select *Allow Individual Staff Spacing* as you did before on page 1.

    c.   Drag the system up so the top system margin is flush with the page margin.

    d.   Press **Esc** and double-click a staff name.

    e.   **Manual Staff Spacing**. Starting with Trumpet 1, select all of the bottom staff handles from Trumpet 1 down to Drum Set.

    f.   Press **Down Arrow** to adjust the spacing.

    g.   You may want to also adjust the spacing of Trumpet 2 and Trombone 1. Make sure to select the bottom handles for all staves below the staff you wish to adjust.

9. **Adjusting Measure Numbers**. Some of the measure numbers could collide with other items in the score. Select the *Selection* tool (**Esc**). Now you can:

    a.   Drag them to a new position.

    b.   Right-click (**Control-click**) and delete them.

    c.   Double-click a measure number. This will display a handle on all measure numbers. You can drag select several handles and move them together to keep them aligned.

    d.   In Finale 2007–2008, you can also hide measure numbers so that they disappear from the score but not the parts. First select the handle(s), right-click (**Control-click**), and select *Unlink in All Parts*. Then simply press **Delete** to hide them. They will dim, showing that they are hidden, and they will not print).

10. **Individual Expression Positioning**. If you need to adjust the positioning of measure expressions assigned to staff lists, simply drag any of the expressions to adjust them together. If you need to adjust measure expressions individually:

    a.   Select the *Selection* tool (**Esc**) if not already selected.

    b.   Right-click (**Control-click**) on the expression you need to move.

    c.   In Finale 2006, select *Edit Measure Expression Assignment* from the contextual menu; in Finale 2007–2008, select *Allow Individual Positioning*.

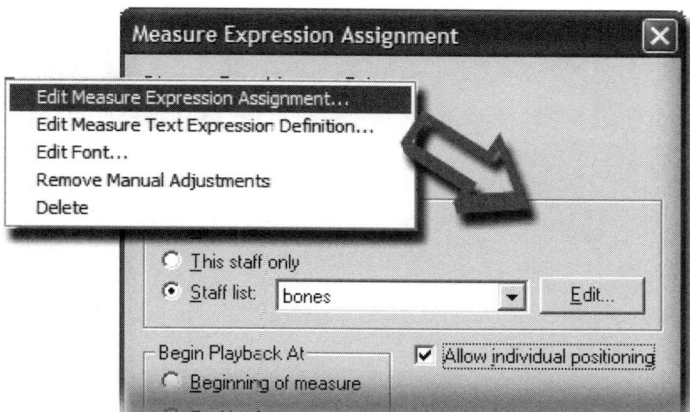

The Measure Expression Assignment dialog

d. In Finale 2006, check the box next to *Allow Individual Positioning*. Click *OK*.

e. Now you can drag these expressions individually.

11. **Positioning Chords**. Finally, adjust the position of the chords in the Piano staff.

a. Press **Esc** and double-click a chord. Positioning triangles appear to the left of the score.

b. Drag the leftmost triangle down. These triangles adjust the chords and fretboards the same way lyrics are adjusted, as taught in the previous project.

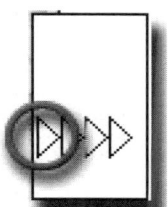

Positioning triangles

PART EXTRACTION IN FINALE 2006

Now we need to print individual parts for each of the instruments. (For Finale 2007–2008, see the instructions in the following section.)

In Finale 2006, part extraction is basically achieved by selecting *File* menu/*Extract Parts*. Click *OK* and Finale will create a new file for each part and extract it with new page formatting. But there are a few more items you may want to know.

1. You may want to create a new folder into which you will place the new files.

a. Create a new folder using the method most comfortable to you for your computer. Give it a recognizable name, such as HS Jazz Band.

2. Select *File* menu/*Extract Parts.*

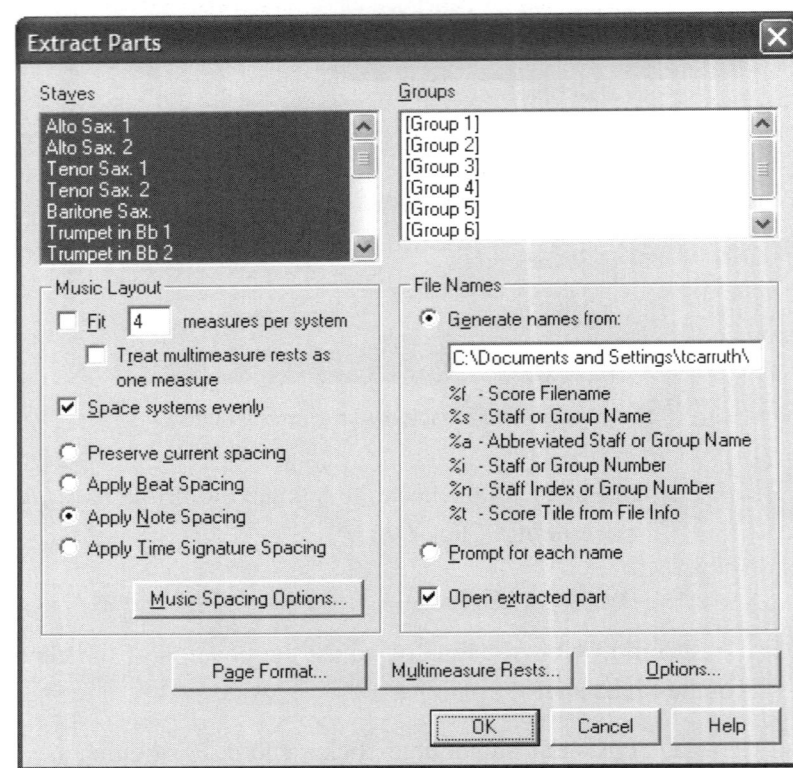

The Extract Parts dialog

3. Under *File Names*, below *Generate names from*, there is a text field for specifying where Finale will place the new files for each part. Do one of the following:

   a. Type the path to the folder into which you would like Finale to place the files. (Be careful to type the path correctly or Finale will not know how to find the specific folder you want.) Finale will automatically create a new filename based on the score name and instrument name.

   b. Click *Prompt for Each Name*. When you click *OK*, Finale will ask you for the filename and where to save the file for each part.

4. Note that you can change many other aspects of the extracted parts via the *Page Format*, *Multimeasure Rests*, and *Options* buttons at the bottom of the dialog.

   a. Click *Page Formatting*. The *Page Format for Parts* dialog appears.

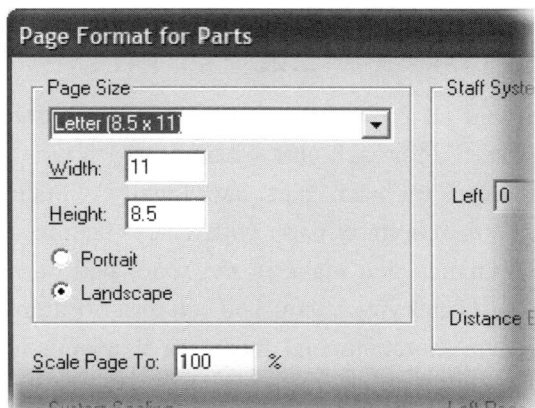

The Page Format for Parts dialog

b. Under *Page Size*, change the orientation from *Landscape* to *Portrait*. Click *OK*.

5. You can select only the staves you want to extract. You can also select groups of staves for extraction. If you simply click *OK*, the Piano part will be split into two files, one for treble clef and one for bass clef. To fix this:

a. In the *Staves* pane of the *Extract Parts* dialog, scroll down to Staff 14 and 15.

The Extract Parts dialog

b. Press and hold **Ctrl/Command** and click these two staves to de-select them.

c. In the *Groups* pane, scroll down to *Piano* and click it.

VIDEO
CLIP 7:7
WORKING WITH LINKED
PARTS (2007–2008)

PART EXTRACTION IN FINALE 2007–2008

In Finale 2006 and all previous versions, part extraction is done by creating a separate file for each part. Changes to a score require you to re-extract and clean up each part individually. Finale 2007–2008 changed the need to re-extract parts with a new feature called *Linked Parts*. Now any change you make in the score will be automatically reflected in the parts and vice-versa. You can turn off items that you do not want linked via the contextual menu for that item (right-click or **Control-click**) and selecting *Unlink in All Parts* from the score. Moving the position of an item in a part will automatically unlink that item from its position in the score. You can re-establish the link from the contextual menu for that item.

In Finale 2007–2008, the score and all of the parts are combined into a single document rather than separate files for each part. You do have the option of extracting each part to a separate document as before, but in general, this is not necessary. You can simply print the parts all from one command.

You can view parts from the *Document* menu or with the shortcut keys described below. You can also create new parts for *divisi* scores. For example, Flute 1 and Flute 2 may be notated in the score on one staff, but can be automatically separated into two individual parts. Or you can create a part for several instruments. For example, you may want to create one part for all of the percussion staves.

To view the individual parts of a score:

1. Select *Document* menu/*Edit Part*. A submenu of available parts appears.

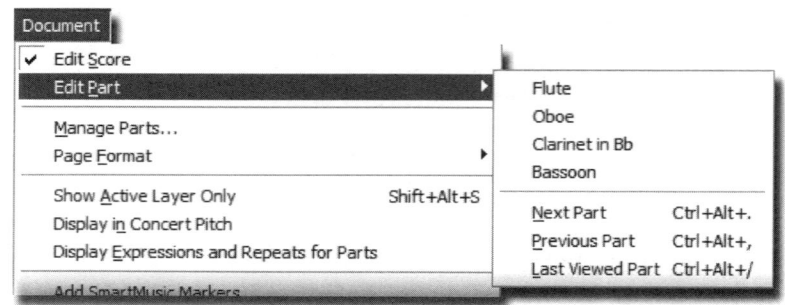

Selecting a part

2. **Note**: If you are opening an older score, the parts have not yet been created. In this case the *Document* menu/*Edit Part* submenu will display *No Parts Defined*.

3. **Defining Parts**. If no parts are defined, select *Document* menu/ *Manage Parts*.

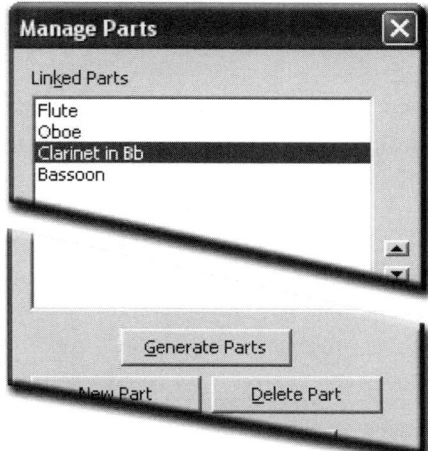

The Manage Parts dialog

4. Here you can simply click *Generate Parts* and Finale will automatically create a part for each staff in the score.

5. Now you can select a part as described above, or try the following shortcut keys. On Windows, press and hold **Ctrl–Alt**; on Macintosh, press and hold **Command–Option**, then press > (the period key) to cycle forward through the parts, < (the comma key) to cycle backwards through the parts. Once you cycle through the parts, the full score is at the top of the cycle.

6. If you need multi-measure rests in the parts, in Finale 2007, click the *Measure* tool. (In Finale 2008, press **Esc** for the *Selection* tool.)

The Measure tool

   a. Select *Measure* menu/*Multi-measure Rests/Create for Parts/Score*. (In Finale 2008, this is in the *Edit* menu.) The *Select Parts/Score* dialog appears.

   b. Click *Check All*. De-select *Score* if needed. Click *OK*.

Editing Parts.

   a. You can make edits to notes, measures, dynamics, shapes, expressions, articulations, and so forth. They will be reflected in the score.

b. Changing the position of an item in the part will not change its position in the score. When you change the position of an item, it will change color, indicating an alteration from its position in the score.

c. Once you change a position of an item it is unlinked from the score. If you want to restore the link:

    i. Right-click (**Control-click**) the item's handle, or select the *Selection* tool and right-click (**Control-click**) the item itself to access its contextual menu.

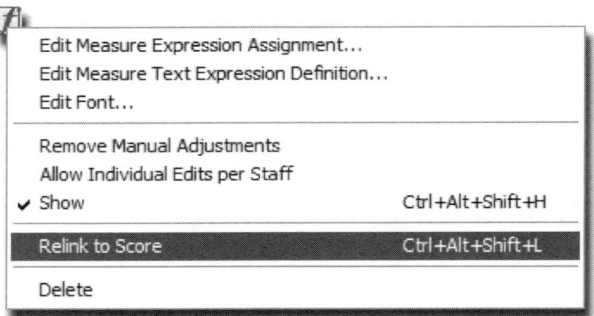

The contextual menu for relinking an item in a part back to the score

    ii. Select *Relink to Score*. That item will move back to the original position established in the score.

d. Make any edits you want to format individual parts. Try some of the edits described in step 6 in the Part Extraction section above.

e. To print the parts, select *File* menu/*Print*. The *Select Score and Parts for Printing* dialog appears.

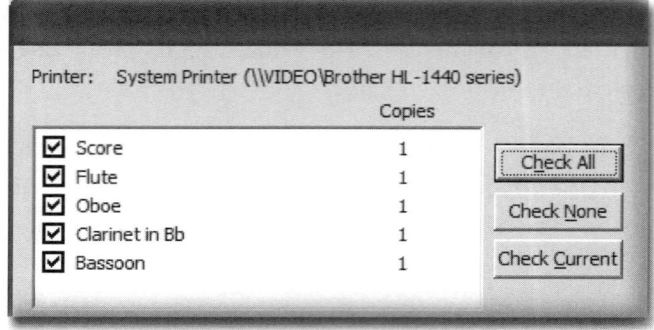

The Select Score and Parts for Printing dialog

f. Note that you can print the score, any part(s), and select the number of copies you like for each part. For this project, simply click *Check All*, then click *OK* to print all of the parts and the score.

8. By default, new scores created in Finale 2007–2008 will show the part name at the top of each part. However, a score created with an older version of Finale will not show these names. You will need to create a score/part name text insert.

a. Select the *Selection* tool (**Esc**) and double-click any text box, such as the score title. This is the same as selecting the *Text* tool from the main palette.

b. While viewing a part, double-click in the upper left corner of the page to create a text box.

c. Select *Text* menu/*Inserts/Part/Score Name*. This will label each part according to the name listed in the *Manage Parts* dialog.

d. If you want to re-position the name in the parts, select the *Selection* tool (**Esc**), press and hold **Ctrl/Command**, and then drag the text to the desired position. Holding **Ctrl/Command** allows you to change the linking behavior. Normally, changing the position in a part unlinks that item from the score. Holding **Ctrl/Command** while dragging maintains the link to the position of this item in the score, which in turn updates the position for all parts.

e. If you need to reposition the text box in the score independently, select *Document* menu/*Edit Score*, then press and hold **Ctrl/Command**, which unlinks to the position in the parts, and drag the text box to the desired position.

f. If you do not want the text *Score* to display in the score, select the *Selection* tool (**Esc**), right-click (**Control-click**) on the text box and select *Unlink in All Parts*. Right-click (**Control-click**) the text box a second time and select *Show* to uncheck this menu item. This will dim the text, reminding you that it is there, but will not print.

The Text tool

THE LINKING OVERRIDE FUNCTION

The **Ctrl** key on Windows and the **Command** key on Macintosh serves as an override key. Holding this key while performing many functions between score and parts will reverse the normal linking effect.

In the example above (step 8), we wanted to move a text box in a part and have it update in the other parts. By default, moving a text box in a part unlinks the position from the score and the other parts. Since the score is what links the parts together, you may want to view the position in the part, but have the score link this position to the parts. Holding the override key while moving this item will do this.

Holding the override key while moving an item in the score would also have the reverse effect by *not* changing the position of the item in the parts.

EXTRA CREDIT SECTION

The linked parts feature in Finale 2007–2008 is very flexible and powerful. You can adjust page layout settings and apply them to all of the parts with one command. As mentioned above, if the score has divisi parts on a single staff, you can have Finale automatically generate separate parts from that staff. You can also create a part made from multiple staves. These instructions apply to Finale 2007b and above. If you do not have at least Finale 2007b, select *Help* menu/*Check for Finale Updates*. Download the update file, then double-click the icon to run the updater.

To create a new part for a divisi staff:

VIDEO CLIP 7:8

CREATING LINKED DIVISI PARTS

Divisi Parts in Finale 2007b–2008.

1. Input notes on a staff for a second part. There are two ways to do this: Either put each divisi part on a different layer, or, in the case of rhythmically identical parts, input both parts as one layer using intervals for the divisi parts. However, you can mix both layers and interval divisi if needed; it just takes a few extra steps to work around. **Note**: If the divisi part starts with a rest in the measure, make sure the rest is visible. Hidden rests will not display in the linked part.

2. Select *Document* menu/*Manage Parts*.

3. Click the part for which you would like to create a divisi part. In this example, we will use the Oboe part. This will set the order of the new part. (**Note**: If you forget to do this, you can use the arrow icons next to the list of parts to change the order of the parts.)

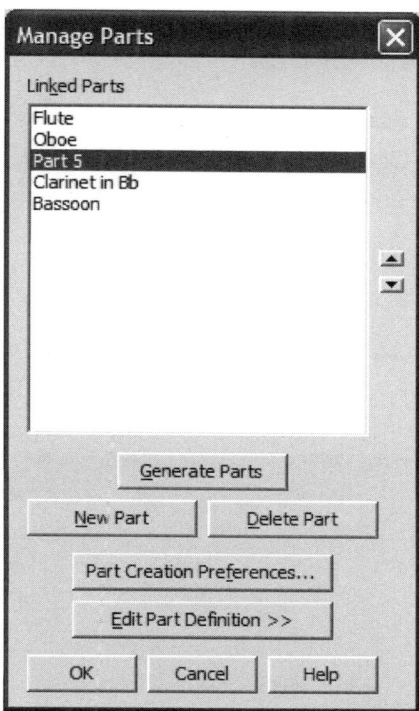

The Manage Parts dialog before expansion

4. Click *New Part*. Note that the name of this new part is called *Part X*, where *X* is the next available part number. Now we will change the name and other attributes of this part.

5. With the newly created part selected in the *Linked Parts* pane, you need to select the instrument or staff that contains the notes for this part. In the *Available Instruments* pane, click the desired staff. In this example, that is the Oboe. Click *Add to Part*.

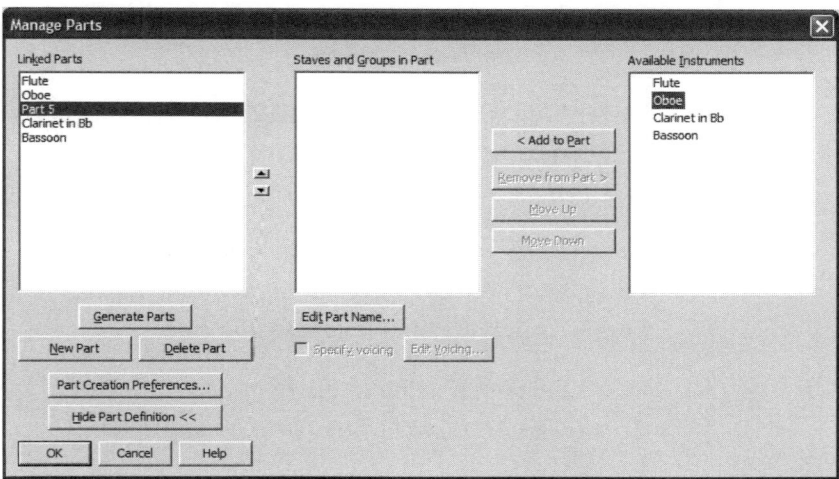

The Manage Parts dialog after expansion

6. Click *Edit Part Name* and type in the name for this part, in this case, **Oboe 2**. Click *OK*.

7. You may want to change the part name of the original oboe part to Oboe 1. Click Oboe in the *Linked Parts* pane, then click *Edit Part Name* and change the name to **Oboe 1**.

8. Now you will need to set the voicing options so Finale will know how to split the divisi parts.

    a. Select Oboe 1 from the linked parts list.

    b. Click *Edit Voicing*.

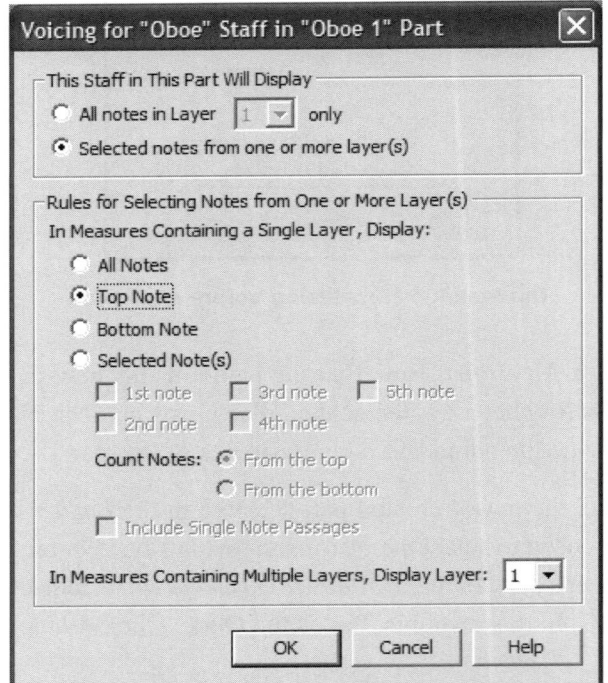

The Voicing dialog

    c. Under *This Staff in This Part Will Display*, click the button next to *Selected notes from one or more layer(s)*.

    d. Under *Rules for Selecting Notes from One or More Layer(s)/In Measures Containing a Single Layer, Display*, click the button next to *Top Note*.

    e. Leave the popup menu to the right of *In Measures Containing Multiple Layers, Display Layer* set to Layer 1.

    f. Click *OK*.

9. Repeat this by selecting Oboe 2 in the *Linked Parts* pane of the main dialog. Click *Edit Voicing* and set the values for Oboe 2 to the following:

   a. Under *Rules for Selecting Notes from One or More Layer(s)/In Measures Containing a Single Layer, Display*, click the button next to *Bottom Note*.

   b. Set the popup menu to the right of *In Measures Containing Multiple Layers, Display Layer* set to Layer 2.

   c. Click *OK*.

It is best to either use layers for all divisi parts or have all parts in one layer rather than mix the two note entry methods. When you create the divisi part using both intervals and layers, you could run into some interesting results, although they are easy to adjust. For example, say you had notes in a measure that applied only to Part 1. This can confuse Finale unless *all* Part 1 notes are in Layer 1 and *all* Part 2 notes are in Layer 2. However, if you do have a need to mix layers and intervals for divisi parts in the score, follow these instructions:

Consider the Clarinet 1 and 2 example below. The second measure is for Part 1 only.

1. Assuming that you have already created the divisi parts as outlined above, now we will alter measure 2 so Finale will know these notes are for Part 1 only and this measure is to be included in a multi-measure rest for Part 2.

2. In the score, select Layer 4 and input a half rest into measure 2. You can hide the rest if you like by selecting it and typing **H** for *h*ide.

3. Select *Document* menu/*Edit Part/Clarinet 2*, or use the shortcut keys to scroll through the parts. (On Windows, use **Ctrl–Alt–<** and **Ctrl–Alt–>**; on Macintosh, use **Command–Option–<** and **Command–Option–>** to cycle through the parts).

The Measure tool

VIDEO
CLIP 7:9

PAGE FORMATTING
FOR PARTS AND
DIVISI CUE NOTES

4. You may need to have Finale re-calculate multi-measure rests. Select the *Measure* tool.

    a. Select *Measure* menu/*Multi-measure Rests*, then *Create for Parts/Score*.

    b. Here you can select any or all parts for which to generate multi-measure rests. Select the Clarinet 2 part, then click *OK*.

MORE THAN TWO DIVISI PARTS

A question that comes up quite often is what to do when working with a score that has more than two divisi parts. For this example, consider a Flute staff with three Flute parts. As long as all three parts are rhythmically identical, as in measure 1 in the example below, this is very easy to do. But when you begin adding additional layers to the score, as in measures 2 and 3, some problems may arise. First, we will split up the parts, then deal with the layer issue.

More than two divisi parts on a single staff

1. Select *Document* menu/*Manage Parts*.

2. Create and name the additional Flute parts as described above.

3. Click *Edit Voicing*.

    a. Click the button next to *Select notes from one or more layer(s)*. Under *Rules for Selecting Notes from One or More Layer(s)/In Measures Containing a Single Layer, Display*, click the button next to *Selected Note(s)*, as shown in the example to the right. Set each of the three parts with the desired voicing, i.e., set Flute 1 to *1st note*, Flute 2 to *2nd note*, etc.

    b. You may want to check the box next to *Include Single Note Passages*, depending on how you would like to handle unison portions of the score for this part.

    c. Set the popup menu to the right of *In Measures Containing Multiple Layers, Display Layer* set to Layer 1 for Flute 1, Layer 2 for Flute 2, and Layer 3 for Flute 3.

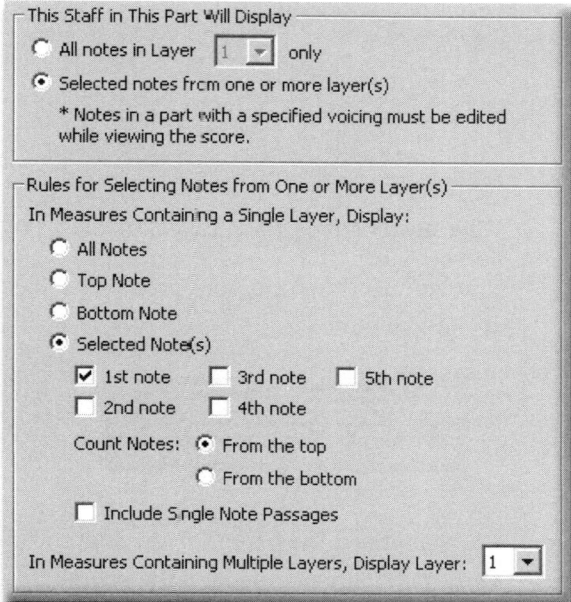

The Edit Voicing dialog

4. Again, if all parts are rhythmically identical and in Layer 1, this is all you need to do. However, if there are places in the score where you need more than one layer in a measure, follow these instructions:

   a. Anytime an additional layer is needed in a measure you will need to use a different layer for each part. This is the reason for the setting in step 3c above. This tells Finale that when there is more than 1 layer in a measure, set each part to the layer specified.

   b. In this example, you may think that you could put Parts 1 and 2 into Layer 1, since they are rhythmically identical, then Part 3 into a separate layer. However, this would result in the Flute 1 part containing both Flute 1 and 2 notes and the Flute 2 part having no notes at all.

   c. Input the notes for Flute 1 using Layer 1. Input the notes for Flute 2 using Layer 2. You may want to flip the notes manually (type **L**) or use the *Mass Edit* tool on Layer 2 only, or specify the stem direction for Layer 2 by selecting *Document* menu/*Document Options/Layers* and specifying how you want Finale to display stemming in multiple layers.

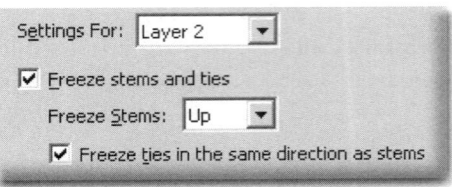

The Document Options/Layers dialog

d. Now the resulting measure probably looks like the example below.

e. You can adjust the beam for the score using *Special Tools*. Adjustments made in the score with these tools are not reflected in the parts. We need to remove or hide the beam in Layer 2.

f. Select the *Special Tools* icon. On Windows, you may need to select *Window* menu/*Advanced Tool Palette*. From the *Special Tool* palette, select the *Beam Thickness* tool.

g. Select Layer 2, then click the measure to display beam handles. Drag a marquee around the handles to select all of them in the measure.

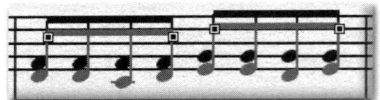

Beam handles selected

h. Press **Up Arrow** several times until the beam dissapears.

i. Now input the notes for the Flute 3 part. Make sure to set the layer setting for stems to freeze down in *Document* menu/*Document Options/Layers*.

The Special Tools icon

The Beam Thickness tool

5. In the third measure of this example, there is a single eighth note in the Flute 1 and 2 part with a flag. Once you input the notes in Layers 1 and 2, measure 3 will look like the example below. You know how to make the beam disappear from step 4 above. The flag will not disappear, so you need to superimpose it over the flag in Layer 1.

6. Using *Special Tools* as described above, click the *Stem Length* tool. With Layer 2 selected, click the measure to display stem handles.

The Stem Length tool

7. Click the handle for the eighth note stem. Change the length of the stem by dragging or pressing **Up Arrow** or **Down Arrow** to position this flag directly over the flag in Layer 1.

8. Add Layer 3. The measure should now look like the example below.

9. **Note**: If you are concerned about the flag in Layer 1 showing, you can use the *Custom Stem* tool in the *Special Tools* palette to eliminate it.

The Custom Stem tool

   a. Select Layer 1 and select the handle for the stem.

   b. Double-click the handle to enter the *Shape Selection* dialog.

   c. Click *Create* to create a new shape.

   d. Click *OK* without creating any shape.

   e. Click *OK* to assign this blank shape to be the new stem and flag for this note. Again, this will only affect the score, not the parts.

CUE NOTES FOR DIVISI PARTS

Previously we discussed using the *Cue Notes* plug-in to create cue notes. Creating cue notes for one of the divisi parts and *not* the other can be somewhat interesting. Here are some tips. Suppose the score looked like the example below. You may want to show some Flute 1 cue notes in the Flute 2 part.

1. Select the notes you would like to use for cue notes using the *Mass Edit* or *Selection* tool.

    a. Select *Plug-ins* menu/*Scoring and Arranging/Add Cue Notes*.

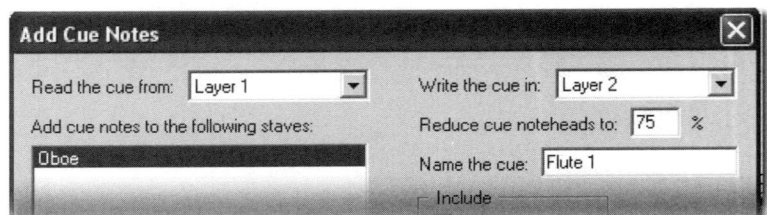

The Add Cue Notes dialog

    b. Select a layer to display in Part 2. For example, as discussed above in divisi voicing, Part 2 was set to display Layer 2 if more than two layers existed in a measure.

    c. In the text field to the right of *Name the cue*, type **Flute 1**.

    d. You will not be able to add the cue notes to the Flute staff, so select another staff for now—Oboe for example.

    e. Click *OK*.

2. Select *Document* menu/*Show Active Layer Only*. In the popup menu in bottom left corner of the screen, select *Layer 2*.

3. Select the *Mass Edit or Selection* tool and then select the cue notes from the Oboe staff (in this example) and drag-copy them to the Flute staff. Now clear the cue notes from the Oboe staff (if you do not want them there).

4. Select *Document* menu/*Show Active Layer Only* again to turn off this mode.

5. Now you will need a new staff style. Select the *Staff* tool, then select the measure with cue notes in the Flute part. Right-click (**Control-click**) in the highlighted area and select *Define Staff Style*.

The Staff tool

> a. In the *Staff Styles* dialog, select *New* and enter a name such as **Hide Layer 2**.

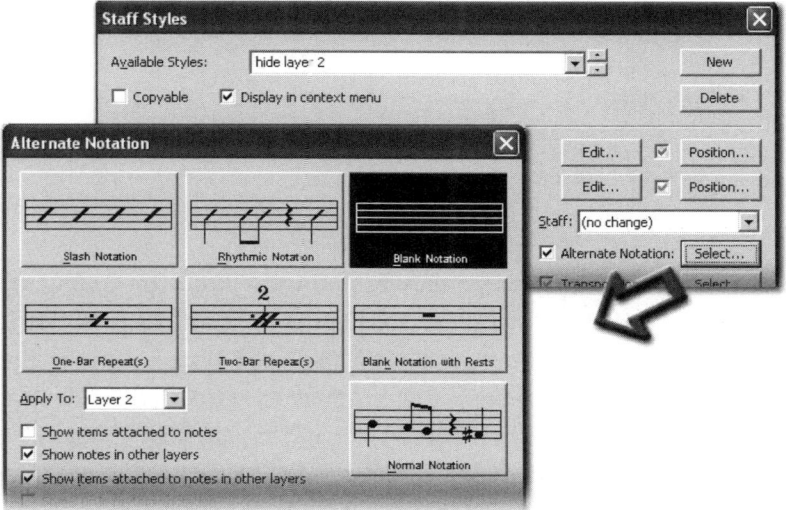

The Staff Styles and Alternate Notation dialogs

> b. Click *Select* next to *Alternate Notation*.
>
> c. Select *Blank Notation*.
>
> d. In the dropdown menu next to *Apply To,* select *Layer 2*.
>
> e. Clear the box next to *Show items attached to notes*. Check the boxes next to *Show notes in other layers* and *Show items attached to notes in other layers*.
>
> f. Click *OK* twice to return to the score.
>
> g. Right-click (**Control-click**) in the highlighted area again and select the new staff style *Hide Layer 2*. This will hide the cue notes in the score. Now you will need to unhide them in the Flute 2 part.

6. Select *Documents* menu/*Edit Part/Flute 2* or use the shortcut keys to scroll to the Flute 2 part.

Shortcut keys for scrolling to parts to edit

7. Select the *Staff* tool, then select the measure in which you want to see cue notes. Right-click (**Control-click**) and select *Clear Staff Style*. This clears the staff style for the part, but not the score.

The Staff tool

PAGE LAYOUT LINKING

Before Finale 2007–2008, formatting parts was time-consuming. You would either have to fix the page formatting on each part individually or take the time to figure out each of the page and system settings, enter them into the *Part Extraction* dialog, then re-extract all of the parts again. This has changed with *Linked Parts* in Finale 2007–2008.

We will do a few page layout functions on one of the parts, then apply this to all of the other parts.

1. Press and hold **Ctrl–Alt–>** (on Windows) or **Command–Option–>** (on Macintosh) to select the Alto 1 part.

2. Select the *Resize* tool.

3. Zoom out to view the entire page.

4. Click in the top left-hand corner of the page.

The Resize tool

5. In the *Resize Page* dialog, in the text field next to *Resize Page To*, enter **90**.

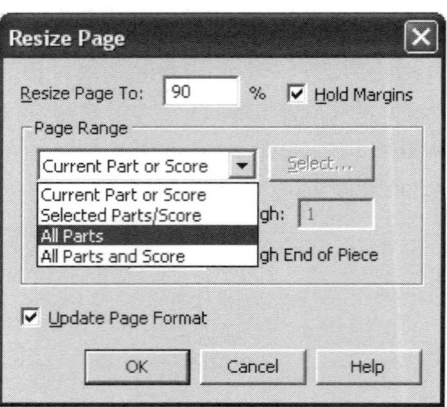

The Resize Page dialog

6. Under *Page Range* select *All Parts* from the dropdown menu.

7. Click *OK*.

8. Now select the *Page Layout* tool and try some other functions.

9. Right-click (**Control-click**) in the middle of the second system and select *Edit System Margins*.

The Page Layout tool

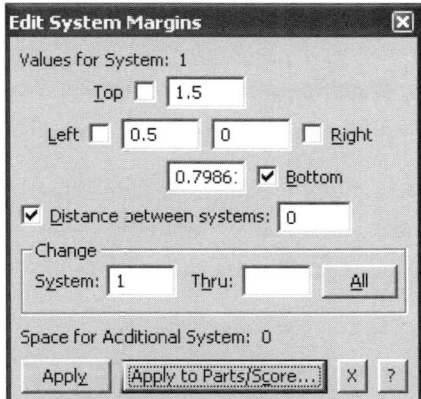

The Edit System Margins dialog

10. Move the dialog to the right so you can edit the margins visually.

11. All we want to change is the bottom margin, so clear the checkboxes next to *Top*, *Left*, and *Right*.

12. Under *Change,* click *All* to select all systems, then, at the bottom of the dialog, click *Apply*. This will change the value in the text field next to *Distance between systems* to 0.

13. Click the bottom-right handle of the top system on the page. Type **Ctrl/Command–A** to select all of the right handles.

The bottom-right system handle

14. Press **Down Arrow** to adjust the bottom margins to achieve the look you want on the parts.

15. In the *Edit System Margins* dialog, click *Apply to Parts/Score*. In the *Select Parts/Score* dialog check *All* then clear the box next to *Score*. Click *OK*. Now these margin settings have been applied not only to all of the systems in the Sax 1 part, but all of the other parts. Click the dialog close box to send it away.

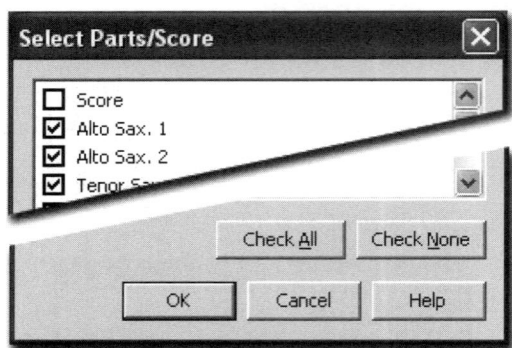

The Select Parts/Score dialog

16. Select *Page Layout* menu/*Page Size*. Note that you can select a new page size, then apply that to the score and/or parts from the dropdown menu in this dialog.

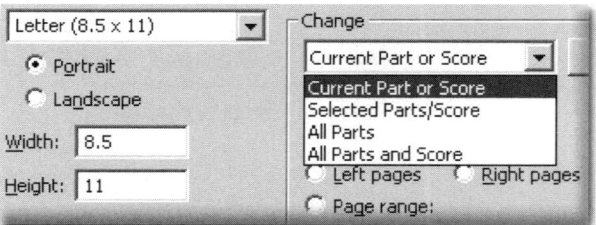

The Page Size dialog

FINAL FORMATS FOR FINALE 2006–2008

1. Before printing, you may want to review each part to make sure that the page formatting is as you want it. There may be a few parts, such as the Drum Set part, with a single measure on the last system that stretches across the page.

2. **Moving Measures**. Select the last measure with the *Mass Edit* or *Selection* tool.

3. Press **Up Arrow** to move the measure to the system directly above.

4. I want more measures on the last system in the Trumpet 1 part.

   a. Click the last measure in the second-to-the-last system and press **Down Arrow** to move the measure down a system.

The Mass Edit and Selection tools

5. **Adjusting Repeat Brackets**. I want to move the ending brackets up a bit in the first Trombone and Trumpet 1 parts because they are colliding with the notes.

    a. Press **Esc**.

    b. Double-click a repeat or repeat bracket.

    c. Drag a box around all of the repeat handles to select them.

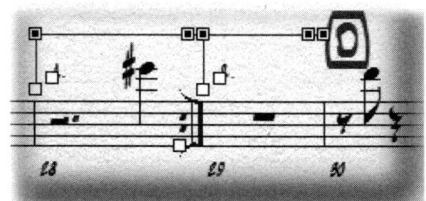

Moving repeat brackets

    d. Press **Up Arrow** to nudge the brackets higher.

    e. You may want to select all but the bottom handles and just position the top of the brackets to keep from moving the feet away from the staff.

6. Save all changes to each part.

PRINTING THE SCORE AND PARTS IN FINALE 2006

1. To print the score, select the score file from the *Window* menu if it is open, or re-open it from the *File* menu.

2. Select *File* menu/*Print* (or type **Ctrl/Command–P**).

    a. In the *Print* dialog, change the *Page Orientation* to *Landscape*.

    b. Print the score.

3. **Printing the Parts**.

    a. If the parts are not all open, open all of them from the *File* menu.

    b. Type **Ctrl/Command–P** and change the *Page Orientation* from *Landscape* to *Portrait*.

    c. Click *OK* and print the first file.

    d. For the balance of the files:

    i. Type **Ctrl/Command–P** to print the next file.

    ii. Type **Ctrl/Command–W** to close this file.

    iii. The next part will show. Repeat these steps (d-i and d-ii) until all of the parts have been sent to the printer.

PRINTING THE SCORE AND PARTS IN FINALE 2007–2008

Because of the *Linked Parts* feature, you can print the score and as many copies of the parts as you like. However, since the score is printed using a landscape page orientation and the parts are printed using portrait orientation, make sure to print the score and the parts separately. Finale will not automatically change the printer page orientation for the parts and the score.

LIBRARIES AND DEFAULT FILES

In this score we created several new items such as chord suffixes, expressions, and *SmartShapes*. You may want to save these settings in a new default file so they will be available next time you create a score using the *Jazz Font*.

Note: If you are using Finale in a lab, you should check with your teacher or lab assistant before changing the default files. It is *not recommended* that you change default documents on a computer others will be using.

1. Items created in a score can be saved in a *library* and then opened in another file. When a library is opened in another document, only the items that are new to that document are loaded so that the new file will not have duplicate items.

2. **Creating Libraries**. Select *File* Menu/*Save Library*. The *Save Library* dialog appears.

3. Here you can specify what items you want to be saved as part of the library. In this document we created chord suffixes, text expressions and *SmartShapes* (lines). Select the types of elements you want to save in the library.

4. Click *OK* and give the library a name.

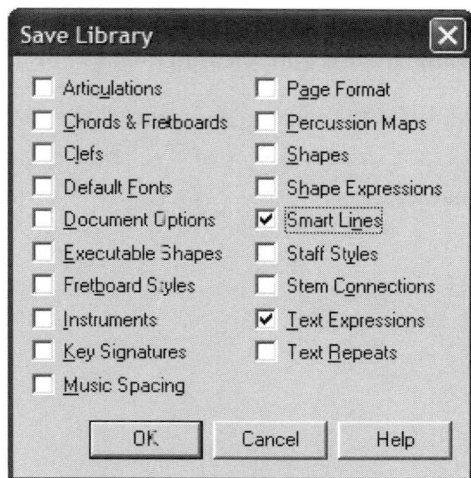

The Save Library dialog

5. **Creating a New Default File.** Start a new document with the *Setup Wizard*. Do not type anything into the first page; leave title, composer, etc., blank.

6. On the *Document Setup Wizard – Add or Delete Instrument(s)* page, select *Empty Staves* and *Treble Clef Staff*.

7. Click *Next* until you get to the fourth page of the dialog. Select *Maestro Font* or *Jazz Font*, depending on which default file you want to change. Click *Finish*.

8. **Loading Libraries.** Select *File* menu/*Load Library*.

9. Select the library you just created and click *Open*.

10. *Metatools* do not save with Libraries; if you would like to save your *Metatools* to the default file, assign them now. (Transposition *Metatools* 6–9 are program-specific and do not need to be re-assigned. They are not part of the default document.)

11. **Saving a New Default File.** Select *File* menu/*Save As*. On Windows, change the file type to *Finale Template File*.

12. Navigate to the location of your current default files. Generally this is found in the Finale 2007 or 2008/Components Files folder.

13. Click the file you want to replace, either Maestro or Jazz. **Note:** You may want to stop and change the name of this file (prefix the file with the letters **OLD** is one suggestion) so you can return to it if needed, since the next step *will* overwrite it.

14. Save the new file using the correct file name, either *Maestro Font Default* or *Jazz Font Default*.

15. If you ever want to return to the original file, delete the new file from the Components folder and rename the original with its original name.

CHAPTER 8

PERCUSSION SCORES

Concepts covered in this chapter:

- Percussion Notation
  - Percussion Input
  - Percussion Maps
  - Altering Percussion Maps for Previously Entered Notes
- Staff Styles
  - Editing and Creating Staff Styles
  - Hide Staff—Stemless Notes
- Staff Names
  - Editing Full and Abbreviated Staff Names
- Measure Numbers
  - Editing, Removing
- Changing Noteheads
- Removing Automatic Word Extensions
- Hints for Note Input in Triple Meter
- Creating a Floating or Ossia Measure
- Using the Text Tool
- Exporting and Importing Graphics
- Mixing Pitched and Non-Pitched Percussion on a Staff
  - Assigning Independent Sounds to Layers in the Same Staff
- Adjusting Beaming Patterns
- Changing Stem Direction for a Region
- Stem Control (Short Stem Alterations)
- Splitting Measures
- Creating a Coda
- Creating Percussion Playback from a non-percussion staff

PROJECT FILE PDF: PERCUSSION SCORE

Whether you ever plan on creating a percussion score or not, this project has many important concepts that will assist you in other projects. As shown from the list above, there are many procedures that are important beyond the needs for percussion scores. **Note**: It is advisable to understand the previous chapters before attempting this score.

CHOOSING INSTRUMENTATION

Using the *Setup Wizard* to create a score is certainly familiar to you by now, but you need to take care when selecting instruments for percussion parts. There are different instrument groups from which you can select instrument staves that seem to be the same staff and sound. Make sure to follow these instructions to make this score creation easy.

1. In Finale 2006–2007, in the *Setup Wizard*, enter the title, composer, and copyright. *Make sure* to set the page size to *Landscape*. (In Finale 2007–2008, leave the parts page orientation set to *Portrait*.)

    a. In Finale 2008, select *Create New Ensemble,* then the *Band (Maestro)* document style. Input the text information on page 3 of the *Setup Wizard.*

2. On page 2 of the *Setup Wizard,* make sure *SmartMusic SoftSynth* is selected from the dropdown menu, then select these instruments from the listed groups:

    a. Pitched Percussion—Xylophone.

    b. Drums—Snare Drum.

    c. Marching Percussion—Quad Toms.

    d. Marching Percussion—Snare drum.

    e. Marching Percussion—5-line bass drum.

    f. Drums—Drum Set.

3. Use the up and down arrow buttons next to the score list to adjust the score order as shown in the example below. Click *Next.*

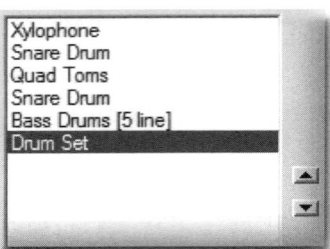

Setting up percussion instruments in the Setup Wizard

4. In Finale 2008, set the title and other text inserts. Click *Next.*

5. Set the time to *6/8* and the key to *D minor.* In Finale 2006–2007, click *Next.*

6. Set the tempo marking to ♩ = 125.

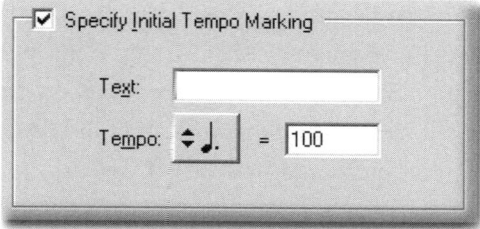

Setting the tempo marking

7. Click *Finish* to complete the blank score.

Before putting in notes, we need to change some staff names and change the measure numbering system. This will make it easier for you to keep track of where you are and what you are selecting. Make sure you are in *Page View*.

1. **Changing Staff Names.** Press **Esc** and right-click (**Control--click**) on the staff name *Xylophone*.

2. Select *Edit Full Staff Name*.

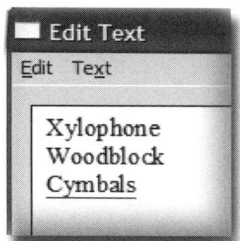

Editing the staff name

 a. Add the names *Woodblock* and *Cymbals* to this name.

 b. Type **Ctrl/Command–A** to select all of the text.

 c. Change the font size to 11-point, either by selecting *Text* menu/*Size*, or using the shortcut keys taught previously, **Ctrl/Command–Shift–<**.

 d. Make sure you de-select all of the text, then click *OK*. (There is a bug in Finale 2007–2008 that makes all staves disappear if you delete all of the text, re-type new text, or have all text selected when you exit the dialog.)

3. Drag the staff name to position it as shown in the PDF example or press **Up Arrow** to move it.

4. Using the steps above, change both of the Snare Drum staff names as shown in the finished example. Do not change the font size.

Teacher, I Have a Question

How do you keep from dragging an item horizontally when you only want to move it vertically? **Shift-drag**. This will constrain the movement vertically or horizontally, depending on the order of the **Shift** key. If you click the item then press and hold **Shift**, you can only drag vertically. If you press and hold **Shift** *before* you click the item, you can only drag the item horizontally.

5. **Changing the Abbreviated Staff Name.** Go to page 2 of the score by typing **Ctrl/Command–Page Down**.

   a. Press **Esc** and right-click (**Control–click**) on the staff name *Xyl*.

   b. Select *Edit Abbreviated Staff Name*. Type the new, abbreviated name.

   c. Change the text size as you did above.

   d. Change the abbreviated staff names for both of the snare drum staves as shown in the finished score.

6. **Changing Measure Numbers.**

   a. Go to page 2, press **Esc** and double-click on a measure number or select the *Measure* tool.

   b. Select *Measure* menu/*Measure Numbers/Edit Regions*. (In Finale 2008, select *Measure* menu/*Edit Measure Number Regions*.)

   c. As we did in the previous project, under *Positioning & Display,* click the button next to *Show Every ___ Measures Beginning with Measure ___* and enter **1** in each text field. (In Finale 2008 this is already set.)

The Measure tool

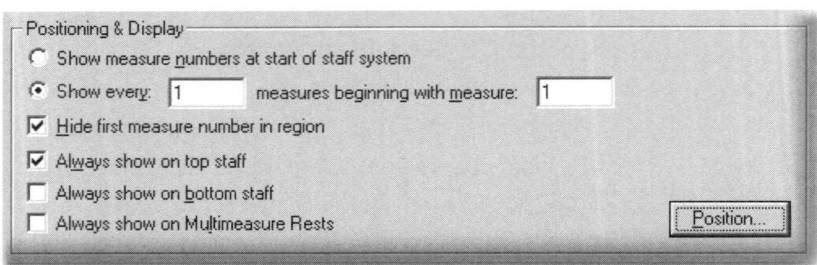

The Measure Number dialog

   d. In Finale 2008, next to *Always Show On*, check the box next to *Top Staff* and clear the box next to *Exclude Other Staves*.

e. In the bottom-right of the dialog, click *Position*. The *Position Measure Number* dialog appears.

f. If needed, drag the 0 above the staff in this dialog to the position shown in the example below.

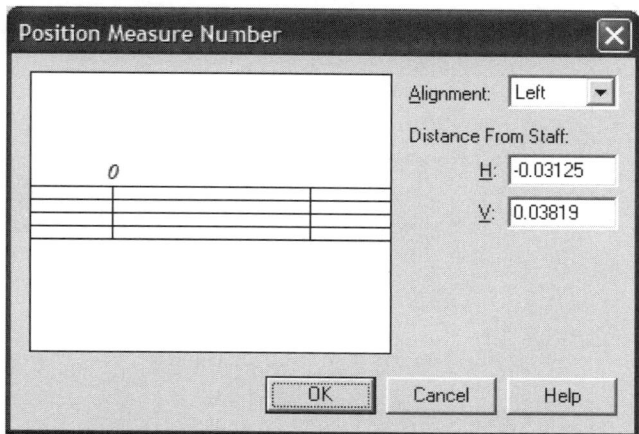

The Position Measure Number dialog

g. Press *OK* to return to the score.

h. Note that in the initial release of Finale 2008 there is a measure-positioning bug. The measure numbers do not show where you positioned them in the *Position Measure Number* dialog until *after* you input notes. Always make sure you have the latest release of your Finale version. To check for updates:

   i. Make sure you are connected to the Internet.

   ii. Select *Help* menu/*Check for Finale Updates*.

   iii. This will tell you if you have the latest update. If not, you will be directed to the Finale website to download it.

EXTRA CREDIT SECTION

The Staff tool

MORE ON MEASURE NUMBER POSITIONING AND DISPLAY

1. **Displaying Measure Numbers on a Staff.** Press **Esc** and double-click on a staff name or select the *Staff* tool.

   a. Double-click a measure in the Quad Toms staff.

   b. In the *Staff Attributes* dialog, under *Items to Display*, select *Measure Numbers*.

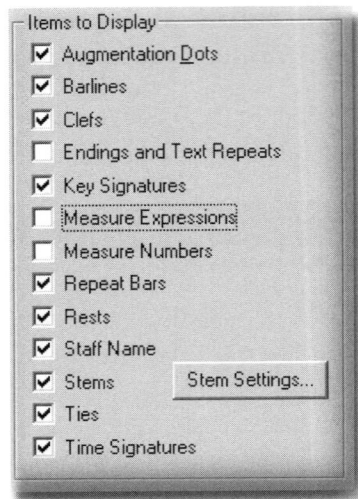

The Staff Attributes dialog

c. Click OK.

d. **Note**: Clearing the checkbox next to *Measure Numbers* will remove measure numbers for all staves *except* the top staff. Why? Because in the *Edit Measure Number Regions* dialog accessed previously we checked the box next to *Always Show On Top Staff* under *Positioning & Display* (see the previous section). Clear this checkbox to prevent measure numbers from showing on the top staff.

2. **Displaying or Removing Measure Numbers in a Region.** Since *Measure Numbers* is under *Items to Display* in the *Staff Attributes* dialog, you could create a staff style to change the staff attributes for a select region. We have used and edited staff styles before; you will learn more about this later on.

   a. **Quickly Removing Measure Numbers in a Region**. Press **Esc** and double-click a measure number.

   b. Drag a marquee around the measure numbers you want to remove.

   c. Press **Delete**.

   d. **Note**: In Finale 2007–2008, this action hides the measure number. The number will still display on the screen as a dimmed object, but will not print. This is because measure numbers are linked to the parts.

3. **Moving Measure Numbers in a Region.**

   a. Press **Esc** and double-click a measure number.

   b. Drag a marquee around the measure number handles you want to position.

   c. Click-drag one of the handles or press **Up Arrow** or **Down Arrow** to nudge the numbers to the desired position.

Before you input the notes for the Xylophone part, you may want to change rest behavior. Since the time signature is 6/8, there are several dotted quarter rests. To have Finale automatically select a dotted rest when filling the measure with rests, do this:

1. In Finale 2006, select *Options* menu/*Quantization*. In Finale 2007–2008, select *MIDI* menu/*Quantization Settings*.

2. In the *Quantization Settings* dialog, click *More Settings*.

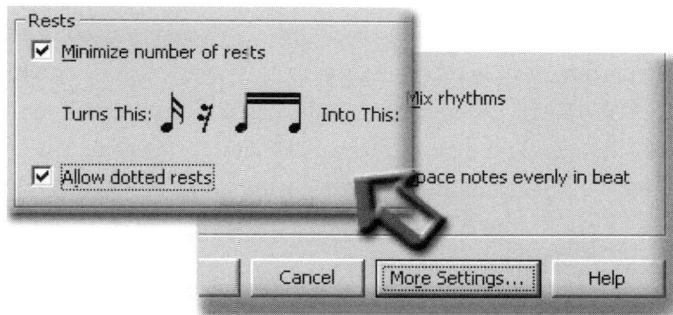

The More Quantization Settings dialog

3. Under *Rests*, check the box next to *Allow dotted rests*. Click *OK* twice to return to the score.

4. In Finale 2008, there are two choices for dotted rests: *Allow Dotted Rests in Simple Meters* and *Allow Dotted Rests in Compound Meters*. For now, check the box next to *Allow Dotted Rests in Compound Meters*.

5. Once you have returned to the score, input the notes for the Xylophone part up to measure 9. For now, do not put any notes in measures 9–16 of the Xylophone staff. We will do that later.

VIDEO
CLIP 8:1

UNDERSTANDING
PERCUSSION MAPPING

PERCUSSION MAPPING

Before inputting notes into the Concert Snare or any non-pitched percussion staff, it would be advisable to understand a bit about percussion mapping. (If you do not want to learn about percussion mapping, skip to *Inputting Notes on Percussion Staves* below and follow the instructions to get the project done.)

When you input notes into a regular staff, Finale plays the pitches using the sound designated for that staff. This is controlled by a MIDI channel assignment and program change, as we have seen from previous chapters. There is one sound for each MIDI channel.

All notes playing the Xylophone sound use channel 1

However, non-pitched percussion (non-chromatic percussion) is different. Most synthesizers (especially General MIDI synthesizers, such as the *SmartMusic SoftSynth* we are using) will place many percussion sounds all on one channel and use different key assignments to differentiate between sounds. For example, the Bass Drum sound is MIDI pitch or key number 36. This is the C two octaves below middle C on a MIDI keyboard. (Middle C is pitch number 60.) This is not the staff position on which you would want Bass Drum notes displayed.

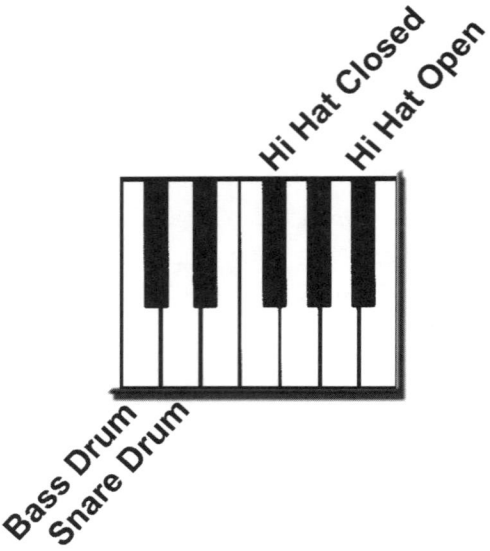

Each key produces a different instrument sound, all on channel 10

In Finale, Bass Drum notes are placed on the first space of a treble clef staff with a percussion clef. When you input a note on the staff, Finale follows a map that designates the correct MIDI key for that staff position. For example, you may place Bass Drum notes on the first space of the staff (the F space in treble clef). However, that is not the correct MIDI pitch for playback of the Bass Drum sound. The percussion map that Finale uses coordinates the staff position with the correct MIDI pitch for playback.

Also, when inputting notes via MIDI, you would play the correct MIDI key for the sound, not the MIDI note as shown on the staff. For Bass Drum, you would play note 36 (two octaves below middle C), but it would display on the staff in the first space. The percussion map coordinates the MIDI key played with the staff position for each instrument or sound.

A percussion map can designate more than one instrument per map. If a percussion staff requires more than one instrument, the map associated with that staff will have several percussion assignments. Finale has many percussion maps pre-created for you. If you create the score using the Setup Wizard, most sounds will be properly mapped for you.

UNDERSTANDING THE PERCUSSION MAP DIALOG

The example on the following page shows a list of sounds in this percussion map, and is labeled to help you understand each section.

A. An asterisk or checkmark in this column indicates that the instrument on this row is active in this percussion map.

B. **MIDI Pitch.** This column shows the pitch on the MIDI keyboard to be played when inputting this instrument.

C. **Playback.** This gives the MIDI pitch Finale will use when playing the note. By default, this is the same as the MIDI input pitch, since you generally use the same key on a MIDI keyboard for input as for Finale playback.

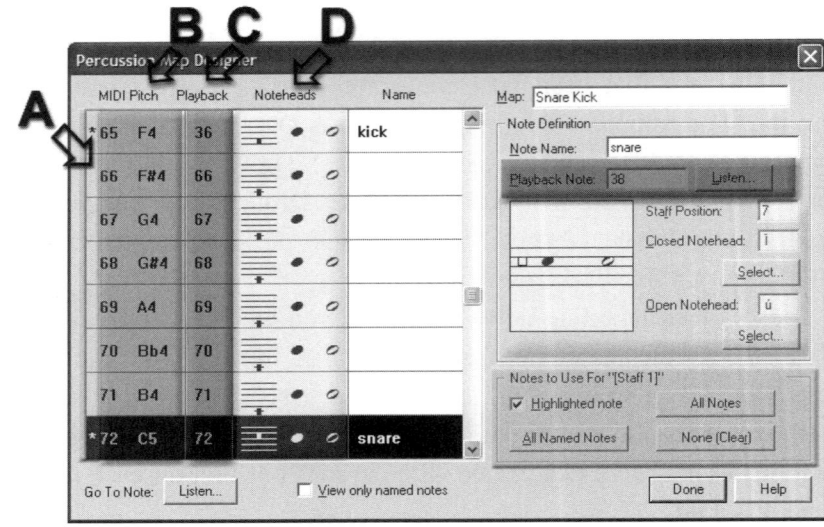

The Percussion Map Designer dialog

D. **Noteheads.** This column shows notehead type and staff position. Staff position controls two functions:

    a.   Placement of the note on the staff.

    b.   The pitch to type if not using MIDI input.

Each instrument shown in the left pane of the dialog can be modified with the controls to the right. To change information for an instrument, click the instrument row in the left pane, then change the settings to the right as follows:

1. Playback is changed by entering a new value in the *Playback Note* text field. You can type a pitch number if you know it, or click *Listen* and play a key on the MIDI keyboard.

2. Notehead type is controlled by the *Closed Notehead* and *Open Notehead* text fields. It is generally easier to click *Select* below each text field and visually locate the notehead you want. Finale fills in the text field with the correct character.

3. Under *Notes to Use For "[Staff 1]"* there is a checkbox next to *Highlighted note* and three buttons: *All Notes, All Named Notes,* and *None (Clear)*.

ACCESSING THE PERCUSSION MAP

1. If you have a MIDI keyboard, it is very helpful to activate the *MIDI Thru* setting for the staff you want to edit.

a. Click the *Simple Entry* tool in the *Main Tool Palette*.

b. Type **Ctrl/Command–Down Arrow** to go to the desired staff—in this case, the Concert Snare staff.

c. Now the keyboard is active on the MIDI channel and Patch number for this percussion set.

2. Press **Esc** and right-click (**Control–click**) on the staff name Concert Snare. Select *Edit Staff Attributes* from the contextual menu.

3. To the right of *Notation Style* there is a popup menu that says *Percussion*. Click *Select* to the right of this popup menu.

4. Note that the highlighted percussion map this staff is using is *Snare Drum*. Click *Edit*.

There are two basic ways to input notes into a score: manually (clicking a note on the staff, typing pitches, scanning, etc.) or via MIDI.

INPUTTING NOTES ON PERCUSSION STAVES

VIDEO CLIP 8:2

INPUTTING PERCUSSION NOTES, ALTERING A PERCUSSION MAP

Manual Note Entry. The information above in *Understanding the Percussion Map Dialog* will help you see that the Side Stick sound in this percussion map is placed on the center line, or the B line of the treble staff. If you use *Simple Note Entry* to type the pitch on the staff, this is the note you would input for the Side Stick sound. Now click the *Acoustic Snare* row in the *Playback* section. Note that it, too, is on the center line (treble clef B) of the staff. The question is, How do you specify which sound (and notehead) you want when you type or place a note on the center line of the staff?

Note that the MIDI pitch 37 is for for Side Stick and 38 is for Snare. When you type a pitch on this staff position, the default sound is Side Stick because it is the lowest MIDI pitch of the two notes. Finale defaults to the lowest MIDI pitch when two or more sounds are assigned to the same staff position.

In this case, you could type a B while entering notes, then use the plus key (**+** the equal sign key) to select the next sound assigned to that staff position. The plus (**+**) and minus (**–** the hyphen) keys cycle through all of the sounds (and noteheads) assigned to the same staff position.

MIDI Note Entry. If you input using a MIDI device, play the pitch or key listed in the *MIDI Pitch* column of the *Percussion Map Designer* dialog. In this example you would play the C♯2 key two octaves below middle C to input the Side Stick notes. You would use the D2 key just above this C♯ to input notes for the Snare sound.

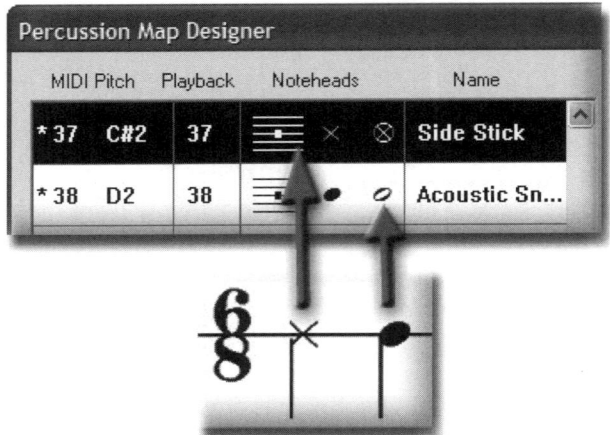

The Percussion Map Designer dialog

EDITING THE PERCUSSION MAP

As shown in the graphic above, the left column displays the percussion map info for each MIDI note. Once a MIDI pitch is selected in the left column you can use the settings on the right side of the dialog to change information.

In this dialog, you can change the staff position for a MIDI pitch, the notehead for both closed and open noteheads, the playback note to access a different sound, and—*very important*—enable or disable this MIDI pitch in this percussion map.

Inputting or copying disabled notes on this staff may yield strange results:

1. Finale might play a sound other than what you want.

2. The note might display several ledger lines above or below the staff.

3. The notehead for this sound may be different than the one you assigned.

In this percussion map, the only two MIDI pitches that are mapped are 37 and 38. This is designated by the asterisk or checkmark to the left of each MIDI pitch. To enable or disable a MIDI pitch, select the MIDI pitch from the window on the left, then clear the checkbox to the left of *Highlighted note* on the right side of the dialog. Note that this adds or removes an asterisk or checkmark next to the MIDI pitch on the selected row in the left pane.

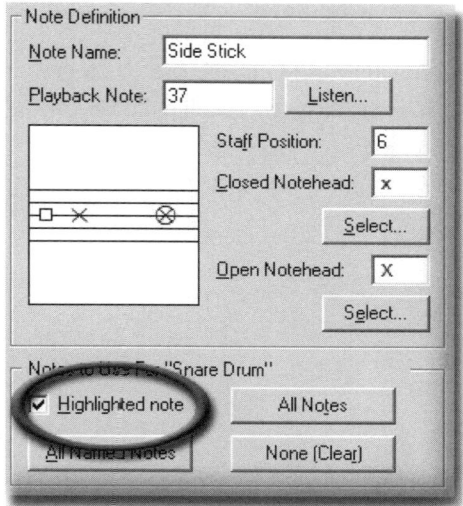

The right side of the Percussion Map Designer dialog

Turning Off the Side Stick. In this score there are no Side Stick notes in the Concert Snare staff, so we can disable that sound in the percussion map. This makes the default note (lowest note) the Acoustic Snare. Now you can manually enter a treble clef B and get a snare sound without having to use the plus (the equal sign) key.

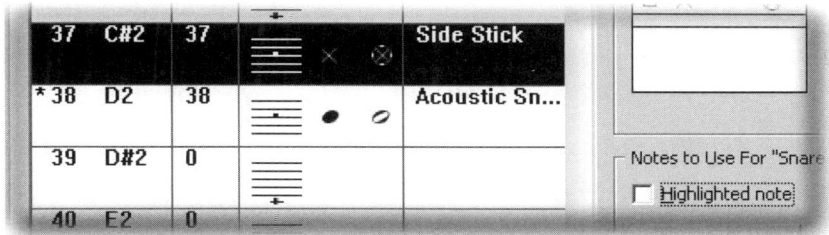

Disabling the Side Stick MIDI pitch

1. In the *Percussion Map Designer* dialog, click the Side Stick row to highlight it.

2. Clear the checkbox next to *Highlighted Note*.

3. Note that the asterisk or checkmark next to MIDI note 37 is gone.

4. Remember, if you are using MIDI input, this step is not necessary because you can input the correct note directly by playing it on the MIDI keyboard. If you want Acoustic Snare, play note number 38 (D) on your MIDI keyboard.

Now we want to change the staff position assignment for Acoustic Snare. We also want to add a second staff position for the Acoustic Snare to designate left and right hands when playing.

1. Select the Acoustic Snare row (MIDI pitch 38).

2. On the right side of the dialog, there is a graphical representation of the staff position (two noteheads, one filled, one open, and a positioning handle). Drag the handle down to the A (second) space on the staff. This will change the staff position value to position 5.

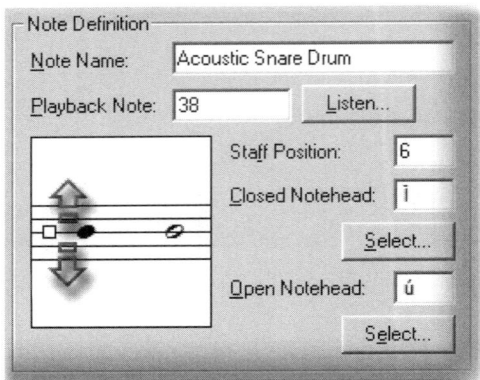

Changing the staff position of a notehead in the Percussion Map Designer dialog

Now we will add another staff position for the snare drum.

1. Select the row for MIDI pitch 40.

2. Check the box next to *Highlighted Note* to enable this pitch.

3. In the text field to the right of *Note Name,* enter **Snare LH** to remind you of the purpose of this note assignment.

4. Under *Closed Notehead* click *Select.*

5. Scroll to notehead 53 and double-click it. (You can also assign a notehead for open noteheads, but there are no open noteheads in this staff.)

6. Drag the handle next to the notehead to the C (third space) position on the staff (staff position 7).

7. In the text field next to *Playback Note,* enter **38** so that this MIDI note will use the same sound as the other note for Snare Drum.

8. Click *Done*, then *Select*, then OK to return to the score. You are now ready to input notes on the Concert Snare staff.

Now with the discussion of percussion maps out of the way, we will enter the Concert Snare part. Above you changed the Concert Snare percussion map to have two staff positions: one above the center line and one below the center line. Here are a few more *Simple Note Entry* features that you may not have discovered yet.

- Press **Right Arrow** at any time to move to the next measure. Finale will complete the previous measure by filling it with the necessary rests.

- This score has many changes in rhythmic value. If you input the wrong note value, simply press and hold **Alt/Option,** then the correct note value to change the note or rest to the correct value before going on.

- We have used some navigation functions before; here are some points to review.

  - **Ctrl/Command–Down Arrow** selects a single note in a chord or moves from one staff to the next.

  - **Ctrl/Command–Right Arrow** moves to the next measure (and **Ctrl/Command–Left Arrow** moves to the previous measure) without selecting each note or rest in that measure.

Teacher, I Have a Question

When I input a note on the MIDI keyboard, why does it sometimes appear two octaves below the staff on ledger lines? Any pitch you input via MIDI that is not enabled on the percussion map will show on the staff as the correct placement for that pitch. So if you are inputting notes on the Snare staff in the example above and play MIDI pitch 36 (C), it shows two octaves below the staff because the actual pitch of MIDI pitch 36 is the C two octaves below middle C. (The Bass Drum sound is not mapped in this Snare Drum map.)

NOTE INPUT

1. **Concert Snare Staff.** Press **Esc** and double-click on the first note in the Xylophone staff. Now type **Ctrl/Command–Down Arrow** to move the cursor to the Concert Snare Staff.

2. **Lock in the Augmentation Dot.** Since this staff has several dotted notes and rests, it is best to lock in the augmentation dot. Type **Ctrl/Command–.** (the decimal key on the numpad). On laptop computers, type **Shift–.** (the decimal key on the numpad) to enable the dot.

3. Now press **5** for quarter note and **0** for the rest, then type or play the notes for the Concert Snare staff up to measure 11. Make sure to turn off the augmentation dot using **Ctrl/Command–.** or simply double-tap a duration key.

4. **Note**: Do not be concerned about stem directions. We will deal with that issue later on.

5. Remember, if you are using a MIDI keyboard for input, use the MIDI pitches assigned in the percussion map as shown in the example below. (The snare sound for MIDI pitch 40 will be different during input, but since we assigned it to play back using key 38, it will sound fine during playback.)

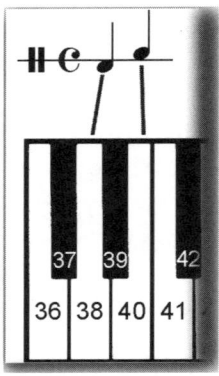

Snare Drum MIDI pitch assignments

6. In measures 11 through 15, you have the perfect opportunity to input accents as you input the notes.

    a. Input the third sixteenth note in measure 11.

    b. Press ***** (the *multiply* key) on the numpad or **~** (the tilde key) on laptop computers.

    c. Press **A** for accent.

    d. Press **0** for rest and go on to the next set of sixteenth notes.

7. Do not worry about the beaming of the sixteenth notes for now; we will fix that later.

8. **The Quad Drum Staff.** Input the notes for the Quad Drum staff.

    a. The MIDI pitches happen to be the same notes as displayed in the staff. The exception to this is the x notehead on the E (fourth) space. Use the F key (MIDI pitch 77) on the MIDI keyboard to input that note.

b. When entering notes, type the pitches as shown in the example below. Press **E**, then **+** (the equal sign key) once for the x notehead.

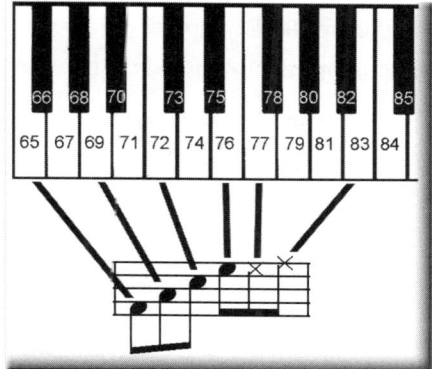

c. Measures 14–15 have some rim notes. Either type **F** or use MIDI pitch 83 (B) as shown on the Rowloff® marching percussion map above.

d. Remember, measure 17 (the coda) is a copy of measure 16. Also, both measures are a rhythmic copy of measure 17 in the Concert Snare staff. You may want to copy and re-pitch the notes.

e. Again, do not be concerned with stem direction right now.

9. **Marching Snare Staff.** Type or play the note on the staff.

a. **If Typing the Notes.** Type the pitch as shown on the staff. However, if you want to hear the left and right snare sounds (yes, there is a difference), you will need to press **+** (the equal sign key) twice for the right snare sound.

    i. You can input the grace notes by changing a regular note to a grace note (type **Alt/Option–G**), or you can lock in grace notes using **Ctrl/Command–G**. You can also click them in with the mouse after the regular notes are input as we did in the previous project.

    ii. Starting in measure 7, you will need to change to a rim shot sound. To do that, press **+** (the equal sign key) once to activate that sound and notehead as you type the note.

iii. In measures 14–15 you need to input the stick click notes. Type **F** as shown.

b. **If Playing the Notes on a MIDI Keyboard**.
Reference the Rowloff® percussion map diagram in the example below for the Snare Drum sounds.

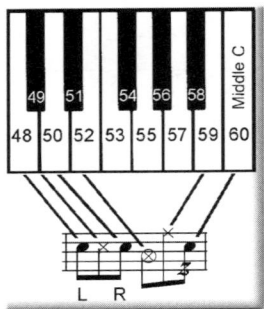

The Rowloff® Percussion Map dialog

i. For left-hand snare, use MIDI pitch 48, the C below middle C.

ii. For right-hand snare, use MIDI pitch 50, the D below middle C.

iii. For left-hand rim (x notehead), use MIDI pitch 49, the C♯ below middle C.

iv. For the stick click notes in measures 14–15, use MIDI pitch 59, the B below middle C.

v. For the Gok (the strange notehead on the A line for us non-percussion people), use MIDI pitch 52, the E below middle C.

vi. The articulation shortcut key (*Metatool*) for the roll (three slashes on the note) is **8** in the numrow (not the numpad). After inputting that note:

1. Type ***** (the *multiply* key on the numpad) or **~** (the tilde key on laptop computers).

2. Press **8** for this articulation.

c. **Ties Versus Slurs.** In measures 3 and 9 there is a tied note with a roll articulation. This figure should be played by rolling for the duration of the dotted quarter note with a final hit on beat 1 of the next measure. A tied-from rolled note will not sound correctly. The best thing to do in this case is to use a slur in place of a tie. This gives the visual appearance of a tie and the correct sound at the same time.

   i. Select the *SmartShapes* Tool, then the *Slur* tool, or press and hold **S**.

   ii. Double-click the first note in the tie.

The Slur tool

d. **Buzz Roll.** There is a buzz roll articulation in measure 5. This articulation can be accessed from the *Articulation* palette by typing ***** (the *multiply* key on the numpad) or **~** (the tilde key on laptop computers) and then pressing **Enter** in *Simple Note Entry* mode, or by using the *Articulation* tool.

   1. Playback of the buzz roll is not automatic. This buzz roll is a completely new sound, not just a MIDI roll.

   2. If you are inputting notes by typing, type the C pitch, then press **+** (the equal sign key) six times.

   3. For MIDI users, the buzz roll key is Middle C (60).

10. **Entering the Sticking.** The L and R "sticking text" in the Marching Snare staff are created using lyrics. This is the easiest and fastest way to do sticking. The only problem you will run into is automatic word extensions. You could use the selection tool and click on word extensions to remove them, but there are many scores for which you may not want word extensions for lyrics because you are using the lyric tool for some other text besides lyrics. So tell Finale *not* to use automatic word extensions.

   a. **Removing Word Extensions in a Document.** Click on the *Lyrics* Tool. Select *Lyrics* menu/*Lyric Options*.

The Lyric tool

b. In the *Document Options — Lyrics* dialog, click *Word Extensions* in the lower-right corner.

The Word Extensions dialog

c. In the *Word Extensions* dialog clear the checkbox next to *Use Smart Word Extensions*.

d. Click *OK* to return to the *Document Options* dialog but *do not* close it.

e. **Changing the Default Fonts.** Change the font for lyrics before entering the sticking text with the *Lyrics* tool.

f. In the left pane of the *Document Options* dialog, click *Fonts*.

g. To the right of the *Lyrics* dropdown menu, click *Select Font* (on Macintosh, *Set Font*).

h. Change the font to Arial 10–point and click *OK*. (the example uses Arial, not Arial Black or Arial Narrow.)

i. Click *OK* to return to the score.

11. Now enter the sticking text in the Marching Snare staff using the *Lyrics* tool.

12. **Bass Drum Staff.** Type or play the notes as shown on the staff.

a. **Typing.** The default sound for the center line (B) is the Bass Drum rim sound using an x notehead. You will need this for measures 14–15. So you will need to press **+** (the equal sign key) once to activate the Unison Bass Drum sound and the normal notehead.

b. **MIDI input.** If using MIDI, refer to the MIDI note chart in the example below.

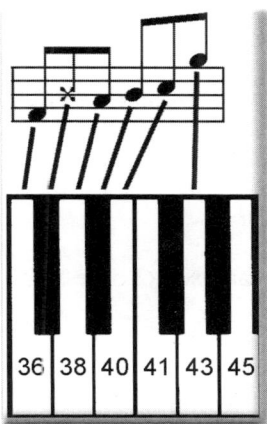

MIDI Bass Drum pitch assignments

 i. Bass Drum 5 is the note on the F space. On the MIDI chart, this is key 36, the C two octaves below middle C. This happens to be the same key for the Bass Drum sound in the General MIDI map.

 ii. The bass drum on the **A** key is Bass Drum 4, key 38 (the D).

 iii. The x notehead is the bass drum rim on the center B line. This is key 37, C♯.

 iv. See if you can find the other keys on the map.

13. **Drum Set Staff.** This staff uses the General MIDI percussion mapping. However, the default GM map uses the same staff position and the same notehead for both closed and open Hi Hat. I prefer to differentiate the open and closed Hi Hat by using different noteheads. Also, there is no Side Stick sound in this staff. To simplify inputting the Snare Drum part with the *Simple Note Entry* method, we should disable Side Stick from the percussion map.

 a. Access the *Percussion Map Designer* dialog as described above. Here is a quick reminder:

  i. Press, **Esc**, right-click (**Control–click**) on the staff name *Drum Set*. Select *Edit Staff Attributes*.

VIDEO CLIP 8:3

ADDITIONAL HYPERSCRIBE TOPICS

ii. Click *Select* next to Percussion.

iii. Click *Edit*.

b. Click on MIDI pitch 46, *Open HH*.

c. Under *Closed Notehead*, click *Select*.

d. Select notehead symbol 122.

e. Click *Select*.

f. Scroll up and select Side Stick, MIDI pitch 37.

g. Clear the checkbox next to *Highlighted Note*.

h. Click *Done, Select,* and *OK* to return to the score. But there is a faster way to return to the score.

i. **Exiting Multiple Dialogs.** Type **Ctrl/Command–Enter** (on Macintosh, type **Ctrl/Command–Return**). This will automatically select all of the active close buttons and return you to the score.

14. The Drum Set staff has notes that are stemmed both up and down. All of the cymbals are upstemmed and Bass Drum and Snare are downstemmed. Use Layer 1 for upstemmed notes and Layer 2 for downstemmed notes.

a. You may want to record this staff using HyperScribe. After you record the notes for Layer 1, you can select Layer 2 and record the notes for that layer as Layer 1 plays back. Layer 1 will not be recorded over by recording layer two.

b. **Using a Metronome in Triple Meter.** If you want to use HyperScribe, you will need to change the metronome to be either eighth note or dotted quarter note. Playing to a quarter note metronome is going to feel quite strange in 6/8 time.

i. Click on the *HyperScribe* tool. (If the message about turning off HP comes up, simply click *Ignore* or *Do not show again*).

ii. Select *HyperScribe* menu/*Beat Source/Playback and/or Click*.

The HyperScribe tool

    iii. **Note**: Finale 2008 has a choice of *Use Playback Tempo* or *Use This Tempo*. Select *Use This Tempo*.

    iv. Change the *Beat Equals* note duration to either eighth or dotted quarter.

The Beat Equals portion of the Playback and/or Click dialog

    v. Click *Listen*. Tap a single note on the MIDI keyboard several times to calculate the tempo at which you would like to record, or simply enter the tempo for the beat value you selected in the *Use This Tempo* text field.

        1. For an eighth note value, you may want a tempo of 160 to 190.

        2. For a dotted quarter note, perhaps 60–80.

        3. **Note**: This is only the recording tempo. The playback tempo is not determined here.

        4. Click *OK* to return to the score.

c. **Disabling Tempo Marking.** If you want to use HyperScribe to input these notes, follow the next set of instructions; otherwise, skip letter D below.

At the beginning of this score we used the *Setup Wizard* to create a tempo marking for the score. Now it may get in the way. The tempo control of the expression at the beginning of the score will override the recording tempo you selected. You will hear the count-off clicks at the desired recording tempo, then Finale will see the tempo expression and adjust to that as you begin recording.

    i. Press **Esc** and right-click (**Control–click**) on the tempo expression.

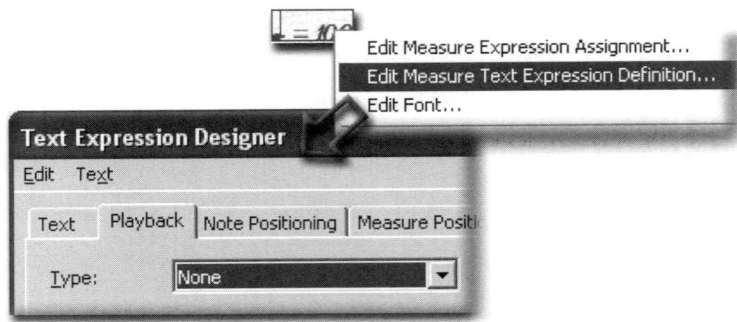

ii. Select *Edit Measure Text Expression Definition*.

The Playback tab of the Text Expression Designer dialog

iii. Click the *Playback* tab.

iv. Change the Type from *Tempo* to *None*. Click *OK*.

d. Follow the General MIDI reference map to input the correct notes.

i. For non-MIDI input (typing, etc.), type the notes as shown in the score for Bass Drum and Snare Drum in Layer 2.

ii. In the reference map below, to input the Ride Cymbal (diamond notehead on MIDI pitch 53), input an F on the top line, then press **+** (the equal sign key) three times. (Yes, this takes some time; MIDI input is faster.)

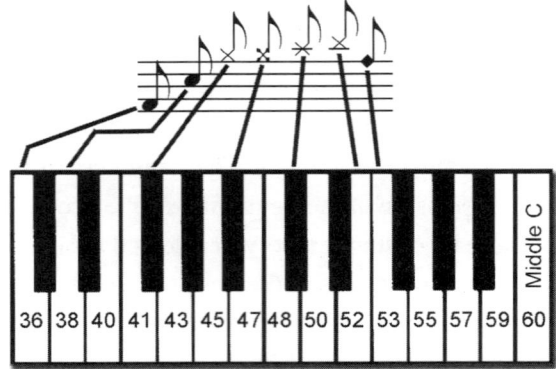

A drum kit reference map

iii. For the open Hi Hat (thick x notehead on MIDI pitch 46), type the G on the top space, then press **+** (the equal sign key) once.

iv. For the closed Hi Hat (thin x note head on MIDI pitch 42), type the G but do not press **+** (the equal sign key).

v. The Crash Cymbal is the A on the first ledger line above the staff (MIDI pitch 49).

vi. The China Crash is the B above the first ledger line above the staff (MIDI pitch 52).

e. If using MIDI for input, either the *Simple Note Entry* method or HyperScribe, follow the General MIDI key map above. See if you can find the correct keys. Look at the Drum Set legend on the finished example to see what notes you will need.

i. Here is a list of MIDI pitch numbers and instrument sounds assigned to them.

INSTRUMENT	MIDI PITCH NO.	KEY
Kick (Bass Drum)	36	C
Snare Drum	38	D
Closed Hi Hat	42	F♯
Open Hi Hat	46	B♭
Bell Ride Cymbal	53	F
Crash Cymbal	49	C♯
China Cymbal	52	E

f. **Note**: Do not delete the extra measures at the end of the score. You are not quite finished inputting notes. You will need these extra measures for the next part of this project.

g. **Note**: If using HyperScribe for input, you may notice strange noteheads for cymbal notes until you stop recording.

h. One last note on HyperScribe: Remember to set the Quantization settings to eighth note as the smallest value, no tuplets, and no Voice 2. Review the Hyperscibe section in Chapter 4.

VIDEO
CLIP 8:4

CREATING THE DRUM
SET LEGEND GRAPHIC

CREATING THE DRUM SET LEGEND

The Drum Set legend at the top of the score is a type of floating measure. Here we will discuss one of three ways to create an ossia or floating measure. This is an easy way to create a floating ossia measure, but not very flexible if you need to alter it later. Another way to create an ossia measure is using the *Ossia* tool. In this project we will create a graphic from the score, then import the graphic. This is the easiest method.

1. First, save the document on which you are working. If you have not saved it before, this will prompt you to create a filename. If you have already saved and named the file, saving again will overwrite the file as it was the last time you saved. Do not save the document again until prompted later in these instructions.

2. Go to measure 20 in the Drum Set staff.

3. Input the notes shown in the example below.

Notes for the Drum Set legend

4. Press **Right Arrow** to go to the next measure. Press **Left Arrow** and hide each rest by selecting it and pressing **H** for hide.

5. Press **Esc** and right-click (**Control–click**) in measure 19 and select *Invisible Barline*. (In Finale 2008, select *Barline/Invisible*).

6. Double-click on the measure number (20) and press **Delete**. (In Finale 2007–2008, this will dim the measure number, letting you know it is hidden. However, it will not print or save as part of the graphics file).

7. Select the *Staff* tool (or access the staff tool by pressing **Esc**, then double-clicking on the staff name Drum Set).

8. Select measures 18–19.

The Staff tool

9. Right-click (**Control–click**) the highlighted measures and select *Hide Staff*. You may also want to hide measures 18–20 in the Bass Drum staff.

10. Select measure 20. Right-click (**Control–click**) with the *Staff* tool in measure 20 and select *Stemless Notes*.

USING THE TEXT TOOL

1. Click the *Text* tool in the *Main Tool Palette*.

2. Just below the Bass Drum staff, Double-click to add a text box.

3. Type the text as shown in the example below. Press **Enter** or **Return** to move to the next line as you normally would in typing.

The Text tool

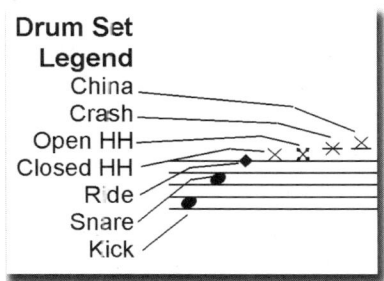

Text for the Drum Set legend

4. Type **Ctrl/Command–A** to select all of the text.

5. Select *Text* menu/*Font*.

6. Change the font to Arial and the size to 9–point. Click *OK*.

7. Select *Text* menu/*Justification/Right*. Note the shortcut key to the right of this menu item.

8. Select the text *Drum Set Legend* by click-dragging over the text. We need to make this text bold. Use one of the methods below.

   a. Select *Text* menu/*Style/Bold*.

   b. Type **Ctrl/Command–Shift–B**.

9. Press **Esc** and drag the text next to the staff.

10. For extra credit, you can use the *Line* tool (click the *Line* icon in the *Smart Shapes* tool palette) to draw lines from the noteheads to the appropriate text.

   a. Zoom in on measure 20.

   b. Select the *Smart Shapes* tool, then the *Line* tool.

The Smart Shapes tool

   c. Input lines by click-dragging from notehead to matching text.

      1. Make sure that the cursor arrow does not point to the Bass Drum staff. If you hide the Bass Drum staff, lines assigned to it will disappear.

The Line tool

d. For lines with angles, draw two separate lines.

e. Once a line is selected, press **Tab** to select the different handles on the line and use arrow keys to nudge the line into position.

The Graphics tool

EXPORTING AND IMPORTING GRAPHICS

1. Select the *Graphics* tool. (On Windows, select *Window* menu/ *Advanced Tool Palette*.)

2. Double-click on the score and drag around the text box and notes as shown in the example below. When you release the mouse, this will place a dotted marquee around the selected area. (**Note**: Sometimes when using the *Graphics* tool for the first time, you may need to select this a second time for the dotted marquee to stick.

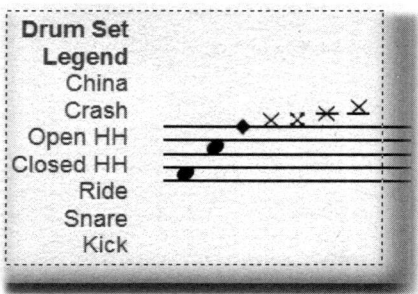

Moving the text in the Drum Set legend

3. Select *Graphics* menu/*Export Selection.*

4. The selection can be saved in a number of formats. For now, simply select *TIFF* from the *Type* dropdown menu and *300* from the *Resolution* dropdown menu, then click *OK.*

5. Name and save this file to the desktop (or a location of your choosing). For this exercise, this is a temporary file you can delete later.

6. **Multiple Undo.** I realize that you just did a bunch of work, but now it is time to undo everything you just did.

7. Select *Edit* menu/*Undo/Redo List.*

8. In the *Select Edit(s) to Undo* column scroll down and click on *---document saved---.*

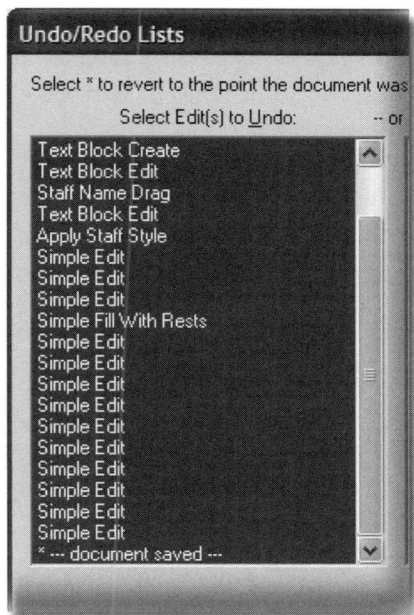

The Undo/Redo Lists dialog

9. Click *OK*. This will undo everything you did up to the last time you saved.

10. **Importing Graphics.** Return to Page 1.

11. Select the *Graphics* tool.

12. Scroll to the top of the page 1 and double-click in the top left-hand corner of the page.

The Graphics tool

13. In the *Place Graphics* dialog, navigate to the desktop and select the graphic that you just created. Click *Open*.

14. Double-click on the graphic and set the scale percentage to 75% for both the H and V settings. Click *OK*.

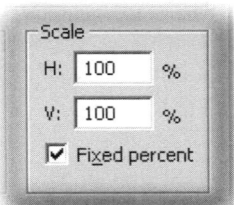

The Scale section of the Graphic Attributes dialog

15. Press **Esc** and drag the graphic to position it as shown in the finished example.

16. If the text box *Score* is visible on the first page of the score, you can drag the graphic over it to hide it, or you can use the *Selection* tool, to right-click (**Control–click**) and deselect *Show* from the contextual menu.

17. **Note**: This graphic may not look great on the screen (remember, screen resolution is only 72 dpi, but you just saved and loaded a 300 dpi graphic), but will look great when you print it.

18. Now you can save the document. Type **Ctrl/Command–S** for save. Generally this will save over the previously saved version unless you haven't saved the document at all, in which case Finale will prompt you for a filename and location for the saved file.

VIDEO
CLIP 8:5

MIXING PITCHED
AND NON-PITCHED
PERCUSSION

MIXING PITCHED PERCUSSION AND NON-PITCHED PERCUSSION

Return to the Xylophone staff. As you recall, this is also a Woodblock and Cymbals staff. In measure 9 we need to change to a single line staff and Woodblock percussion map. In measure 13 we change to a five-line percussion staff and assign a percussion map for Marching Cymbals on this staff.

The MIDI channel for the Xylophone staff is currently set to channel 1 for all layers. We are going to use Layer 2 for Woodblock. The Woodblock needs to be on a non-pitched percussion channel (10, 26, 42, 58, 74, 90, 106, 122 are the non-pitched percussion channels) and use Program Change 1, which is the GM percussion patch. We will use Layer 3 for the marching cymbals on another non-pitched percussion channel using Patch 2. Program Change 2 is the Rowloff® Marching Percussion patch.

1. **Setting Separate MIDI Channels to Different Layers in the Same Staff.** Select *Window* menu/*Instrument List*.

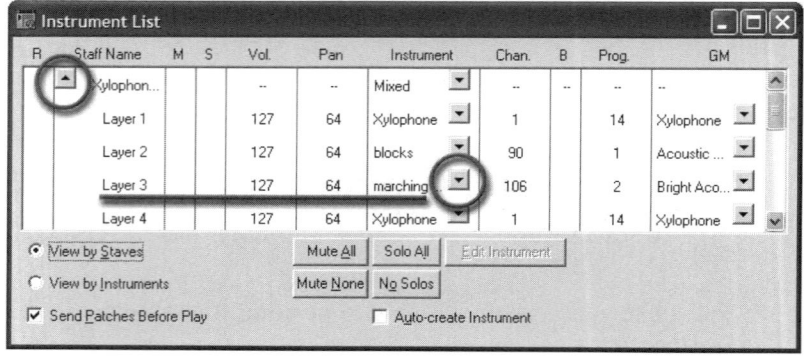

The Instrument List dialog

2. Click the *Expand* arrow next to *Xylophone* in the *Staff Name* column.

3. On the Layer 2 row arrow next to *Xylophone* in the *Instrument* column click to open a dropdown menu. Scroll up in the menu and select *New Instrument.*

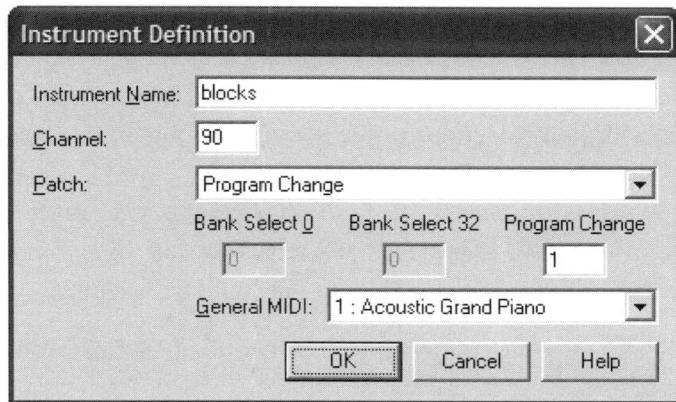

The Instrument Definition dialog

4. In the *Instrument Name* text field, enter a name for the new instrument, such as **blocks.** In the *Channel* text field, enter **90**.

5. In the *Program Change* text field (not the *Patch* dropdown menu that displays the *Program Change* item), enter **1.** Click *OK.*

6. Follow steps 3–5 again on the Layer 3 row.

   a. Create a new instrument.

   b. Enter **Marching Cymbals** for the instrument name.

   c. Set the channel to **106**.

   d. Set the Program Change to 2. Click *OK.*

7. Click the close box to return to the score.

EDITING AND CREATING STAFF STYLES

Previously you selected the *Staff Attributes* dialog. There you can change attributes of the staff for the entire score. A *Staff Style* is the way to alter staff attribute settings for a region of the staff.

When editing or creating a staff style, you will notice that clicking a checkbox will alternate between three states. On Windows, these states are dark checkmark, light checkmark, or no checkmark. On Macintosh, they are checkbox with checkmark, checkbox with line, and cleared checkbox.

A dark checkmark (Windows) or cleared checkbox (Macintosh) indicates that you want to override the setting in the *Staff Attributes* dialog.

For example, if the global staff attributes setting shows a checkmark next to *Stems* in the *Items to Display* area, you could turn them off with no checkmark (Windows) or cleared checkbox (Macintosh) in a staff style. If the staff attributes had no checkmark (Windows) or a cleared checkbox (Macintosh) next to *Stems,* then a staff style could turn them on with a dark checkmark (Windows) or a checkmark (Macintosh). A staff style will have no effect if there is a light checkmark (Windows) or checkbox with line (Macintosh); the setting will remain as designated by the staff attributes setting.

You will need to change the staff attributes at measure 9 using a staff style as you have in previous projects. The staff style *Percussion: 1–line Staff* will work, but we will edit the staff style slightly.

The Staff tool

1. Select the *Staff* tool or press **Esc** and double-click on the staff name.

2. Select measures 9–11. In Finale 2008, this is a good place to try out the new measure region select.

   a. Click on measure 9, then press **Ctrl/Command– Shift–Right Arrow**. Continue holding **Ctrl/ Command–Shift** and press **Right Arrow** repeatedly until all of the additional measures you want to include are selected.

3. Right-click (**Control–click**) in the highlighted area and select *Percussion: 1-line Staff.*

4. Right-click (**Control–click**) in the highlighted area again and select *Define Staff Styles.*

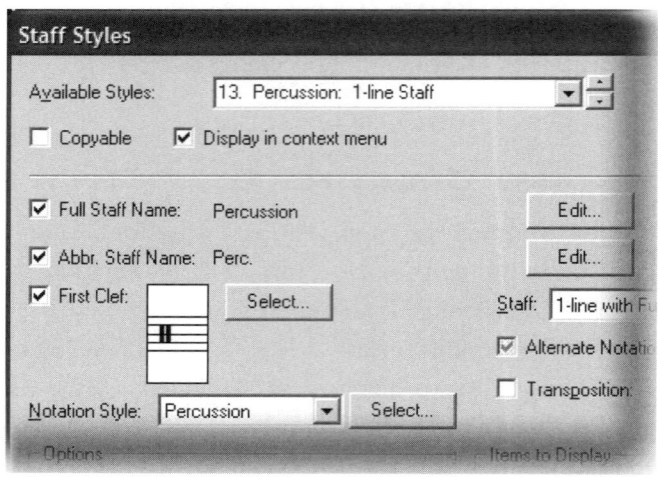

The Staff Styles dialog

5. In the *Available Styles* dropdown menu, select *Percussion: 1–line Staff.*

6. Click *Select* next to the *Notation Style* dropdown menu.

7. Select the Woodblocks percussion map. Click *Edit.*

8. Click *View Only Named Notes.* This will show only pitches 76 and 77. (They are the only named MIDI pitches).

9. Click pitch 76 *High Woodblock.*

10. Click *Highlighted Note* to enable it in the map if it is not already enabled.

11. Click *Select* under *Closed Notehead* and double-click notehead symbol 121. As before, there are no open noteheads in this score.

12. Repeat steps 9–11 for MIDI pitch 77: *Low Woodblock.*

13. Click *Done,* then *Select.*

14. In the *Staff Styles Designer* dialog, under *Items to Display,* de-select *Key Signature* (a cleared checkbox).

15. If you like, you can also change the staff name abbreviation to reflect what is being played. Of course, this will only show if the measures with the new staff style start a new system.

16. Click *OK* to return to the score.

CREATING A NEW STAFF STYLE

The staff style we need for the cymbal part has not been created.

1. Select the *Staff* tool or press **Esc** and double-click the staff name.

2. Click measure 12 on the Xylophone Staff.

3. Right-click (**Control–click**) measure 12.

4. Select *Define Staff Styles.*

5. Click *New* to the right of the *Available Styles* dropdown menu.

6. In the *Style Name* text field, enter a name for this staff style, such as **Marching Cymbals.**

7. Under *Items to Display* clear the checkbox next to *Key Signature.*

8. Under *Independent Elements,* put a dark checkmark (Windows) or a checkmark (Macintosh) in the checkbox next to *Notehead Font.*

9. Click *Select* next to *Notehead Font*.

10. Select *Maestro Percussion*. Click *OK*. (In general, percussion maps use this font for noteheads.)

11. Click the dropdown menu next to *Notation Style* and select *Percussion*.

12. Click *Select* to the right of this dropdown menu.

13. Select *Percussion Map Crash Cymbals* (channel 10, patch 2).

14. Click *Edit*. Scroll down to MIDI pitch 44. Enable all four cymbals by clicking *All Named Notes* under *Highlight Notes*.

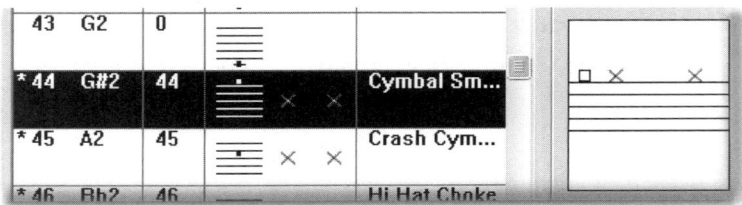

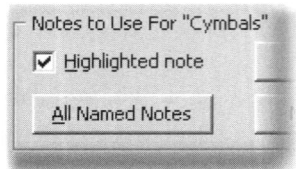

Enabling the cymbals in the Percussion Map Designer dialog

15. Click on MIDI pitch 44 and change the *Staff Position* to the top line (*Staff Position 10*).

16. Click on MIDI pitch 45 and change the *Staff Position* to the C space (*Staff Position 7*).

17. Click on MIDI pitch 46 and change the *Staff Position* to the A space (*Staff Position 5*).

18. Click *Select* under *Closed Notehead*. Change the notehead to symbol number 116, a triangle notehead. Click *Select*.

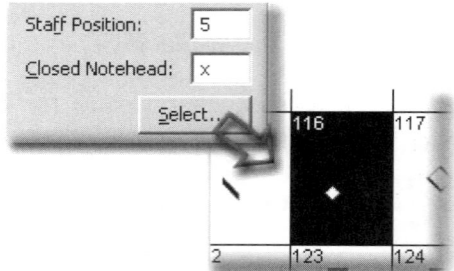

Selecting a triangle notehead

19. Click on MIDI pitch 47 and change the *Staff Position* to the F space (*Staff Position 3*).

20. Click *Select* under *Closed Notehead*. Change this notehead to symbol number 90 (a circle with an x in the middle). Click *Select*.

21. Click *Done,* then **Ctrl/Command–Enter** (on Macintosh, **Ctrl/Command–Return**) to return to the score.

22. Select measures 12–16. Right-click (**Control–click**) in the highlighted area and choose the newly created staff style *Marching Cymbals*.

23. **Note**: I am not advocating these noteheads or staff positions for percussion staves. The intention here is to give you some experience in editing the percussion map.

24. **Changing Clefs.** Press **Esc** and double-click on the last note in measure 8 of the Xylophone staff.

    a. Press **Right Arrow** to move to measure 9.

    b. Type **Alt/Option–C** for *clef*. Press **Enter.**

    c. Select the percussion clef. Note the option for placing the clef after the barline. If you prefer, you may select this option.

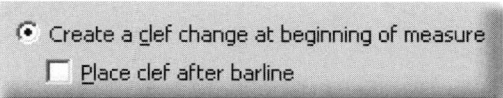

The Place clef after barline option

    d. Once you have selected the options you want, click *OK*.

25. **Optional Method for Changing Clefs in Finale 2008**. The instructions in step 24 will work in Finale 2008; however, you may find the following method faster and easier to remember.

    a. Press **Esc**. Right-click (**Control–click**) in measure 9.

    b. Select *Change Clef.*

    c. Select the correct clef and click *OK*.

Teacher, I Have a Problem

I selected 4/4 or common time and I still get eighth notes beamed together in groups of four. The exception to the rule in Finale is 4/4 time. The default setting in *Document Options/Beaming* is to beam four eighth notes together in 4/4 time. You can change this setting before you input notes if you wish. If you select it after changing meters, you will need to use the mass edit re-beam music function. (In Finale 2008, select the *Selection* tool (**Esc**) and select *Utilities* menu/Rebeam).

Now you can finish inputting the notes on the Xylophone staff. Remember to put the Woodblocks in Layer 2 and the Marching Cymbals in Layer 3. Also note that you can copy measure 17 from the Snare staff and re-pitch it.

If you are using MIDI input, note that we have altered the percussion map for Marching Cymbals. The GM percussion map for did not show the Woodblock settings. The map in the example below shows which key to use for each note. If you are inputting by typing, simply type the position on the staff. Since these are the only notes in these maps, there will be no need to type **+** (the equal sign key).

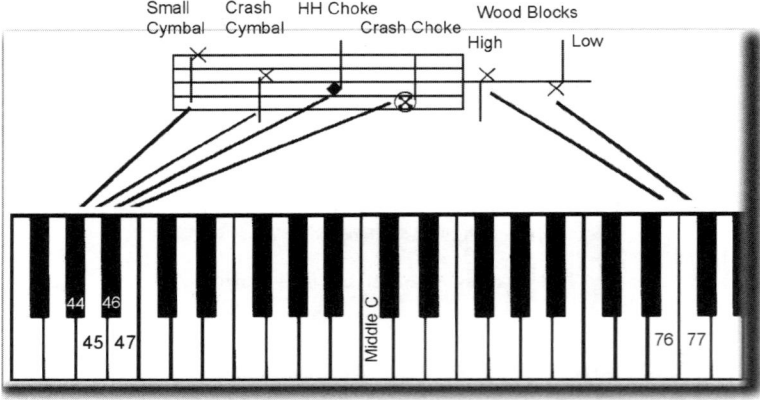

Percussion map with Woodblock key assignments

ADJUSTING BEAMING GROUPS

Finale uses the time signature to determine how notes are to be grouped with beams. Generally, Finale beams notes based on the size of the beat selected in the time signature. In 6/8 time, you could set the time signature to six eighth-note beats, which would result in the upper example on the following page. A 6/8 time signature of two dotted-quarter-note beats would result lower example on the following page.

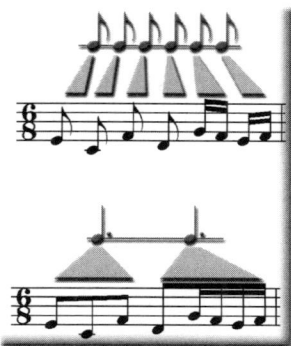

6/8 beaming examples

Finale's default for 6/8 is two dotted-quarter-note beats (the lower example). You can change time signature beaming attributes *before* you input notes. In the *Time Signature* dialog, you can set one time signature to control the meter and beaming and a separate time signature for display. (Click *Options* in the *Time Signature* dialog. Complex beaming shown in the example below is covered below).

Setting a different time signature for display

We have already input notes for the Concert Snare staff. In measures 11–15, you may notice that the beaming is quite different in the finished example than the beaming that Finale provided when you input the notes. You can alter these beams independently or for a region.

INDIVIDUAL SIMPLE NOTE BEAMING CONTROL

1. Press **Esc** and double-click on a notehead or rest to select it.

2. Select the first rest in measure 11 of the Concert Snare staff.

3. Press **/** (the forward slash key on the numpad above **9** or on the question mark key [**?**] to the left of the right-hand **Shift** key) to break the beam.

4. Press **Right Arrow** to move forward.

5. Correct each beam group by selecting the desired note to break or to join a beam. If the note is not beamed, pressing **/** (the forward slash key) will beam it to the note to the left. If it is beamed, it will break the beam to the note to the left.

Of course, this is time-consuming; but there is a faster way.

REGIONAL BEAMING CONTROL

1. Select measures 12–15 of the Concert Snare staff using the *Mass Edit* or *Selection* tool (press **Esc**).

2. Right-click (**Control–click**) in the highlighted area and select *Rebeam/Rebeam to Time Signature*. (In Finale 2008, select *Utilities* menu/*Rebeam/Rebeam to Time Signature*.)

3. In this dialog, you are presented with the basic time signature controls available in the *Time Signature* dialog.

4. Change the time signature to 3/4 (three quarter-note beats). This beams the notes as shown in the finished score but leaves the real time signature as 6/8. Click *OK*.

5. Save your work.

EXTRA CREDIT
SECTION

COMPLEX BEAMING CONTROL

If you need to beam notes in a less traditional way to emphasize rhythmic groups, try this exercise:

1. Start a new blank document. Set the time signature to 4/4.

2. Input a couple of measures of eighth notes.

3. We will beam the first measure as in the example below.

4. Select the first measure with the *Mass Edit* or *Selection* tool (press **Esc**).

5. Right-click (**Control–click**) in the highlighted area. Select *Rebeam/Rebeam to Time Signature*. (In Finale 2008, select *Utilities* menu/*Rebeam/Rebeam to Time Signature*.)

6. Click *Composite*.

7. Set the dialog settings as shown in the example below.

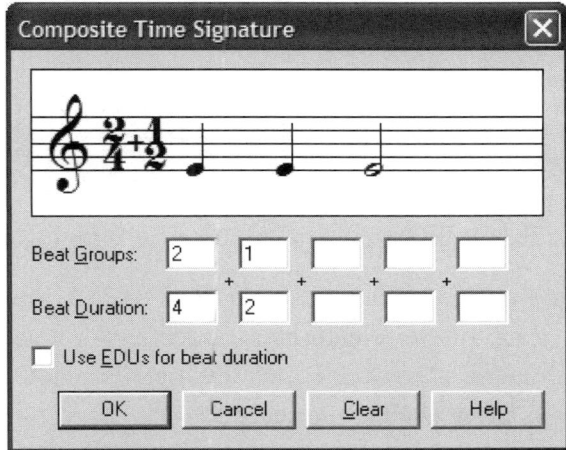

The Complex Time Signature dialog

8. The composite time signature settings allow you to have several beat groups of different types. Here we have set two quarter-note beats (two *Beat Groups* with a *Beat Duration* of four—think of the numerator and denominator of a time signature) plus one half-note beat. (one *Beat Group* with a *Beat Duration* of two).

9. Press *OK* in each dialog (or **Ctrl/Command–Enter** [on Windows] or **Ctrl/Command–Return** [on Macintosh] to exit all dialogs with one keystroke) to return to the score.

10. The second example in this exercise is a bit more complex. Note the example below.

11. Select the next measure and repeat steps 5 and 6.

12. In the *Composite Time Signature* dialog, click *Clear* to clear the previous setting.

13. Here we need one quarter-note beat followed by two dotted-quarter-note beats. Or as shown in the example below, one group of two eighth notes and two groups of three eighth notes.

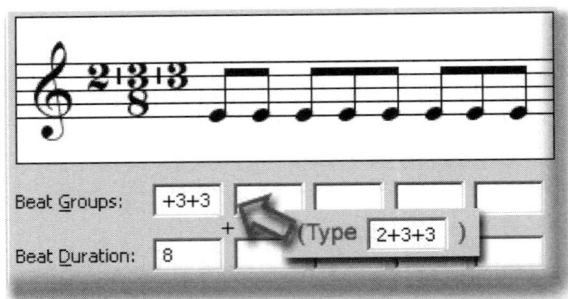

14. In the first *Beat Duration* text field, type **8** for eighth notes.

15. In the first *Beat Group* text field, type **2+3+3.** This will result in a group of two eighth notes, three eighth notes, and three eighth notes. (The *Beat Group* text field is small, but you can enter as many numbers as needed.)

16. **Note**: The only time you need to use another *Beat Duration* text field is if you select a different *Beat Duration*.

17. Return to the score to see the effect on the beaming.

18. Close this test file to return to the project.

BACK TO THE PROJECT

FORMATTING

In previous projects we learned how to move measures and lock systems. Moving a measure *does* lock the system, but systems can also be locked manually. If measure 17 is on the page 4, move it to page 3.

1. Select measure 17 with the *Mass Edit* or *Selection* tool (press **Esc**).

2. Press **Up Arrow**.

3. If this measure is already the last measure of system 3, then simply press **L** (on windows) or **Command–L** (on Macintosh) to lock this system.

Now delete all of the extra measures.

1. Select measure 18 with the *Mass Edit* or *Selection* tool (press **Esc**).

2. Type **Shift–Right Arrow.** (In Finale 2008, type **Shift–End**).

3. Press **Delete**.

CHANGING STEM DIRECTION

In previous projects we changed stem direction by using the typing **L** (for *flip*) in *Simple Note Entry* mode. This changes stem direction for individual stems. In percussion scores we often want to change stem direction for a region.

1. Use the *Mass Edit* or *Selection* tool (press **Esc**) to select the entire Marching Snare staff by clicking to the left of the staff.

2. Right-click (**Control–click**) in the highlighted area and select *Utilities/Freeze Stems Up*. (In Finale 2008, select *Utilities* menu/*Stem Direction/Up*.)

3. Change the other regions that require a change in stem direction.

SHORT STEM CONTROL

After flipping stems, you will notice the articulations that are positioned on the stem may be positioned too low. This is because the stem has been altered to be a short stem. Finale will automatically shorten some stems that have been flipped. If you change the short-stem setting, you will not need to adjust each of the articulations.

1. In Finale 2006, select *Options* menu/*Document Options*. In Finale 2007–2008, select *Document* menu/*Document Options*.

2. Click *Stems* in the menu to the left.

3. Change the value for *Shortened Stem Length* to match the value for *Normal Stem Length*. The default should be 0.29167 inches. (An easy way to do this is to click in the *Normal Stem Length* text field and press **Ctrl/Command–A** [select *all*], then **Ctrl/Command–C** [*copy*]. Then click in the *Shortened Stem Length* text field, and press **Ctrl/Command–A** [select *all*], then **Ctrl/Command–V** [*paste*].)

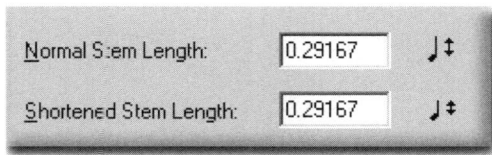

Stem length settings

4. Click *Apply,* then *OK*.

5. You should not need to adjust articulations after changing this setting. If you feel you need to do so, change articulation position with the *Selection* tool. Remember: you can double-click on an articulation using the *Selection* tool and then select several articulation handles and move them together.

Moving multiple articulations

VIDEO CLIP 8:6

SPLITTING MEASURES— CREATING A CODA

SPLITTING MEASURES

In measures 8 and 10 there is a dashed barline to indicate a subdivision of the measure. This is easy to do with the *Split Measure* plug-in.

1. Select the *Mass Edit* or *Selection* tool (press **Esc**).

2. Make sure that *Edit* menu/*Select Partial Measure* is turned on. (This is not needed in Finale 2008.)

3. Select the first three eighth notes in measure 8 of the Xylophone staff.

4. Select *Plug-ins* menu/*New Plug-ins for Finale 2006/Split Measure*. In Finale 2007–2008, select *Plug-ins* menu/*Measures/ Split Measure*.

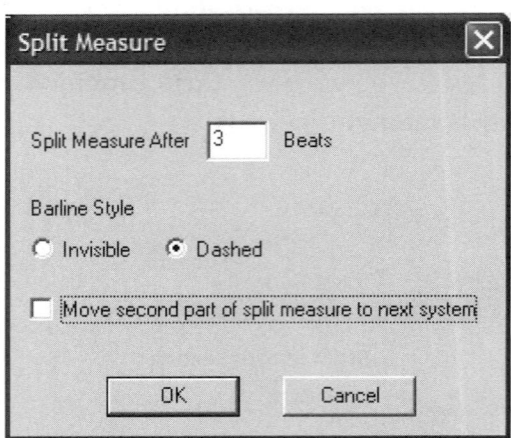

The Split Measure dialog

5. The split setting has already been determined by the selection you made.

6. Under *Barline Style* click *Dashed.*

7. Clear the checkbox next to *Move second part of split measure to next system.*

8. Click *OK.*

9. Repeat these steps for measure 10. When you are done, you may want to turn off *Edit* menu/*Select Partial Measures* if you prefer automatic selection of full measures.

This plug-in is very helpful for splitting a measure across a system. For example, in hymnals and other vocal music, it is common to keep lyric phrases together. *Split Measures* allows each system to have its own pickup measure by using the *Invisible* barline setting and selecting *Move second part of split measure to the next system.*

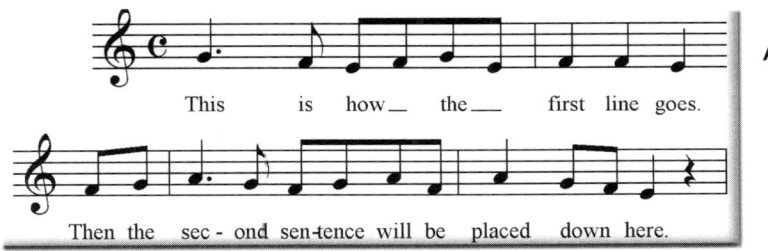

Split measure at the beginning of the second system of a hymn

CREATING A CODA

Creating a Coda that plays correctly can be a tricky procedure in notation software. Finale has made this very easy with a *Coda System* plug-in.

1. Use the *Mass Edit* or *Selection* tool (press **Esc**) to select measure 17.

2. In Finale 2006, select *Plug-ins* menu/*New Plug-ins for Finale 2006/Create Coda System.* In Finale 2007–2008, select *Plug-ins* menu/*Measures/Create Coda System.*

3. I like a bit less space for the system break, so I set the value for *Horizontal Space Before Coda* to 0.4 inches.

4. Check the box next to *Create "To Coda" in Measure* and enter **12** in the text field to the right.

5. In the lower part of the dialog, click *D. S. al Coda.* Check the box next to *Create Segno* and enter **5** in the text field to the right of *in Measure.* (This is the measure to which Finale will repeat during playback.)

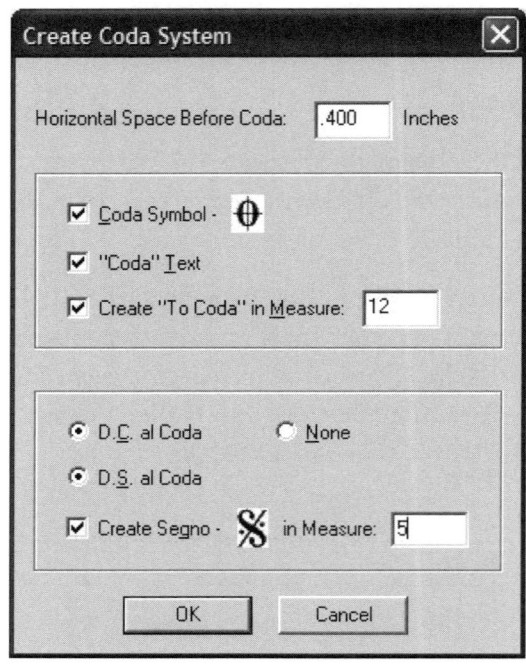

The Create Coda System dialog

6. Click *OK.* Finale not only displays the coda information in all three measures correctly, but it splits the system, aligns it to the previous system, and creates all of the playback parameters for you.

7. **Note**: This plug-in works well most of the time. However, it has been reported to have an intermittent bug. Sometimes system formatting can go awry. If this is the case, follow these instructions to fix the problem after clicking *OK* to run the plug-in:

    a. Select the *Page Layout* tool.

    b. Right-click (**Control–click**) on system 3, or select *Page Layout* menu/*Edit System.*

    c. In the text field to the right of *Left,* enter **0**; in the text field to the left of *Right,* enter **2**. Click *Apply.*

    d. Click on system 4—the coda system.

    e. Change the settings to *Left:* **7.7** (inches) and *Right*: **0**. Click *Apply.*

The Page Layout tool

f. Click the close box to close the dialog. Use the system margin handles to re-position further if needed.

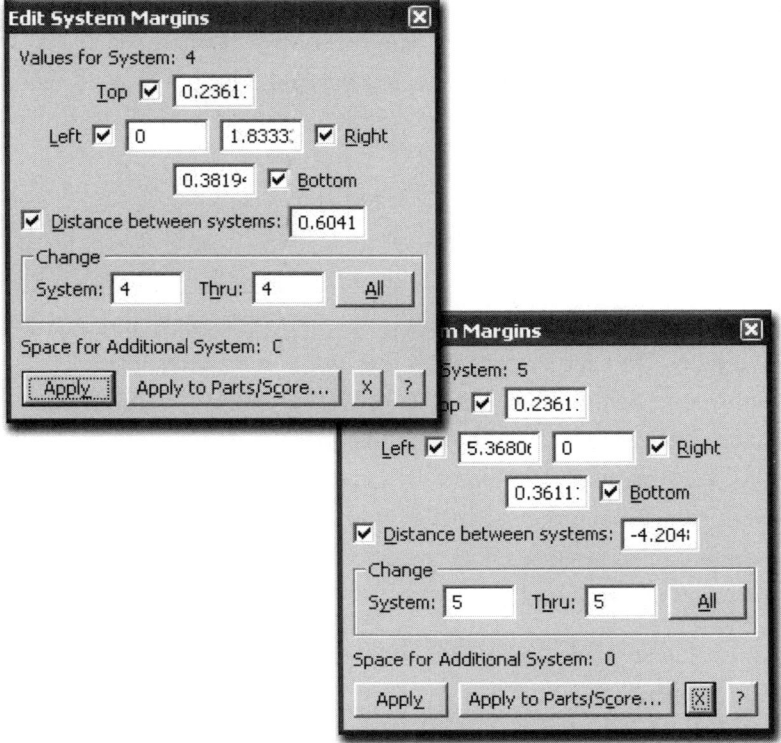

The Edit System Margins dialog

8. This is optional, but I do not like a measure number on the first measure of the Coda. To remove the measure number for all staves:

a. Press **Esc** and double-click on the measure number in measure 17.

b. Drag a box around all of the measure numbers in measure 17 in all staves.

c. Press **Delete**. (Remember that this hides the number in Finale 2007–2008.)

9. You may also want to reposition the repeat text. You can do this easily with the *Selection* tool. (Keep in mind that you can double-click with the *Selection* tool on any repeat text.) Drag a box to select the handles of all the repeat text you want to position, then use the arrow keys to position them together.

CREATING EXPRESSIONS

A few hairpins and expressions need to be added to this score. You may want to do this for practice. You should know how to do this by now, but review previous chapters if you need help. Remember, it is always faster to duplicate an existing expression and edit it. You will also need to create the expressions for the Woodblock and Cymbals text.

FINAL FORMATTING

The systems are too close to the top of the page on pages 2–3. Simply select the *Page Layout* tool, click in the middle of a system, and drag it down a bit. On page 3, only drag the first system, not the coda system. It will move automatically as you move the main system on page 3. If you are concerned about having the same positioning on all pages, Select *View* menu/*Rulers and Grids* to ensure that you place systems the same distance from the top of the page.

Finally, it is always a good practice to lock systems before performing a spacing command.

1. Select the entire score with the *Mass Edit* or *Selection* tool (press **Esc**).

2. Type **L** for lock.

3. Type **3** or **4** in the numrow for the desired spacing. (In Finale 2008, type **4** for *Note Spacing* or **5** for *Beat Spacing*.)

PERCUSSION PLAYBACK

The default for *Human Playback* is the *Standard* setting. In the previous jazz chart, we changed the *Human Playback* to a *Jazz* setting. When playing marching percussion specifically, it is correct to play grace notes very quickly. Rolls need to be interpreted correctly. The overall feel is quite different than the *Standard Human Playback* function.

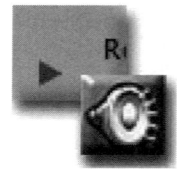

The Speaker icon and Expand button

1. In the *Playback Controls* palette, click the *Speaker* icon (on Windows) or *Expand* (on Macintosh).

2. In the dropdown menu to the right of *Human Playback Style*, select *Marching Band*.

3. There is some additional control for rolls in the HP preferences settings. In Finale 2007–2008, click *HP Preferences*. In the *Human Playback Preferences: "Default Prefs"* dialog, click *Ornaments & Tremolos* in the left pane.

4. Be sure to set the tempo expression at the beginning of the score to *Type: Tempo* if you turned it off previously to record to HyperScribe.

    a. Right-click (**Control–click**) on the tempo expression.

    b. Select *Expression Definition.*

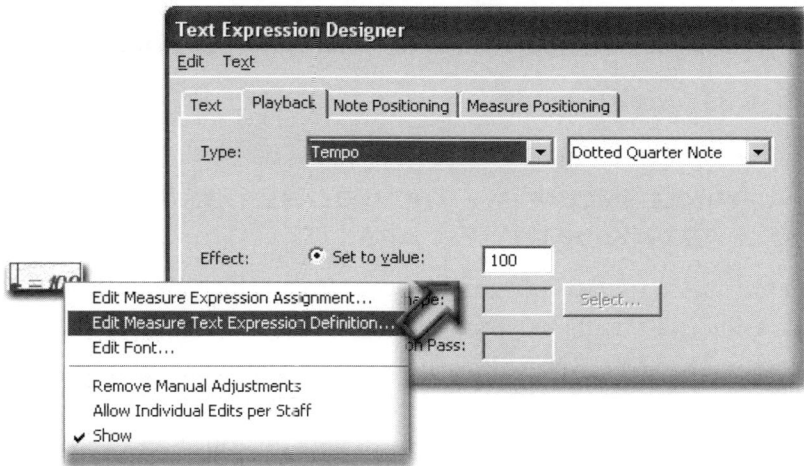

Setting the text expression type to Tempo

    c. Select the *Playback* tab.

    d. In the dropdown menu to the right of *Type,* select *Tempo.*

ADJUSTING ARTICULATION PLAYBACK

Articulations automatically affect the playback of the score when using *Human Playback;* however, you can alter articulation settings. If you change an articulation setting, for example, for accents, the change affects all accents throughout the score. If you need an accent with different playback parameters for a certain section, you can duplicate the articulation, edit the newly created expression, then place the new expression where you need it.

1. Press **Esc** and right-click (**Control–click**) on an accent.

2. Select *Edit Articulation Definition.*

3. In the *Articulation Designer* dialog, under *Playback Effect,* select *Change Key Velocity* from the dropdown menu. You can alter the strength of the accent in playback by entering a non-zero number.

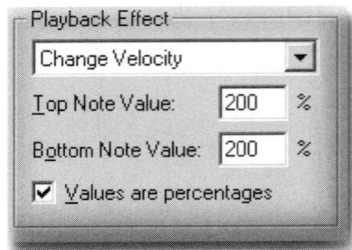

The Playback Effect portion of the Articulation Designer dialog

MAPPING NOTES PREVIOUSLY INPUT ON A STANDARD STAFF

You may have a score, or receive a score from someone else that has a percussion staff with playback set incorrectly. Since the notes are already in the score, you will need to map the notes that are placed on the staff, not the MIDI input notes.

Start a new document to experiment with this function.

1. In the *Launch Window* click *Default Document.*

2. Click *Quarter Note* in the *Simple Entry* palette.

3. Type **Alt/Option–K** to change the key to F major.

4. Input two measures of quarter notes, alternating first-space F and third-space C (the staff positions for bass and snare drums) as shown in the example below.

At this point you have a percussion staff with the equivalent of a bass and snare drum part that was input into the treble clef with no percussion map. Now we will assign the proper playback for these notes.

5. Select the *Mass Edit* or *Selection* tool (press **Esc**). Select the entire staff by clicking to the left of it. Transpose the notes up by three diatonic steps (up a perfect fourth) using the *Mass Edit* menu or the transpose *Metatool* keys. (In Finale 2008, *Metatool* 7 is programmed to be up a step.) Since percussion maps do not follow key transpositions, adding a percussion map to this staff will change the notes diatonically to the key of C. Transposing the interval before assigning the percussion map is the easiest way to fix this problem.

6. Select the *Staff* tool.

7. Select the entire staff by clicking to the left of it.

8. Right-click (**Control–click**) in the highlighted area and select *Percussion: 5-line Staff.*

> 09. Standard 5-line Staff
> 10. 1-line Staff: Full Barline
> 11. 1-line Staff: Short Barline
> 12. Hide Staff
> 13. Percussion: 1-line Staff
> 14. Percussion: 5-line Staff
> 15. Note Shapes

The Staff tool contextual menu

9. Right-click (**Control–click**) again in the highlighted area and select *Define Staff Styles.* This takes you to the *Staff Styles* dialog. Select *5-line Percussion* from the *Available Styles* drop-down menu. Note some of the settings in this staff style, such as *Ignore Key Signature* and *Independent Elements: Notehead Fonts.*

10. Click *Select* to the right of the *Notation Style* dropdown menu.

11. Choose the percussion map you want. For this project, click *Create.*

12. Enter a name in the *Map Name* text field. For this project, **Kick/Snare** is a good choice.

13. In this project, the only notes that are already on the staff are MIDI pitch 65 (in the F space) and 72 (in the C space). As a reference, remember that middle C is MIDI pitch 60.

14. Click on note 65 in the *MIDI Pitch* column on the left side of the dialog.

15. Check the box next to *Highlighted Note* on the lower-right side of the dialog to enable it on the percussion map.

16. In the graphic to the left of *Staff Position,* drag the handle next to the notehead up to the F space on the staff.

17. If you like, you can enter a name for this note in the text field to the right of *Note Name* box so that it will display in the *MIDI Pitch* list. I used the name *kick.*

Adjusting the staff position in the Percussion Map Designer dialog

18. Enter **36** in the *Playback Note* text field, since that is the correct General MIDI pitch number for Bass Drum if you're using a GM synth like Finale's *SmartMusic SoftSynth*. If you are using the Rowloff® or the GPO sounds, the Bass Drum could be assigned to a different note.

19. **Note**: If you do not know the correct playback note, you could play notes on the MIDI keyboard (if channel 10 is active) until you hear the sound you want. Then click *Listen* to the right of the *Playback Note* text field and press the key associated with that sound.

20. Repeat steps 10–15 for MIDI pitch 72, placing it on the third space of the staff (C in treble clef) and assigning the playback note to a value of 38 for Snare Drum. Make sure to check the box to the left of *Highlighted Note* so this pitch is active in the percussion map.

21. Click *Done, Select,* and *OK* to return to the score.

22. Make sure that this staff is set to MIDI channel 10, and Program Change 1. Previously you have used the *Instrument List* to do this. There is another quick way to make channel and program changes.

    a. Select *Window* menu/*Mixer* (note the key shortcuts shown in the menu to access this command).

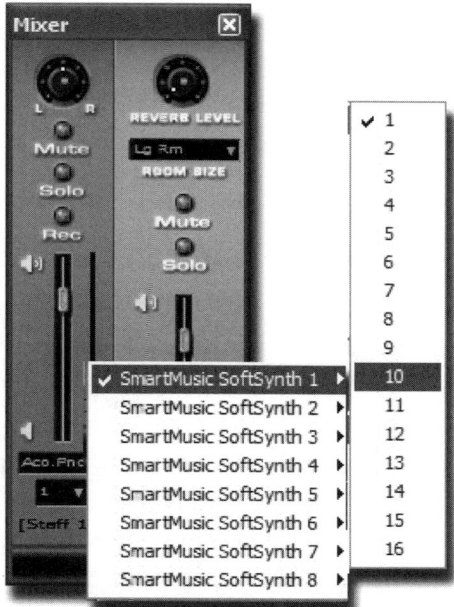

The Finale Mixer

b. This mixer works like the *Studio View* mixer. Note that program change 1 (*Aco. Pno.*) is already selected.

c. Click on the box with 1 in it. From the dropdown menu, select *SmartMusic SoftSynth 1,* then select *10* for channel 10.

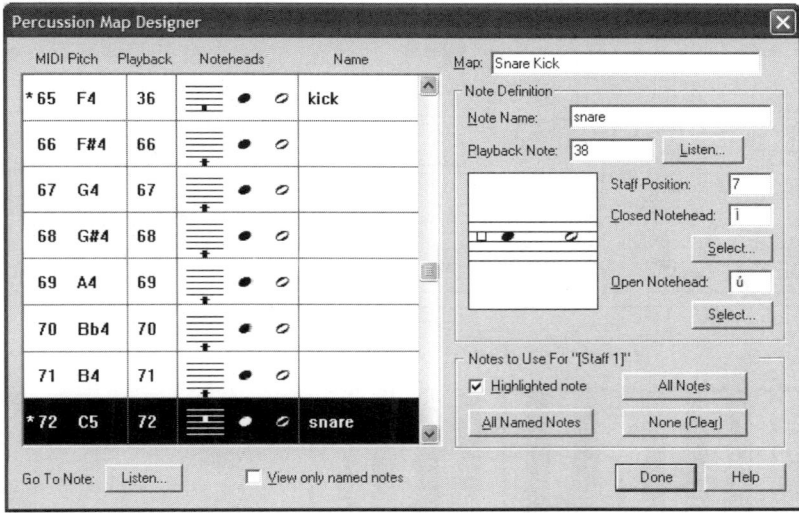

The Percussion Map Designer dialog

Note: It may be faster to create a new percussion staff and copy the notes into the percussion staff, then delete the old staff. Remember:

- The notes still may not be mapped correctly. You may need to go back and remap the pitches shown on the staff.

- If the concert key is not C, you should transpose the notes to the correct interval before copying them. Follow steps 1–3 above.

REFERENCE PERCUSSION MAPPING

Below are two percussion map references. These show the default staff and MIDI pitch settings for the percussion maps in Finale. The first diagram shows General MIDI percussion mapping. If you are using any of the marching percussion sounds from the *Setup Wizard,* then use the second diagram for Rowloff® marching percussion mapping.

In some percussion maps you may need to enable sounds by checking the *All Named Notes* button in the *Percussion Map Designer* dialog.

If you are inputting notes via MIDI, simply play the correct note number as shown on the keyboard diagram. If you are inputting notes manually (via mouse click, typing letters, scanning, copying, etc.), input the notes on the staff as shown. Then use **+** (the equal sign key) to designate the sound and notehead assignment you desire. In these mapping diagrams you will notice that some sounds have multiple plus signs. For example, the Cymbal (bell) sound has three plus signs. This indicates how many times you need to press **+** (the equal sign key) to select that sound if inputting manually.

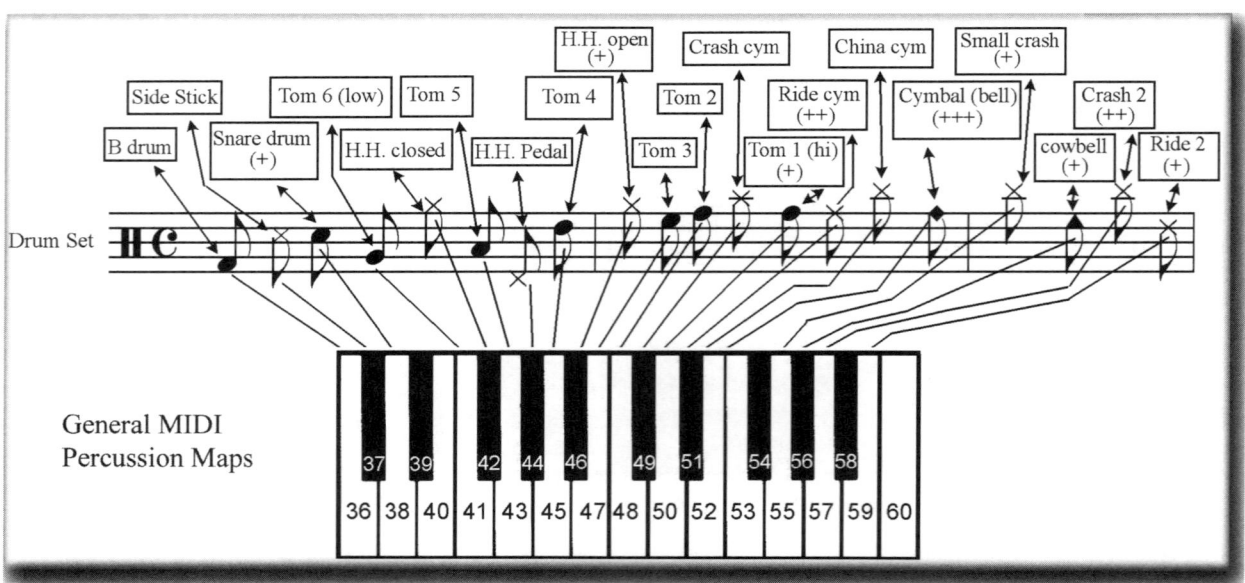

General MIDI Percussion Maps

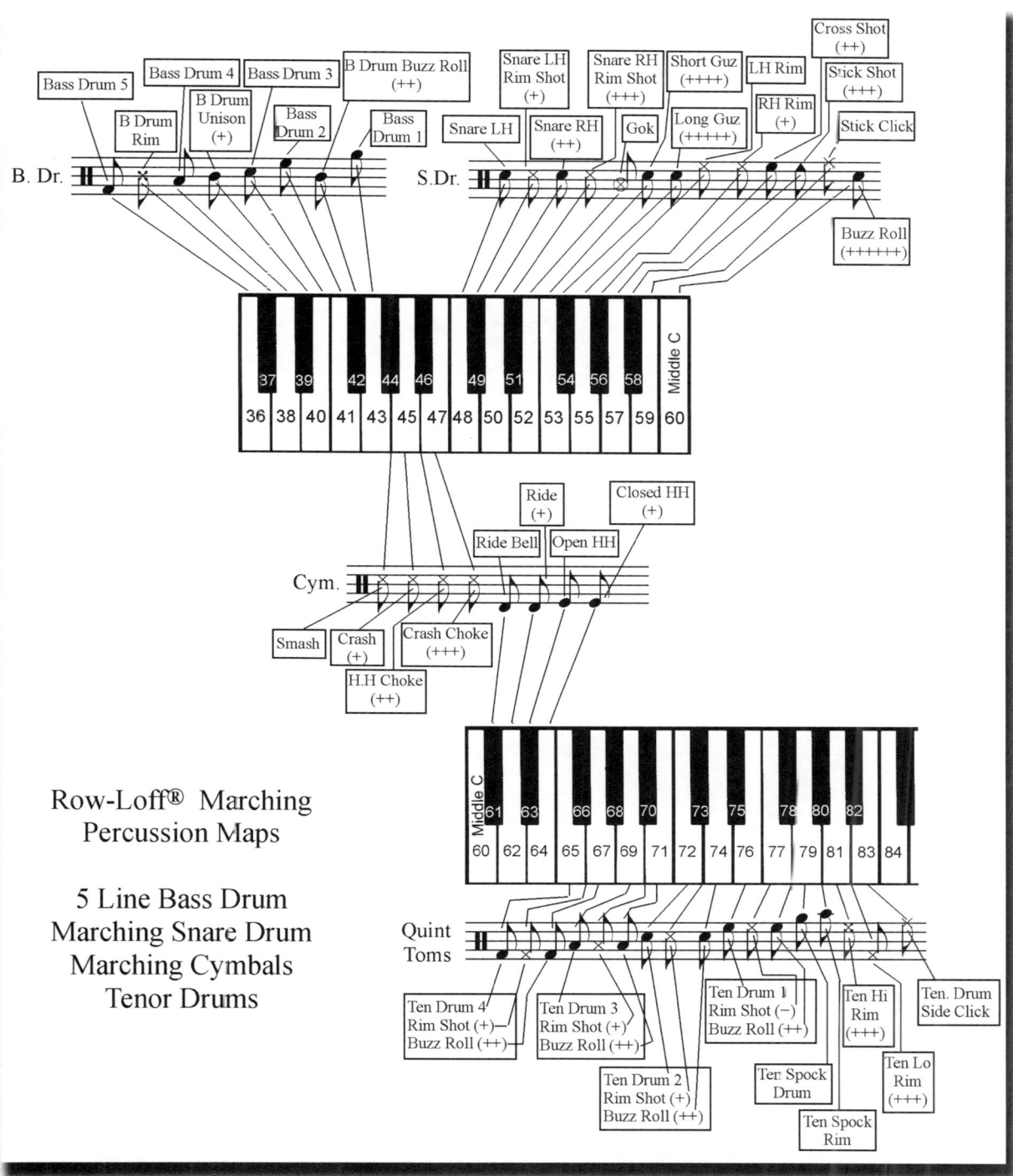

Rowloff® Marching Percussion Maps

CHAPTER 9

CREATING TESTS, WORKSHEETS, AND EXERCISES

Concepts covered in this chapter:

- Using Finale NotePad
- Education Templates
- Exercise Wizard
- Systems
    - Inserting and Deleting
    - Positioning
    - Optimizing
- Time and Key
    - Altering
    - Custom Time Graphics
    - Hiding and Showing
- Staff Styles
    - Applying
    - Creating and Editing
    - Custom Staves
    - Colored Note Heads
- Measure Attributes
    - Barlines
    - White space
    - Adding and Deleting measures
- Note Positioning
- Shape Designer
-Creating and Editing shapes
- Special Noteheads
- Text boxes
    - Text Inserts
    - Enclosures
-Moving and Alignment
- Grids and Guidelines
- Articulation
    - Creation
    - Duplication and Edit of Shapes

INTRODUCTION TO WORKSHEETS AND EXERCISES

Even if you do not ever anticipate making a worksheet, this chapter has very helpful information on page layout, custom graphics, and more. Using the concepts that you have been introduced to in previous projects, it will be easy to create a worksheet or exercise sheet.

Note: It is advisable that you understand the previous chapters before attempting this project. If you are creating an exercise sheet with scales, arpeggios, intervals, and rhythmic training, then Finale has over 50,000 easily accessible exercises built into the *Exercise Wizard*.

Finale can automatically generate exercises for each of the instruments in your ensemble, complete with correct time and key signatures, clefs, appropriate ranges, and automatic page layout. You select the exercise parameters, choose a list of instruments for your ensemble, then click *Print* and the entire project is done for you.

With this in mind, this project will focus more on creating a worksheet in Finale. There are two ways to create worksheets: One is to create the entire worksheet in Finale. However, if the project requires a lot of text formatting and few musical examples, it may be best to create the musical examples you need in Finale and import them into a word processing program.

If the worksheet has several musical examples and little text, it is easy to create the entire project in Finale. Doing this has two advantages: First, if you want to alter the musical examples later, you do not have to recreate them and import them into a word processor a second time. But more important is the flexibility of creating a worksheet that students can open in Finale NotePad in order to answer questions. This is a great way to get students to start using a notation program.

Finale NotePad is free software, available on the web (www.finalemusic.com). Students can download this software and create their own music. Finale NotePad has some limitations, but can open any Finale file regardless of how complex. This makes it perfect for use with worksheets, since what students can access is limited.

The worksheet we will create in this project is specifically designed to show different ways that questions can be answered using NotePad.

Some music educators have even used Finale to create worksheets that have hidden answers in the file. Then the students use NotePad to answer the questions, return the completed file to the teacher. The teacher then opens the file in Finale and "unhides" the answers, allowing easy comparison of correct vs. incorrect answers. The first question we will create is an example of this.

Worksheets are different than regular musical scores. Finale by default has many useful automatic features that are wonderful for creating musical scores, but are not useful when creating worksheets. For this reason, Finale has several templates that are formatted with the correct defaults for creating worksheets. These worksheet templates turn off features such as cautionary time, key, and clef changes, system limitations on placement, and other options not conducive to creating worksheets. They also have additional elements that make worksheet creation faster

Note: The worksheet on which this project is based is not designed not to be an actual worksheet. You likely would not put all of these topics on a single worksheet. The project is designed to introduce several formatting concepts to assist you in creating the worksheet you would like to do.

WORKSHEET PROJECT

Formatting the Template

1. Select *Launch Window/Templates.*

2. Select the *Education Templates* folder, then the file named *2-Measure Examples.*

    a. In Finale 2008, you can also enter page text, change key and time signatures, and set the number of measures for the file using the last two pages of the *Setup Wizard.*

3. Make sure you are in *Page View* (check this in the *View* menu). This template contains a text block with instructions for use. Select the *Selection* tool, click once on the instruction text below *Today's Assignment,* and press **Delete**.

First, lay out the systems as you need for this project.

1. Select the *Page Layout* tool.

2. Zoom out to see the page (**Ctrl/Command– –** [the hyphen key]).

3. This template has five systems; we need seven. All but the top two systems need two staves.

    a. With the *Page Layout* tool selected, right-click (**Control–click**) on system 4 (the single bass clef system).

    b. Select *Delete System.*

VIDEO
CLIP 9:1

FORMATTING THE
TEMPLATE

The Page Layout tool

c. Again right-click (**Control–click**) on the new system 4.

d. Select *Insert System.*

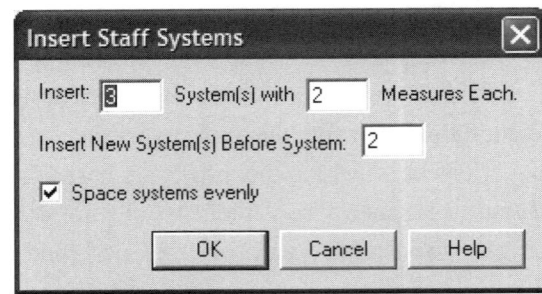

The Insert Staff Systems dialog

e. Enter **3** in the *Insert* text field. Enter **2** in the *System(s) with* text field. Click *OK.*

f. Note: There may be more systems on page 2 of this template. You can delete them if you desire.

4. We want to have two systems side by side throughout most of this worksheet, so you will need to make the systems smaller.

a. Click on the lower-right margin handle on the top system.

b. Type **Ctrl/Command–A** to select all of the right margin handles.

c. Press and hold **Left Arrow** until the systems are shortened as shown in the example below.

The lower-right margin handle

d. Click anywhere outside a system to de-select the system handles.

5. Drag the top system to the left of the page.

6. Drag system 2 up and to the right of system 1.

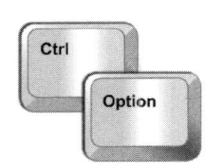

7. To keep other systems from moving as you move a system, press and hold **Ctrl/Option** as you drag the system.

8. Continue dragging the other systems as shown in the example below.

9. System 5 needs four measures rather than two.

    a. Press **Esc** and right-click (**Control–click**) on system 5, measure 2.

    b. Select *Insert Measures* (In Finale 2008, select *Insert Measure Stack*). Enter **2** in the *How Many Measures?* text field. Click *OK*.

    c. Select the *Page Layout* tool.

    d. Select the lower-right margin handle of system 5 and drag to the right or press and hold **Right Arrow** to move the system to the right until the system reaches the right page margin.

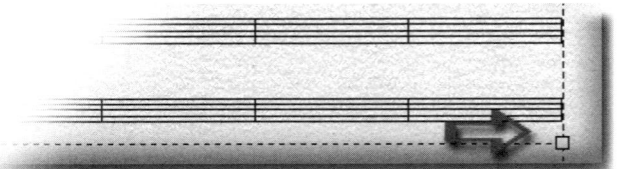

Moving the system margin to the right

10. Drag system 6 to the left as shown above.

11. The last system may remain on page 2 by default. Select page 2 typing **Ctrl/Command–Page Down.** (In Finale 2008, you can press **Page Down** without **Ctrl/Command**.)

12. If the last system is not off the page, drag it into position.

13. Drag system 7 up until it is off or above the page. Release the mouse and the system will be forced to page 1.

Dragging the last system up to move it to page 1

14. Select the *Selection* tool (press **Esc**) and drag the text boxes into position as shown in step 8.

15. If the systems are not already locked, lock all of the systems so music spacing will not affect measure layout. (I'm sure you remember how to do this.)

    a. Select the *Mass Edit* or *Selection* tool (press **Esc**) and then press **Ctrl/Command–A** to select *all*.

    b. Press **L** for *lock*. (On Macintosh, press **Command–L.**) (In Finale 2008, press **L** to *lock* or **U** to *unlock* systems without **Ctrl/Command**.)

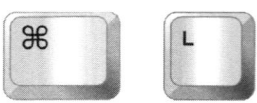

Note: Throughout this chapter, measures will be referred to as "system 1, measure 1," or "system 5, measure 3," even though Finale counts the measure, in this worksheet as 1–14. This will help you know which measure we are discussing. Each of the following sections deals with the creation of one example or system. All measure references are directed to the system on which we are focusing at the time. You will never need to work on system 1, measure 1 when you are creating Example 5.

Creating Example 1, System 1

Now you are ready to create the first example. The first measure contains eight whole notes.

VIDEO
CLIP 9:2

CREATING EXAMPLE 1

Question 1

System 1, measure 2 can be deleted. As you will recall, the procedure to delete a measure is:

1. Zoom in on system 1, measure 1. (**Ctrl/Command–+** [the equal sign key]).

2. Press **Esc** to go to the *Selection* tool. Right-click (**Control– click**) on measure 2.

3. Select **Delete.** (In Finale 2008, make sure to double-click the measure to select a measure stack, then right-click [**Control–click**] and select *Delete Measure Stack*).

4. The key signature needs to have two flats.

    a. Right-click (**Control–click**) on measure 1 and select *Edit Key Signature.* (In Finale 2008, select *Key Signature* then the list of keys).

    b. Select the key of B♭ (two flats) and click OK.

5. Change the time signature to make room for eight whole notes in measure 1.

    a. Right-click (**Control–click**) again in measure 1.

    b. Select *Edit Time Signature* (In Finale 2008, select *Time Signature.*)

    c. Set the meter to eight whole notes (8/1).

d. Set the *Measure Region* as measure 1 through 1.

e. Click *OK*.

6. Now you need to hide the time signature.

   a. Again, with the *Selection* tool still selected (press **Esc**), right-click (**Control–click**) in measure 1 and select *Edit Measure Attributes*.

   b. You have used the *Measure Attributes* dialog before. Take note of some of the other functions available in this dialog. They are very useful when creating worksheets.

   c. Select *Always Hide* from the dropdown menu to the right of *Time Signature*. Click *OK*.

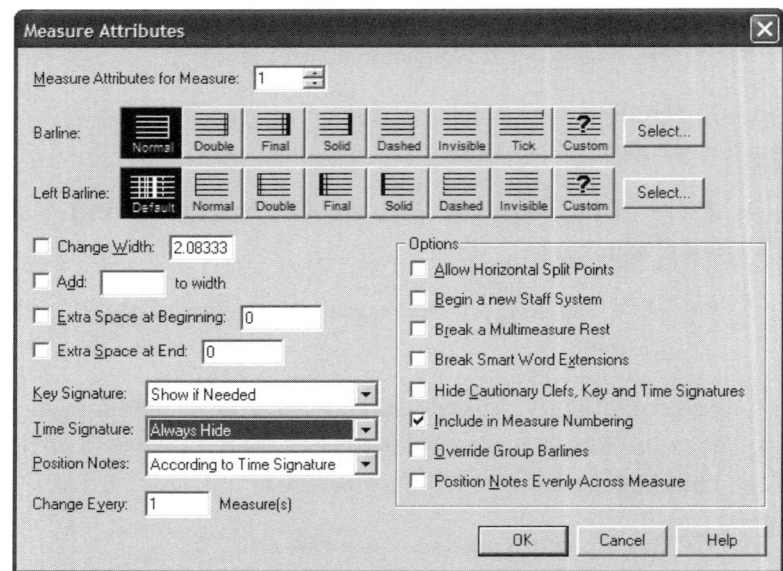

The Measure Attributes dialog

7. Input the eight whole notes required.

8. Remove the bass clef staff from this system using *Optimize Systems* as we did before.

   a. Select the *Page Layout* tool.

   b. Right-click (**Control–click**) on the first system and select *Optimize Staff Systems*.

   c. Make sure the dialog is set as shown. This is the default setting for this action. Click *OK*.

The Page Layout tool

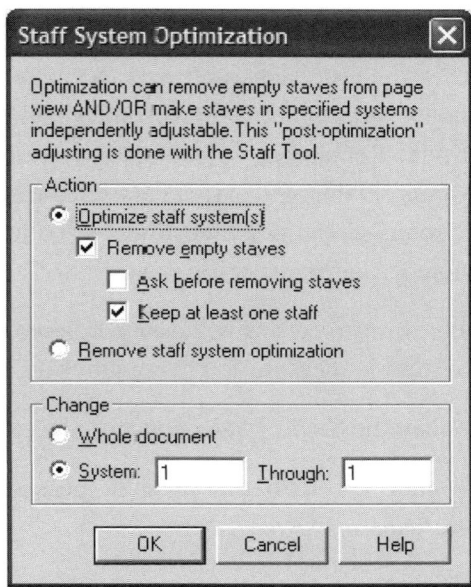

The Staff System Optimization dialog

9. Performing this optimization may re-position other systems. Simply drag system 2 down and all other systems will adjust accordingly. (Do not use **Ctrl/Option** to move this system. You want only all lower systems to move.)

10. Save your work.

Colored Noteheads

Optional: In Finale 2008, colored noteheads are possible. Each chromatic pitch can be a different color. This is very useful for elementary education. In the *Setup Wizard,* you can select Boomwhackers® or Chromatone® instruments in the pitched percussion area. This will automatically create diatonic colored noteheads that match those instruments as well as load the sounds for these instruments.

1. Select *Document* menu/*Document Options/Notes and Rests* to manually alter the colors assigned to noteheads.

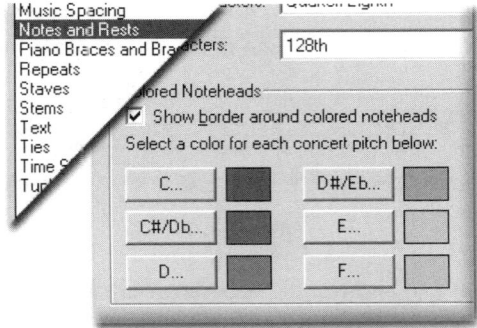

The Colored Noteheads section of the Notes and Rests pane of the Document Options dialog

2. In this dialog, click a note name, then select a color.

3. Once this is done for each pitch, you can assign a staff to have colored notes either in the *Staff Attributes* dialog or by creating a Staff Style. Remember, selecting colored noteheads in the *Staff Attributes* dialog will assign colored noteheads throughout the entire score. Creating a Staff Style will allow you to assign colored noteheads for a specific region.

The Staff tool

    a. For this project we will assign colored notes only to system 1, measure 1. This requires a Staff Style.

    b. Select the *Staff* or *Selection* tool (press **Esc**).

    c. Right-click (**Control–click**) in measure 1 and select *Define Staff Style*.

    d. Click *New* and enter a name for the style, such as **Color Noteheads.**

    e. Click *Define* to the right of *Color noteheads*. Make your choices, then click *OK*. Make any other changes you want to include in this staff style in the main *Staff Styles* dialog and click *OK*.

The Color noteheads Define button in the Staff Styles dialog

    f. Right-click (**Control–click**) in measure 1 and select the new Staff Style *Color Noteheads* that you just created.

Creating Example 2

System 2, Example 2 appears to have eight counts. In measure 1 you will change the time signature to accommodate this. In this example, hide the barline between the two measures; change the key to E♭ minor; input the notes and two hidden rests as shown in the example below.

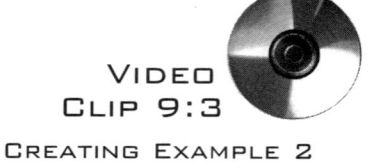

Video Clip 9:3

Creating Example 2

Question 2

1. Press **Esc** and right-click (**Control–click**) on the key signature in system 2, measure 1.

2. Select *Other* or *Edit Key Signature* and change the key to E♭ minor.

3. Under *Measure Region,* enter *Measure* **2** *Through* **3**. Click *OK*.

4. Input the notes E♭ through B♭.

5. Press **0** (zero, not letter "oh") to input a quarter rest. Press **H** for *hide.* (This will dim the rest in note input mode.) Repeat this for the next beat.

6. Input the final E♭ on beat 4.

7. Press **Esc** and right-click (**Control–click**) on system 2, measure 1.

8. Select *Invisible Barline.* (In Finale 2008, select *Barline/Invisible Barline.*)

9. Right-click (**Control–click**) again on system 2, measure 1. Select *Edit Measure Attributes.* When trying to create a seamless look between two measures, you may want to remove space at the end of the first measure so that there is no extra space between notes from one measure to the next.

10. In the text field to the right of *Extra Space at End,* enter a negative number to subtract space from this measure. Enter **-0.05** (inch).

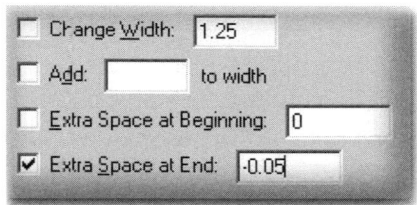

The Measure Attributes dialog

   a. In Finale 2008, you can adjust space at the beginning and end of a measure visually rather than with numeric values. To do this, select the *Measure* tool.

   b. Select *Measure* menu/*Show Measure Spacing Handles.* Since this is a program preference, this is the only time you have to turn this on.

   c. Now note the handles at the bottom of the beginning and end of each measure. Click in a bottom handle press **Left Arrow** or **Right Arrow** to adjust the amount of space.

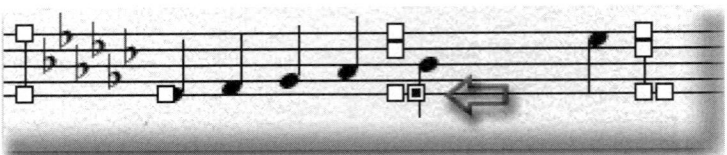

Measure Spacing Handles

11. Before exiting the *Measure Attributes* dialog, set the time signature to *Always Hide*. (If you do not see the *Measure Attributes* dialog because you used the Finale 2008 instructions above, you will need to open the dialog. Select the *Selection* tool (press **Esc**) and right-click (**Control–click**) in the measure and select *Edit Measure Attributes*.

12. Optimize this system. Review optimization above if needed. Since staff 2 of this system is already hidden, optimizing the system will have no visual effect.

　　a. **Note:** You may think that this system does not need to be optimized because the bass clef is hidden using a Staff Style. In this type of page layout where systems are side by side, it can be difficult to select measures when they are overlapping other systems. That is why it is best to remove the staff by optimizing the system.

13. After optimizing the system, you can drag system 3 down to position it as desired. Once again, save your work.

Creating Example 3

Example 3 (Question 3) has a hidden staff and custom staves. You will change the time signature to 3/4 and use Layers 1 and 2 for the answers in both staves.

VIDEO
CLIP 9:4
CREATING EXAMPLE 3

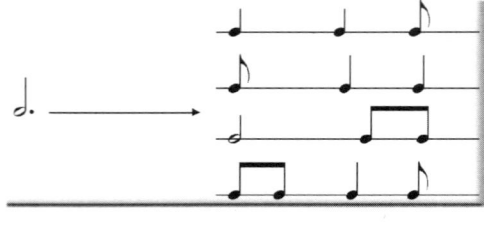

Question 3

1. Press **Esc** and right-click (**Control–click**) on the time signature in system 3, measure 1.

2. Select *3/4*.

3. Input a dotted-half F three ledger lines below the treble staff.

4. Input the other notes shown in the example below. Use Layer 1 for black notes above the staves, Layer 2 for red notes below the stave. Do not worry about any extra rests.

5. Select the *Mass Edit* or *Selection* tool (press **Esc**); select measure 2 on both staves.

6. Right-click (**Control–click**) and select *Utilities/Freeze Stems Up*. (In Finale 2008, select *Utilities* menu/*Stem Direction/Up*.)

7. Select the *Page Layout* tool.

8. Right-click (**Control–click**) on system 3 and select *Optimize Staff System*.

9. Select the *Staff* tool. Drag the bottom handle of the bass clef staff up to position the notes evenly as shown in the example above.

10. Press **Esc** and right-click (**Control–click**) in system 3, measure 1; select *Edit Measure Attributes*.

11. Select *Invisible* on the *Left Barline* row. Click OK.

The Page Layout tool

The Staff tool

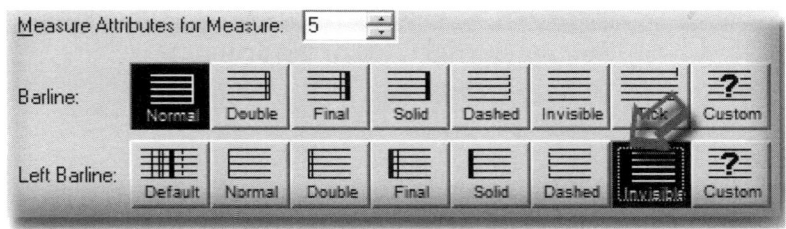

The Barline section of the Measure Attributes dialog

Select the *Mass Edit* or *Selection* tool (press **Esc**); select measure 1 in the treble staff.

12. Select *Plug-ins* menu/*Note, Beam, and Rest Editing/Ledger Lines (Hide)*.

The Special Tools tool

The Stem Length tool

The Staff tool

13. The dotted-half note in measure 1 has a very long stem due to the fact that it is on a lower ledger line. To shorten this stem:

   a. Select the *Special Tools* tool. (On Windows, select the *Advanced Tools* palette.)

   b. Select the *Stem Length* tool.

   c. Click system 3, measure 1, top staff.

   d. Click-and-drag the stem handle or click once and press **Down Arrow** to shorten the stem.

14. Select the *Staff* tool; select system 3, measure 1, both staves.

15. Right-click (**Control–click**) on the highlighted area and select staff style *21. Notes Only*.

16. The staff style you will need for example 3, measure 2 is not created.

   a. Select the *Staff* tool.

   b. Select example 3, measure 2, both staves.

   c. Right-click (**Control–click**) on the highlighted area and select *Define Staff Styles*.

   d. Click *New* at the top of the *Staff Styles* dialog and enter a name in the *Style Name* text field. I named mine *23. Top and bottom only*.

   e. Under *Items to Display*, clear the checkboxes next to *Rests* and *Barlines*.

   f. Select *Other* in the dropdown menu to the right of *Staff* (on the right side of the dialog).

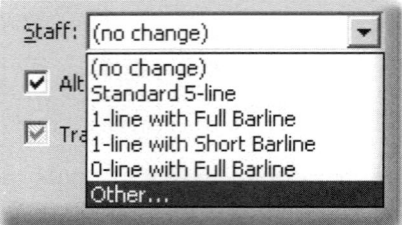

The Staff dropdown menu in the Staff Styles dialog

   g. The *Staff Setup* dialog appears. Here you can create a custom staff.

   h. Click *Custom Staff*.

i. Add a staff line above the staff and below the staff by clicking on the small box above and below the staff. Now you have a 7–line staff.

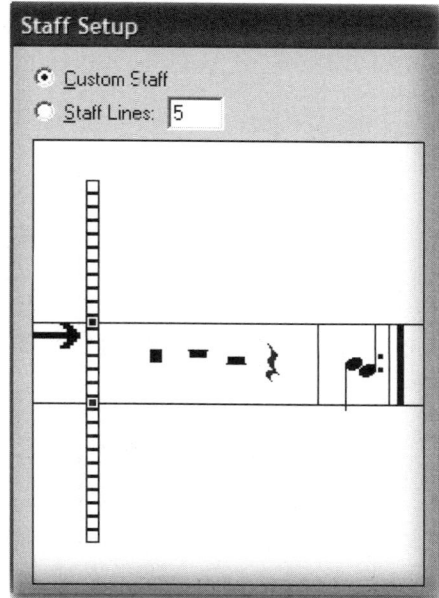

The Staff Setup dialog

j. Deselect the five lines inside of the top and bottom line to create the staff as shown in the example above.

k. Click *OK*, and *OK* in the previous dialog to return to the score.

17. With measure 2 of this system selected, right-click (**Control–click**) in the highlighted area and select the new staff style you created. I called my staff style *23. top and bottom only*.

18. Select the *Shapes* tool. Hold **Ctrl/Option** and click the *Custom Line* tool.

19. Select the line with an arrow on the right end. Click *Select*.

A custom line with a right arrowhead

The Custom Line tool

20. Double-click-and-drag to place the line as shown in the finished example. (Press and hold **Shift** before dragging to constrain the drag to 45° increments. This helps maintain alignment.)

21. If you like, you can move the notes horizontally to make it more challenging for students to pick the correct answer.

The Special Tools tool

    a. Select the *Special Tools* tool (on Windows, access the *Advanced Tool Palette*).

    b. Select the *Note Positioning* tool.

    c. Click on any note on system 3, measure 2.

    d. Drag the handles above the notes slightly to randomize placement.

The Note Positioning tool

Dragging notes with the Note Positioning tool

    e. Select Layer 2 and move the notes in those layers.

    f. Select Layer 1 before starting the next example.

22. Save your work.

Creating Example 4

In system 4, example 4 you will create a new graphic for an interesting time signature. This is a type of time signature used in Kodály and other elementary education music. The heart represents the beat. Also, you will create some articulation shapes (boxes) for students to use in answering questions in Finale NotePad.

VIDEO CLIP 9:5

CREATING EXAMPLE 4

1. Input quarter notes in the measures in system 4 as shown in the finished example.

2. Press **Esc** (two or three times, since you are exiting *Simple Note Entry* mode), then right-click (**Control–click**) system 4, measure 1. Select *Edit Measure Attributes.*

3. In the dropdown menu to the right of *Time Signature,* select *Always Hide.*

The **Measure Attributes dialog**

4. Hiding the time signature will move the notes to the left. You need to create space for the new time signature symbol. Enter **0.2** (inch) in the text field to the right of *Extra Space at Beginning.* Click *OK.* (Remember, you can do this visually in Finale 2008 using the measure spacing handles discussed in *Creating Example 2* above.)

5. Select the *Expression* tool and double-click on system 4, measure 1.

6. Click the *Shape* button.

The Expression tool

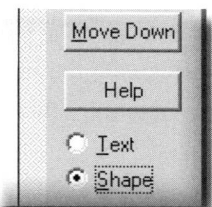

The **Shape button in the Expression Selection dialog**

7. The expression you need is not pre-created. Click *Create.*

8. Click *Select* to the right of the *Shape* text field.

9. The *Shape Selection* palette for this template appears with pre-created shapes. These shapes can be used throughout Finale for expressions, articulations, and more. You can assign one of these shapes to be an expression, but again, the shape you need is not yet created, so click *Create.*

Shape Designer. This is the *Shape Designer* dialog. You can create any type of graphic here. In fact, you can import a graphic to be used as a shape. The *Shape Designer* dialog has several tools.

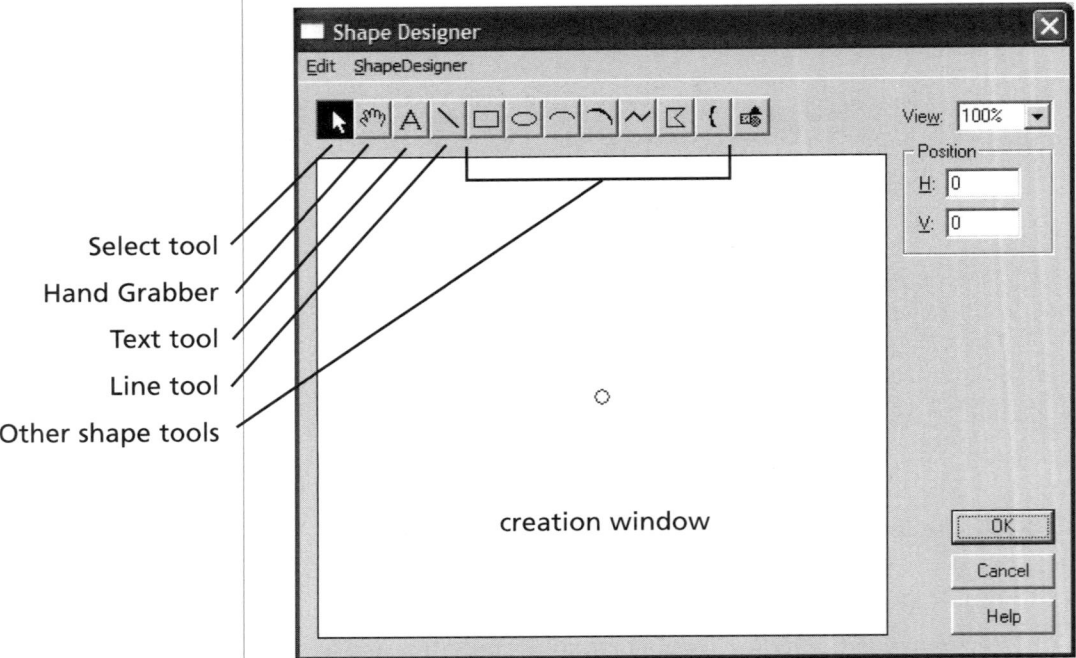

- A *Select* tool to select an item to delete, re-shape or move.
- A *Hand Grabber* to drag the background.
- A *Text* tool.
- A *Line* tool.
- Several other shape tools.

The time signature you need is simply the numeral 3 with a heart under it. If you are an artist, you could create the heart using the *Shape Designer* tools. There are also many symbol fonts available for Windows and Macintosh systems.

Note: If you cannot find a heart in the fonts on your computer, use any symbol for this exercise.

   1. Select *Shape Designer* menu/*Select Font*.

The Font dialog in the Shape Designer menu

2. Change the font to Maestro 24-point. This is the normal size for Maestro font elements. Click *OK*.

3. Select the *Text* tool in the *Shape Designer* dialog (not the *Text* tool in the *Main Tool Palette*).

4. Click in the creation window and type the number **3** near the small circle in the middle of the window.

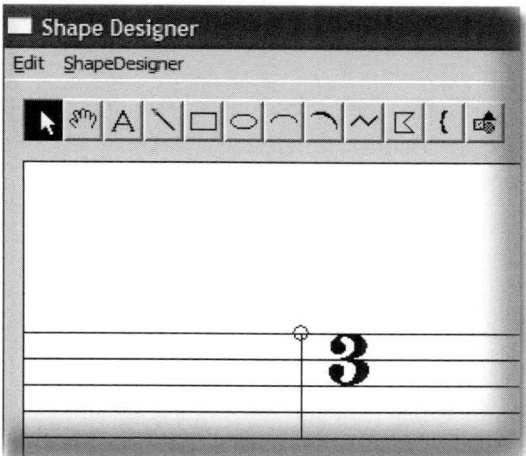

5. Click the *Select* tool (arrow) in the creation window (not the *Selection* tool in the *Main Tool Palette*).

6. Change the *View* value to 200% if you would like to zoom in to position the items as shown.

7. Select *Shape Designer* menu/*Show/Staff Template*. Now you will be able to see size and placement relative to the staff.

8. Drag the 3 to position it to the right of the barline and the circle on the top line of the staff as shown in the example above.

9. Use the *Hand Grabber* tool in this tool palette and drag in the creation window anywhere to position the graphic for viewing.

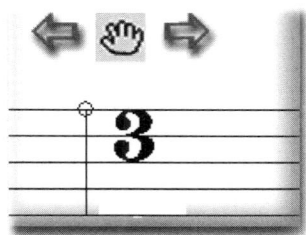

10. **Typing the Heart**.

    a. Repeat steps 1 and 2 to change the font to Symbols 22-point (on Windows) or Zapf Dingbats 20-point (on Macintosh). Click *OK* to return to the designer window.

    b. Select the *Text* tool and click in the creation window to activate a cursor.

    c. On Windows, press and hold **Alt** and type **0169** on the numpad, then release **Alt.** Note: You *must* use the numpad for this function. If you are on a laptop, you will need to hold the **Fn** key and press the key for *NumLk.* Then you can use the alpha keys in the right hand area as the numpad.

    d. On Macintosh, type **Option–2** (2 in the numrow, not numpad).

11. Click the *Select* tool and drag this symbol to place it as shown.

12. Click *OK* to close the *Shape Designer* dialog. Click *Select.*

13. In the *Shape Expression Designer* dialog, deselect *Allow Horizontal Stretching.*

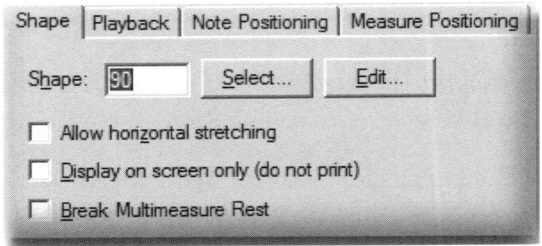

The Shape Expression Designer dialog

14. Return to the score by clicking *OK,* then *Select.* Assign this to *All Staves.*

15. Press **Esc** and position the expression in the time signature area.

16. Save your work.

Teacher, I have a Problem

The number and symbol do not appear to be aligned! Once you create a shape with several elements, you may notice that they do not always appear or they are arranged strangely. This is generally because you didn't deselect *Allow Horizontal Stretching.* This should only be used if the shape is a single element.

17. Note: If you need to return to the *Shape Designer* dialog to alter a shape, use the *Selection* tool. Right-click (**Control–click**) and select *Edit Measure Shape Expression Definition,* then click *Edit.*

18. Use the *Shape Designer* to create a box that students can use to select the correct answer in this example. Students do not have access to expressions in Finale NotePad, but they do have access to articulations. Therefore, for items you do not want students to access, use an expression; for items you *do* want students to access in NotePad, use articulations.

    a. Select the *Articulation* tool. Click the last note in system 4, example 4.

    b. In the *Articulation Selection* dialog, click *Create.*

    c. Under *Symbols,* next to *Main,* click the *Shape* button.

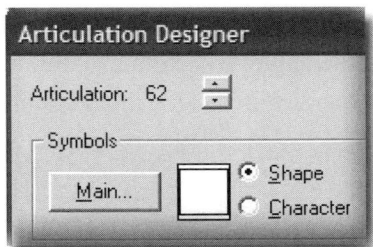

The Articulation Designer dialog

    d. Click *Main.*

    e. In the *Shape Selection* dialog, you are again presented with all of the available shapes in this document. Click *Create.*

    f. Select *Shaper Designer* menu/*Line Thickness/1 pt.*

    g. Click the *Rectangle* tool.

    h. It will be helpful to display the staff template as you did before so you can get an idea of the size of rectangle you are creating. Select *Shape Designer* menu/*Show/Staff Template.*

i.   Click-and-drag in the creation window to create a rectangle.

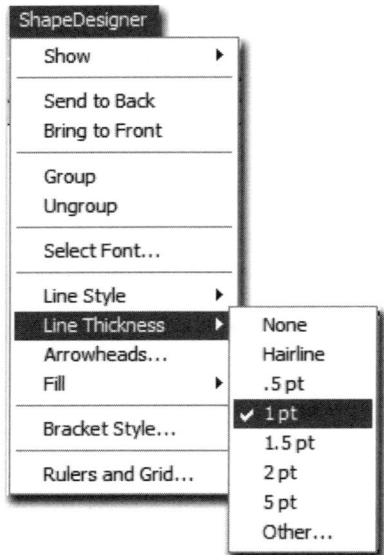

Setting the line thickness in the Shape Designer menu

j.   Click the *Select* tool and move the rectangle closer to the small circle in the center of the creation window. This circle represents the shape's handle position.

k.   Click on the edge of the rectangle (not inside the rectangle) to activate sizing handles. Drag the handles to re-size the rectangle to suit.

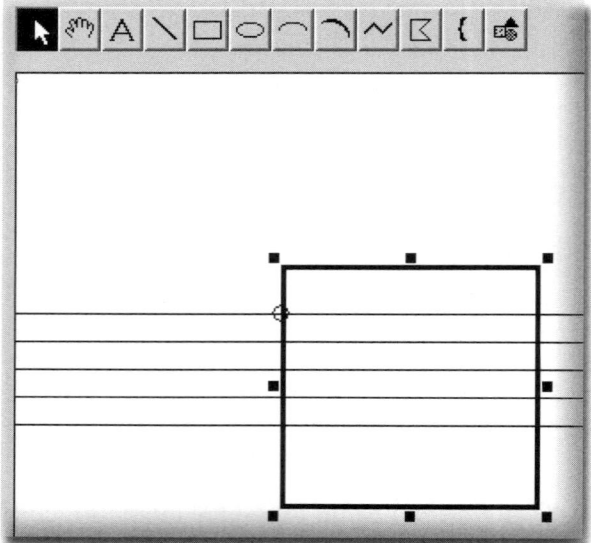

Sizing handles in the Shape Designer dialog

l. When finished, Click *OK* and *Select* to return to the score and assign this new articulation.

m. Double-click the last note in the bass clef and assign this new rectangle shape to that note.

n. Drag the articulations to the left of the page as shown.

19. Select the *Page Layout* tool.

The Page Layout tool

20. Click on the lower-right margin handle in system 4, example 4 and drag or press **Left Arrow** to make the system narrower.

Changing the system width with the Page Layout tool

21. Finally, to challenge the students a bit more, assign the *Stemless Notes* staff style to this system.

a. Select the *Staff* tool.

b. Select system 4, measures 1–2, both staves.

c. Right-click (**Control–click**) and select staff style *16. Stemless Notes*.

The Staff tool

Creating Example 5

In system 5, example 5, we need to add a staff since this example has three staves. Before doing this, make sure that the first four systems are all optimized. This way, as you add the staff to system 5, it will not add the staff to systems 1–4. There is no way to add a staff to a specific system; Finale adds the staff throughout the score. But optimized systems do not display newly added staves.

After this, we will create the notation, assign the *Notes Only* staff style to measures 1 and 3, hide the measures we need to hide, remove the left barline, and finally, position the staves. You have already done all of these functions; this is simply review.

VIDEO
CLIP 9:6

CREATING EXAMPLE 5

1. **Adding a New Staff.**

   a. Make sure that systems 1–4 are optimized. To check, select the *Page Layout* tool and right-click (**Control–click**) in any of the first four systems. Select *Optimize Staves*. You specify a range of systems to optimize more than one at a time in this dialog. (Review optimization in previous chapters if needed.)

 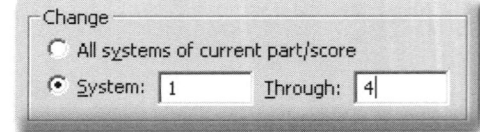

   The Page Layout tool   **The Staff System Optimization dialog**

The Staff tool

   b. Select the *Staff* tool. Click the bass clef staff system 5, measure 1. (This tells Finale where you want to insert the new staff.)

   c. Select *Staff* menu/*New Staves*. Enter **1** in the *Number of Staves* text field and click *OK*. (**Note:** You could also select *Staff* menu/*New Staves with Setup Wizard*. This would allow you to pick a staff formatted with the correct instrument name and clef. In Finale 2008, this selects the correct sound and available MIDI channel. In this project, we just need an additional staff.)

2. This action may push the bottom systems to the next page, but do not worry; this will be fixed later on.

3. Select the *Selection* tool (press **Esc**) and right-click (**Control–click**) system 5, measure 1. Select *Time Signature/4/4*.

4. With the *Selection* tool still selected, change the bass clef in system 5, measure 1 to a treble clef.

5. Input the notes as shown in the top staff of system 5, measure 1.

6. Select the *Mass Edit* or *Selection* tool and copy system 5, measure 2 to measure 1, staff 2. (If you like, you can copy it to all of the other measures in this system, then simply re-pitch the notes in the other measures.)

7. Finish inputting the notes in system 5. Input notes in the top staff of measure 4, then copy them to the measure 3, staff 2.

8. Select the *Page Layout* tool. Right-click (**Control–click**) on system 5 and select *Allow Individual Staff Spacing*.

The Page Layout tool

9. Select the *Staff* tool. Position the bottom handles of staves 2 and 3 so they are quite close, as shown in the example below.

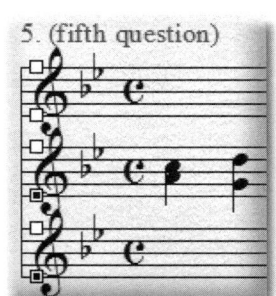

The Staff tool

10. Select the *Mass Edit* or *Selection* tool and select all measures in system 5.

11. Right-click (**Control–click**) in the highlighted measures and select *Utilities/Freeze Stems Up*. (In Finale 2008, select *Utilities* menu/*Stem direction/Up*.)

12. Select the *Staff* tool. Double-click on staff 2.

13. Under *Options*, clear the checkbox next to *Display Rests in Empty Measures*. This will affect all measures of all systems because this is a staff attribute, not a staff style. For this project, that will be fine, since there are no empty measures that will need rests in them. Click *OK*.

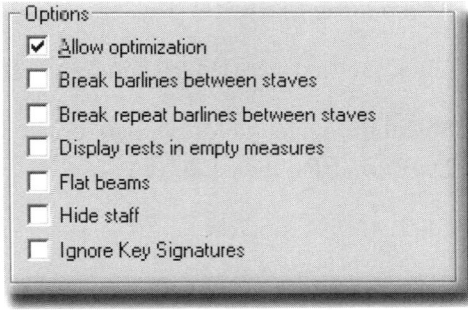

The Staff Attributes dialog

14. Select all four measures of staff 2. Right-click (**Control–click**) on the highlighted area and select staff style *21. Notes Only.*

15. With the *Staff* tool still selected, click on system 1, measure 1.

16. Right-click (**Control–click**) on the measure and select staff style 12. *Hide Staff.* Repeat this for the other three measures in this system that need to be hidden.

17. When you apply the staff style to measure 3, staff 2, you will notice the notes crowd to the left. You could re-position each note, but you may end up with undesirable spacing. An easier way is to make use of the extra white space used in example 4.

   a. Press **Esc** and right-click (**Control–click**) on measure 3 of this system.

   b. Select *Edit Measure Attributes.*

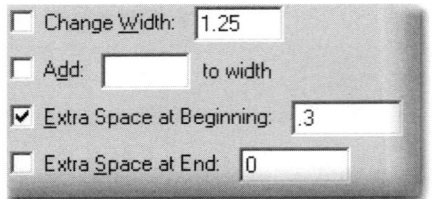

The Measure Attributes dialog

   c. Enter **0.3** (inch) in the *Extra Space/At Beginning* text field. Click *OK.*

   d. Again, this can be done visually in Finale 2008 using the *Measure Spacing Handles* described above in example 2.

18. More articulation boxes are needed for students to select the correct answer in NotePad. Since a rectangle shape has already been created, this can be duplicated and altered.

   a. Select the *Articulation* tool (or double-click using the *Selection* tool on a rectangle in system 4 to access the *Articulation* tool).

   b. Click the first note on system 5, measure 1.

   c. Select the rectangle previously created. Click *Duplicate* (**P**), then *Edit* (**E**).

   d. Click *Main,* as before.

The Articulation tool

e. Note that at the bottom of the displayed shapes, a duplicate of the rectangle shape has been created. Click it once (do not double-click) and click *Edit*.

f. You may want to set the view percentage back to 100% and turn on the *Staff Template* as you did previously.

g. Select the *Select* tool and click on the existing rectangle to activate the sizing handles.

h. Drag the center handle on the right to the right to increase the rectangle's width.

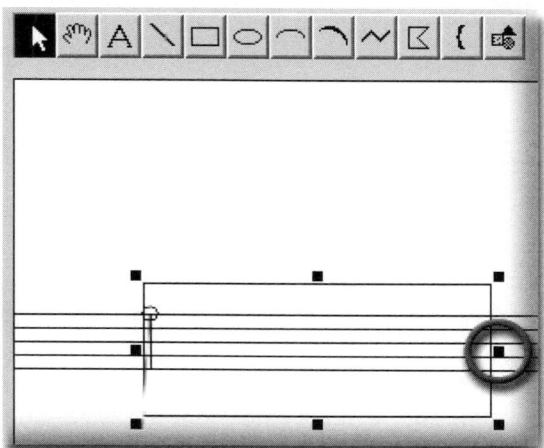

i. Click *OK,* then *Select* to return to the score and assign this articulation.

j. As with the *Shape Expression* discussion, if you need to adjust the shape in the *Shape Designer,* select the *Selection* tool, right-click (**Control–click**), then select *Edit Articulation Definition.* Then click *Main,* then *Edit.*

k. **Note:** You may notice that there is no setting for *Allow Horizontal Stretching.* This is only available for *Shape Expressions.* Generally I would create this type of a shape as an expression so I could stretch it in the score. This is workable because it is a single-element shape. In this worksheet, you are creating this for use in NotePad, so to allow students to access the shape you must use an articulation, since NotePad does not allow expression placement editing.

l. Assign the modified rectangle articulation to the first note system 5, measure 3.

VIDEO
CLIP 9:7

CREATING EXAMPLES
6 AND 7

m. Once again, this is a good time to save your work.

Creating Examples 6 and 7

System 6, containing examples 6 and 7, is very straightforward. However, these examples do show some effective ways to use worksheets with NotePad. Students will use the *Lyrics* tool to type chords above measure A, then will use *Simple Note Entry* to add notes to the existing ones in measure B. Since two different tools are used for chord entry, students cannot erase the chords in measure B, because NotePad does not give users access to the *Chord* tool.

1. If system 6 is on page 2, move system 5 up using the *Page Layout* tool. This will provide room for system 6 on page 1.

2. Press **Esc** and right-click (**Control–click**) on measure A.

3. Select *Edit Measure Attributes.*

4. Set *Time Signature* to *Always Show.* Click *OK.*

5. Change the key signature to C major. (Select the *Selection* tool and right-click [**Control–click**] on the existing key signature.)

6. Change the clef on staff 2 to bass clef. (Select the *Selection* tool and right-click [**Control–click**] on the existing clef.)

7. Input the quarter notes as shown in the example.

8. Select the first note in measure 1, top staff.

9. Press **X** for expression. Press **Enter.**

10. Click *Create.* (On Windows, the shortcut key is **C.**)

11. Press **Shift–A.** Under *Enclosure,* select *Circle* in the *Shape* dropdown menu.

The Enclosure Shape dropdown menu

12. Click the *Note Positioning* tab.

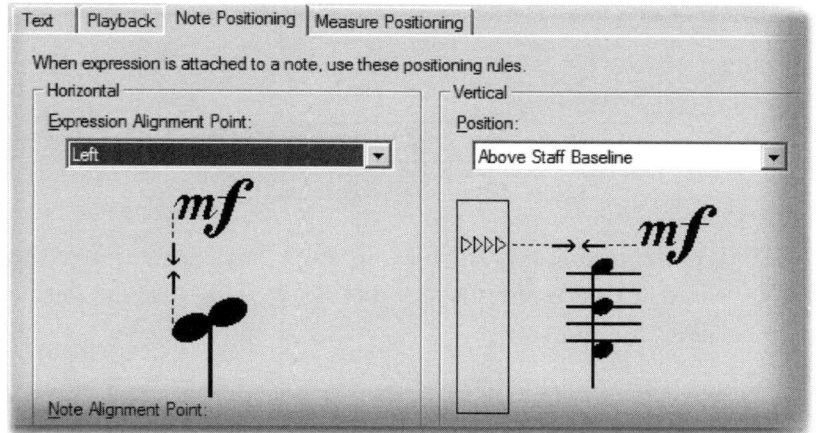

The Note Positioning tab of the Text Expression Designer dialog

   a.   Under *Horizontal,* select *Left* in the *Expression Alignment Point* and *Note Alignment Point* dropdown menus.

   b.   Under *Vertical,* select *Above Staff Baseline* in the *Position* dropdown menu.

   c.   Generally this is already set for Finale expressions. When you created new expressions in earlier chapters, you duplicated an existing expression, then edited it, so there was no need to set this. Now you are ready to examine how to set the default placement of an expression. Note the settings for note-attached and measure-attached expressions. You have just adjusted settings for a note-attached expression.

13. Click *OK,* then *Select* to return to the score.

14. Select the first note in measure B.

15. Press **X,** then **Enter.**

16. Scroll down and select the *A* just created. Click *Duplicate* (**P**), then *Edit* (**E**).

17. Select the *A;* press **Shift–B.** Click *OK,* then *Select* to return to the score.

18. Select the *Chord* tool.

19. Click the first note of measure 2, examples 6 and 7.

20. Input the chords as shown in the example below.

21. Use the positioning triangles in the left margin to move these chords closer to the staff for this system only (use the third triangle from the left).

22. Select the *Lyrics* tool. Click the first note of measure A, top staff.

23. Do not type anything here; simply drag the third-from-the-left positioning triangle to align the lyric baseline with the bottom of the chords that are above the staff. Students will use the *Lyrics* tool in NotePad to enter their answers. This will automatically place the chord names above the staff.

24. Optimize system 6 (see instructions above). After doing this, system 7 should return to the first page, where it was before you added a staff to system 5. If not, use the *Page Layout* tool and drag system 6 up to make room for system 7, then drag system 7 to the appropriate location to the right of system 6.

25. Save your work.

Creating Example 8

Here is a list of steps to complete this last example:

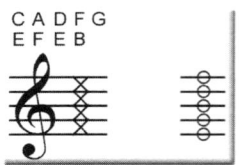

The Chord tool

The Lyric tool

VIDEO
CLIP 9:8

CREATING EXAMPLE 8

- Hide time and key signatures
- Input notes and rests
- Hide a portion of the staff
- Remove barlines
- Optimize the system
- Increase staff size
- Change noteheads
- Position notes horizontally
- Change the staff style to *Stemless*
- Create articulations for students to use in labeling staff lines and spaces.

As a challenge, try this on your own without the following steps. If you are not sure, follow these instructions, but be aware that these steps are not complete. This is part of the process of weaning yourself from this book and remembering what you have learned.

1. Hide the time and key signatures. (Hint: *Selection* tool, *Measure Attributes*. Review steps 1–3 of examples 6 and 7.)

2. Input the notes and rests on the top system as shown in the example above.

3. Optimize the system. (Hint: *Page Layout*, right-click [**Control– click**]. *Optimize.*)

4. Delete the extra measures (Hint: *Selection* tool, right-click [**Control–click**], **Delete.**)

   a. In Finale 2008, double-click the measure to select a measure stack, then press **Delete**. Selecting one measure and pressing **Delete** will only clear the contents of the selected measure, not delete the entire measure from the score.

5. Make the staff larger.

   a. Select the *Resize* tool.

   b. Click to the left of the clef.

   c. Change the size to 250%.

   d. Under *Staff System Range,* enter System **7** Through End of Piece.

   e. Click *OK*.

The Resize tool

6. Make the notes stemless. (hint: *Staff* tool, staff style: *Stemless Notes.*)

7. Hide the staff where the rests are. (Hint: Select *Edit* menu/*Partial Measure Select*, *Staff* tool, select area, select staff style: *Hide Staff.*) Note: In Finale 2008, there is no partial measure select; simply drag a box to select the area.

8. Change the noteheads to x and o.

    a.   There are three ways to change notehead shape:

        i. *Mass Edit* menu/*Change/Noteheads.* (In Finale 2008, *Selection* tool, *Utilities* menu/*Change/Noteheads.*)

        ii. A plug-in. (*Plug-ins* menu/*Note, Beam, and Rest Editing/Change Notehead.*)

        iii. The *Special Tools/Note Shape* tool.

        Since you will need to use the *Special Tool* for positioning, we will use this method. However, if you are changing noteheads for more than one consecutive measure, it is best to use the *Mass Edit* or *Selection* tool or the *Change Notehead* plug-in.

    b.   Click on the *Special Tools* tool (on Windows, use the *Advanced Tool Palette*).

    c.   Click on the *Note Shape* tool.

    d.   Click in the last measure to display the handles next to each note.

    e.   Drag a marquee around all of the handles for the first chord.

    f.   Double-click any of the selected handles.

    g.   Select shape number 192 by double-clicking it.

The Special Tools tool

The Note Shape tool

   h.   Drag a marquee around all of the handles in the second
        chord.

   i.   Double-click on any of the selected handles.

   j.   Double-click on shape number 247.

9. While you have the *Special Tools* palette open, position both
   chords to center them on the staff lines.

   a.   Select the *Note Position* tool.

   b.   Click in the measure.

   c.   Drag the handle above each chord to position it
        horizontally.

The Note Position tool

10. **Creating the Letters Using Articulations**.

   a.   Select the *Articulation* tool (or use the *Selection* tool
        and double-click an existing articulation).

   b.   Click the first chord.

   c.   Click *Create*.

   d.   Click *Set Font* and set the font to Arial 8-point.
        Note: Since we increased the size of the staff, the
        articulations will also increase in size. You can force
        the size of fonts in Finale by choosing *Fixed Size* in
        any of the font dialogs.

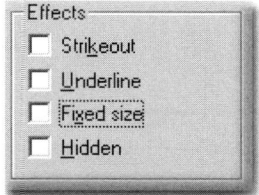

Setting the font size to Fixed Size

   e.   Click *Main;* select the letter *F.*

   f.   Press *Select* and *OK* to return to the score.

   g.   For the next letter, once again click the chord with the
        Articulation tool.

h. Choose the articulation you just created (*F*). Click *Duplicate* (or press **P**), then *Edit* (or press **E**). (The shortcuts are for Windows only.)

i. Click *Main;* select the next letter name: *A.* Click *Select* and *OK* to return to the score.

j. Repeat steps g, h, and i for the remaining letters. Remember, you only have to create an articulation once. Do not create duplicates of E and F.

k. **Note:** This is a great opportunity for Windows users to practice using the shortcut keys: **P** for *Duplicate,* **E** for *Edit,* and **M** for the *Main* button. Then double-click the letter symbol to select it.

11. **Positioning Items.** The articulations you just created would look more professional if they were all aligned as shown in the final example. You can simply drag them with the *Selection* tool, but there is no automatic alignment for articulations. Therefore, it is best to turn on the grid so you can visually align these items.

a. Select *View* menu/*Show Grid.* (In Finale 2008, Select *View* menu/*Grid/Guide/Show Grid.*)

b. Zoom in on the bottom-right corner of the screen to see the grid detail.

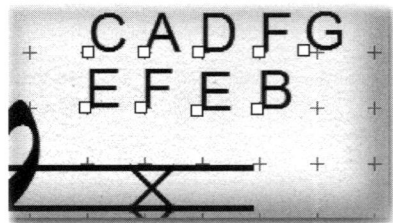

Grid detail

c. Drag letters to align them to the grid.

d. Later we will use a function called *Snap to Grid.* This would be useful for the articulation alignment, but articulations will not snap to the grid because they are note-attached items, and therefore their placement follows note position.

e. You may want to hide the grid after aligning the letter names. Hide it with the same menu command you used to show it.

Finishing the Text

Completing the text boxes and creating new additional text boxes is easy. Select the *Selection* tool; double-click on a text box; select the text you do not want and type to replace it. Below are some special cases of text in this worksheet.

1. In most of the pre-created text boxes, the frame is too large for the small amount of text you are entering. After typing the text, simply drag the bottom of the dotted frame to make it smaller.

2. In question 2 there is a flat (♭) sign.

   a. Type the text up to and including the **E.**

   b. Select *Text* menu/Inserts/*Flat* (note the shortcut key if you use this often).

   c. You can simply press **Spacebar** and continue typing the rest of the text.

   d. If you like, you can make the flat (♭) sign larger and superscript it after inputting all of the text in this text box.

      i. While in text-box-editing mode (typing text mode), click-and-drag over the flat sign to select it.

      ii. Increase the font size using *Text* menu commands or shortcut keys discussed before **(Ctrl/Command–Shift–>)**.

      iii. With the flat sign still selected, select *Text* menu/*Superscript*. Set the value to about **0.05** (inch). Click *OK*.

3. Save your work.

Page Layout and Alignment

A good amount of the page layout work required by this worksheet is positioning systems where you want them. Zoom out and select the *Page Layout* tool, then simply drag a system where you want it. There are a few points to keep in mind:

The Page Layout tool

- Holding **Ctrl/Option** while dragging a system allows you to move a system without affecting the position of other systems.
- If you do not **Ctrl/Option–drag** a system, all systems below the one you drag will move accordingly. This can be a huge benefit.
  - For example, if you drag system 3 (example 3) down, the system to the right of it will move accordingly. Also, all other systems below system 3 will move accordingly.
- As with many items in Finale, you can constrain dragging horizontally and vertically.
  - Press and hold **Shift** before you **click–drag**. This constrains dragging to the horizontal plane.
  - Press and hold **Shift** *after* clicking but *before* dragging an item. This constrains movement to the vertical plane. You will not be able to move the item horizontally.

Finishing the Text Boxes

1. Adjust systems to make room for text boxes.

2. The template had text boxes for questions 1–5 pre-created for you. Text boxes for questions 6–8 need to be created.

   a. If the *Text* tool is not selected, double-click on any text box with the *Selection* tool to activate the *Text* tool.

   b. You can simply double-click on the page and start typing. Finale will automatically make the text box larger as you type. However, it will not automatically wrap the text, since it does not know how large a text box you want. The better approach is in the next step.

   c. Double-click-and-drag to the approximate size you want the text box. (You can always resize it later).

   d. Type text into the box. Finale will auto wrap the text according to the size of the text box.

e. You can also use **Tab** in the textbox as you normally would in a word processing program.

3. Right-click (**Control–click**) on text using the *Selection* tool. Select *Edit Frame Attributes.*

   a. In the *Frame Attributes* dialog, note that text can be attached to a page position or to a measure and staff. If you like, you can attach each text box to the appropriate example, so that if you move the system for that example, the associated text will move with it.

   b. There are a couple of things to remember when doing this: Text attached to measures will resize to the measure. Question 8 would have large text since you increased the size of the staff—unless you specify *Fixed Size* in the *Text* menu.

4. **Text Enclosures.**

   a. Text boxes can also have enclosures around them.

   b. Double-click a textbox with the *Selection* tool.

   c. Click on the page to exit typing mode, then click on the text box handle to select it.

   d. Select *Text* menu/*Standard Frame,* or press **Ctrl/Command–M.**

   e. In the *Standard Frame* dialog, enter a *Line Thickness.* A basic thickness is **0.01** (inch).

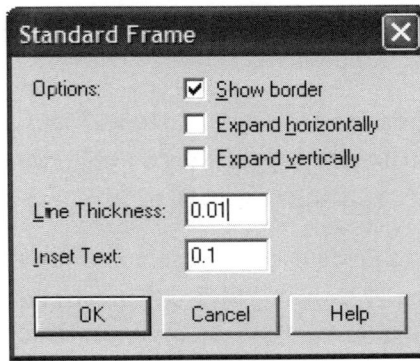

The Standard Frame dialog

   f. Enter **0.1** (inch) in the *Inset Text* text field. This is the amount of space between the text and the enclosure.

Snap to Grid. A quick way to align text boxes is with the *Snap to Grid* function. There are several types of items that will snap to the grid. You can control what items do this.

1. Select *Options* (or *Document*) menu/*Document Options/Grids and Guidelines.*

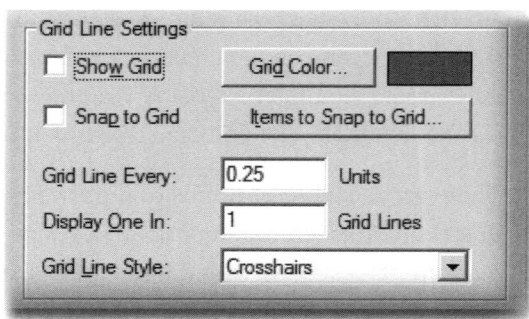

The Grids and Guidelines pane of the Document Options dialog

2. Check the boxes next to *Show Grid* and *Snap to Grid.*

3. Click *Items to Snap to Grid.* This opens a dialog showing what is available to snap to grid and allows you to include the items you would like to snap.

4. You can set the grid size in the *Grid Line Every* text field. The default is 0.25 inch.

5. Adjust these settings as you like, then click *OK* to return to the worksheet.

6. Select the *Selection* tool, then click-and-drag a text box where you want it. As you release the mouse, the text box will snap to the nearest grid point.

7. This is a great way to align questions 3 and 4, and 6 and 8 horizontally. It is also a good way to align text boxes vertically, such as 1, 3, 5, 6 and 7, as well as 2, 4, and 8.

8. The grid cannot be used to align questions 1 and 2 because the frame for text box two is higher than one, due to the superscript flat sign in question 2.

   a. Press and hold **Ctrl/Option** while dragging to temporarily disable the grid.

9. Also, remember that you can select several text boxes to move together by selecting their handles with the *Text* tool.

a.   Double-click a text box with the *Selection* tool.

b.   Drag a box, or **Shift–click** all of the handles of the text boxes you want to position. Then position them by dragging any of the selected boxes, or nudging them with the arrow keys.

CHAPTER 10

MISCELLANEOUS TOPICS

Concepts covered in this chapter:
- Scanning and Editing
- Working with GPO Sounds
- MIDI and Playback Controls (MIDI tool, Spacebar play controls).
- Adjusting Human Playback
- Using Finale NotePad with Students (Letting Students Create Parts for Scores)
- Creating SmartMusic files
- Importing and Exporting MusicXML Files

This chapter covers useful topics that were not part of the projects in earlier chapters. Consider this as valuable reference material.

SCANNING AND EDITING A SCANNED SCORE

Scanning is a feature that *can* make note input very fast. You can use a basic scanner to scan existing music and turn it into a Finale file; then you can edit, transpose, create audio and SmartMusic files, just as with any Finale file. Although there are exceptions to the rule, generally scanning:

- Works only with professionally engraved music
  - Does not work well with music printed in a jazz font
  - Does not work with handwritten manuscript
- Requires an original, not a photocopy
  - Although some users have had success scanning photocopies, they are generally low resolution and do not have the clean detail needed for correct music scanning
  - If you must scan a photocopy, try to make sure the photocopy is high-resolution as possible
- Requires the erasing of rehearsal notes handwritten in the score
  - Sometimes circles and lines drawn on the page can create errors in scanning recognition

The scanning software built into Finale is made by Musitek. It is a reduced version of *SmartScore Pro*. This reduced version of SmartScore will scan:

- Notes (pitch and duration, no grace notes, no triplets or other tuplets)
- Time signatures
- Key signatures (each staff is an independent key signature)
- Page formatting (optimized staves, number of measures per system, number of systems per page)
- Repeats and repeat endings
- A limit of sixteen staves per system (larger scores can be scanned using a work-around)

You can purchase SmartScore Pro for a special price by following the links in the *About SmartScore* dialog. SmartScore Pro can scan most musical items and produces a file that can be imported into Finale. However, I highly recommend that you use the MusicXLM option in SmartScore Pro (version 5) to import into Finale. The new SmartScore Pro X has automated the interface between Finale and SmartScan Pro. Here is a basic list of what SmartScore Pro can scan.

- With SmartScore Pro, clicking on the scanning button in Finale's *Launch Window* opens SmartScore.
- Once a score is scanned with SmartScore Pro, you can simply click the *Open in Finale* button, which looks like the Finale logo. This imports the score into Finale.

SmartScore Pro recognizes all that the reduced version does, plus:

- Grace notes
- Tuplets
- Cross-staff beaming
- 32 staves per system
- Text and lyrics
- Expressions, dynamics, and phrase markings
- Chords and guitar fretboard diagrams

Neither version of SmartScore can scan single-line staves. All percussion parts need to be on 5-line staves to scan properly.

Windows and Macintosh scanning procedures differ slightly. On Windows, Finale has a scanning wizard. On Macintosh, you will need to know how to scan a document as a TIF file. Then you can load the TIF image into Finale and convert it into a Finale file.

WHICH SCANNERS WORK?

In theory, all scanners will work in one of two modes: black-and-white or grayscale. Automatic scanning, accessed by clicking *Scanning* in the *Launch Window*, only works with specific scanning drivers: WIA on Windows; TWAIN on Macintosh. A list of compatible scanners is available at www.smartscore.com

SCANNING WITH A MACINTOSH COMPUTER

Finale 2006–2008. To scan a document on Macintosh, use the scanning software that came with your scanner.

1. Launch the scanning software installed on your Macintosh.

2. Set the scanner to produce either a black-and-white or grayscale TIF image. (This setting may be in the scanning software's advanced settings.) **Note**: In some scanning software, the TIF setting is not available until *after* scanning is done.

3. Set the resolution to 300 dots per inch (dpi). (You can scan at a higher resolution, but 300 dpi is a good general setting. Higher resolutions do not produce much additional accuracy, but substantially increase file size.)

4. Make note of where your scanning software saves the TIF images.

5. Scan each page as a separate TIF image.

6. The scanned image should be in portrait, not landscape, mode. This may require you to rotate the image, depending on how the original was placed on the scanner platen.

7. Preview each page.

8. Most scanning software has advanced controls, which you should access in order to fine-tune your scan.

9. You may want to crop out any unnecessary text or other items you do not want.

10. Generally it is best to darken the image slightly. Some scanning software has a *histogram*—a graph used to visually control the shadows and highlights (dark and light areas) of an image. This is very useful for optimizing the contrast for scanning music.

a. Below is an example of a histogram. Note that the contrast line (the diagonal line) begins at the point at which the image starts to get dark (at the bottom, above the black triangle). If your software does not have a histogram, then adjust the contrast or threshold to make the image somewhat darker. Open the scan in Finale. If you are not happy with the results, then adjust the contrast. This is the most important setting for improving the accuracy of a scan.

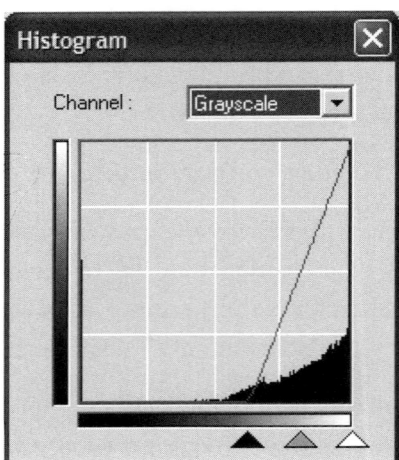

A typical histogram in scanning software

11. After previewing and making adjustments to the image, scan (a separate process from previewing) the page. Repeat this process for each page of the score.

12. Open Finale and select *File* menu/*Launch Window*. Click *Scanning*. The *SmartScore* dialog opens. From here, drop down to the instructions below, Loading the TIF Files for music recognition.

13. **Note**: In Finale 2007 on an Intel Macintosh computer, Finale recommends that you run SmartScore in Rosetta (software built into Mac OS X to allow programs not compiled for Intel processors to run) to allow scanning to work. Subsequent maintenance releases of Finale 2007 fix this. Update to Finale 2007a or higher for this function to work in the Native Universal Binary OS for Intel Macintosh computers.

SCANNING MUSIC WITH A WINDOWS COMPUTER

Finale 2006–2007. Most scanning software for Windows computers is WIA compliant. If so, clicking *Scanning* in the *Launch Window* will start your scanning software. If it does not, follow the instructions above for scanning using a Macintosh.

1. Place the music straight on a flatbed scanner.

2. In the *Launch Window,* click *Scanning.*

3. If your scanning software launches using a simple mode, turning on advanced settings may give you access to some of the following settings.

4. Finale should set your scanning software to 300 dpi resolution and grayscale by default. If it does not, change to these settings manually.

5. Click *Preview* if your software has not automatically created a preview of the music you are scanning.

6. Crop out any items you do not want to scan using the crop tool in your scanning preview window.

7. Unless the original is very thick and heavy in appearance, darken the contrast somewhat as described above in the Macintosh scanning instructions.

8. Click *Scan* to scan this page of music.

9. After scanning the music, Finale will prompt you to scan another page of music. Click *Yes* and repeat the instructions above for each page.

10. After scanning the last page, click *No* when prompted for more pages.

11. A dialog will display informing you that Finale has placed all of the scanned images into a temporary folder on your computer. Click *OK* in this dialog. Finale will display the *SmartScore Lite* dialog.

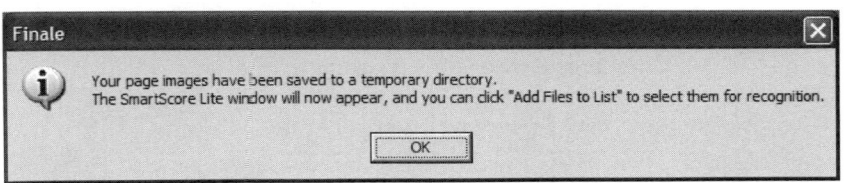

SCANNING IN FINALE 2008

In Finale 2008, the scanning interface changed for those using a WIA-compliant (Windows) or Twain (Macintosh) driver. To make it easier to scan correctly, a common scanning interface was developed that semi-automates scanning. This works on Windows and Macintosh if you have a compliant scanner. If you do not, you will need to scan the music as described in the instructions for Macintosh computers above. Try installing your scanning software, plugging in your scanner, then clicking *Scanning* in the *Launch Window*. A SmartScore advertisement dialog may display. If so, click *OK*. Hopefully you will next see the new scanning interface. If so, then follow these instructions. **Note**: On Macintosh, you may need to deselect *Use PPC Driver* in this dialog to access a Twain-compatible scanner.

1. Place the music on the scanner before you click *Scanning* in the *Launch Window*.

2. Click *Scanning*. A SmartScore advertisement dialog displays. Click *OK*. A command is sent to your scanner to pre-scan the music.

3. After pre-scanning, Musitek calculates the best resolution and sets your scanner to that number of dots per inch. Contrast is also set to -15%, which is a good general setting. However, I sometimes change this setting if the original print is either very light or heavy.

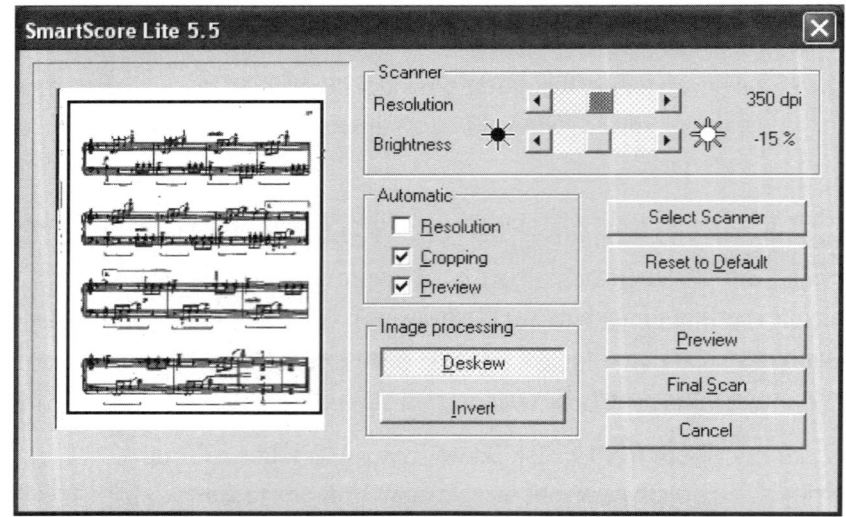

The SmartScore Lite 5.5 scanning interface

4. Crop portions of the page you do not need to scan.

5. Click *Final Scan.* SmartScore scans at the full resolution. (**Note**: pre-scanning creates a lower-resolution preview to enable quicker viewing of a scan. Clicking *Final Scan* initiates the full-resolution scan that Finale will use.)

6. You are given the options of scanning the next page or clicking *Finished.* If you have more pages, set the next page on the scanner *before* clicking the next page option so the scanning software can again do the pre-scan.

7. When finished, click *Finished,* then the follow instructions below.

LOADING TIF FILES FOR MUSIC RECOGNITION

Once you get to the dialog in the example below, you are ready to load the files into Finale. Note the *About SmartScore Lite* button. Clicking that displays a button that links to a Musitek special offer to purchase the SmartScore Pro at a reduced price as mentioned above.

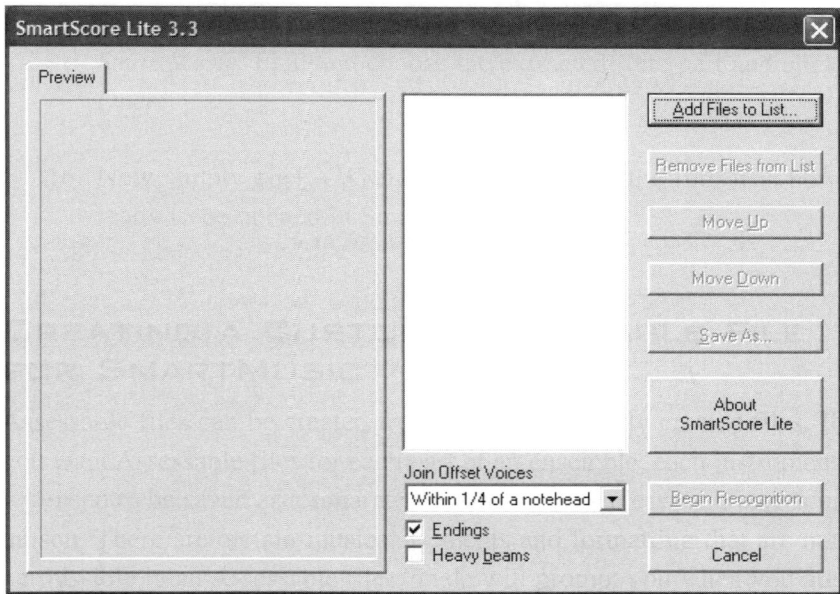

Note: If you are using the new scanning interface in Finale 2008, the files are already loaded for you in this dialog. Simply start with item 5 below.

1. Click *Add Files to List.*

2. On Windows, if you used the scanning wizard in the *Launch Window,* Finale automatically directs the *Open* dialog to the temporary directory where the scanned images were saved. On

Macintosh, or if you scanned the images without the Windows scanning wizard as described above, you will need to navigate to the place where these files are saved, as you would when opening any file on a computer.

3. Select all of the pages that were scanned and click *Open*.

4. Make sure the pages are in the correct order.

    a. If they are not, click on the name of a file in the list. A small preview of the image displays in the *Preview* tab.

    b. Click *Move Up* or *Move Down* to re-position the file.

5. Click *Begin Recognition*. Finale converts the scanned images into a Finale score.

6. Now you can see what notes and music elements Finale has recognized from the scanned image. This is a Finale file, but it may be confusing to work with due to the defaults in this file. To make editing, transposing, and instrument assignments easier, copy/paste the music into a new Finale document. **Note**: Correct any incorrect time signatures before doing the copy/paste. Follow the instructions in the following section on time signatures.

    a. Select the *Mass Edit* or *Selection* tool.

    b. Type **Ctrl/Command–A** to select *a*ll.

    c. Type **Ctrl/Command–C** to copy the score. (Make sure the copy filter is set to *All Items*. In Finale 2008, deselect *Use Filter* if it is selected.)

    d. Type **Ctrl/Command–N** for *n*ew score.

        i. Use the *Setup Wizard* to configure the correct instrumentation and staff order.

        ii. If the top staff of the scanned score is a transposing instrument, select the correct concert key.

        iii. Make sure to select a pickup measure on page 4 of the *Setup Wizard* if needed.

        iv. In Finale 2008, you may want to select the number of measures you need for this score.

The Mass Edit and Selection tools

     v. Finish creating the blank score.

e. Type **Ctrl/Command–A** to select *all*.

f. Use one of these two methods to paste the music into the score:

     i. If the top staff of the score is for a C instrument, simply type **Ctrl/Command–I** for *insert*. This will automatically create enough measures for the score you scanned and copied. You may want to delete extra measures at the end of the score.

     ii. If the top instrument is for a transposing instrument, add enough measures to the new document.

         (a) Select the *Selection* tool.

         (b) Right-click (**Control–click**) and select *Insert Measures*.

         (c) Enter the number of measures needed.

         (d) Paste the music into the score using **Ctrl/Command–V**.

g. Now you can edit, transpose, play, and arrange as you would any Finale file.

Editing the Score from a Scanned Image

Generally, scanning does not do a perfect job of accurately recognizing music, but at least ninety-five percent of the notes (pitches and durations) should be correct. If not, you may want to re-scan and set a different contrast level to increase accuracy. In my experience, ninety percent of the scores I scan come in quite nicely. However, there are always a few scores that are not accurately recognized no matter what changes in settings I make. This is to be expected with all optical character recognition (OCR) software.

Once a score is scanned and converted into a Finale file, you can change notes, transpose, and make other alterations as you have learned in this book. Below are some common scanned-music problems and their solutions.

Correcting will proceed more smoothly if you fit the music to match the number of measures per system in the original using the *Mass Edit* or *Selection* tool. Resize the page to match as well. **Note**: This is not necessary with SmartScore Pro, since it always shows the scanned image on the same screen with the recognized score, making it very easy to follow.

OPTIMIZED SYSTEMS

One of the most common problems in scanning is a score with optimized systems. To refresh your memory, the choral score project utilized optimized systems. System 1 is for Piano only; the next several systems have staves for Soprano, Bass, and Piano; and on page 2, the score opens up to a full set of staves for SATB Choir and Piano. In Finale 2006–2007, a top-down distribution of music to staves is assumed. In Finale 2008, a bottom-up distribution is the default.

In Finale 2006–2007, then, the first staff of scanned music is placed on the top staff of the Finale document; the next scanned staff goes on the next-to-the-top staff of the document, and so forth.

Consider an optimized score for SATB Choir and Piano. If the introduction is for Piano only, then Finale will put the two staves of the Piano introduction (the top two staves on the first system in the original) on the top two staves of the new document, which, in a non-optimized score, would be the Soprano and Alto (in an open-score document) or the treble and bass clef vocal staves (of a closed-score document). You would need to copy the music as placed by Finale from the vocal staves, paste it into the Piano staves, and then clear the music from the vocal staves.

TIES VERSUS SLURS

Slurs are easily misinterpreted as ties due to the similarity in shape. Ties between notes of different pitches will have to be removed. (Fortunately, this is quite easy to do.)

The Mass Edit and Selection tools

1. Select the *Mass Edit* or *Selection* tool.

2. Select the area with incorrect ties.

3. Right-click (**Control–click**) in the highlighted area and select *Utilities/Check Ties*. (In Finale 2008, select *Utilities* menu/ *Check Notation*.)

DOTTED NOTES

Articulations such as staccatos are often mistaken for augmentation dots.

1. Use the *Selection* tool to select a note, press and hold **Alt/Option** plus the correct duration key to remove the dot. For example, to change a dotted-eighth note to an eighth note, press **Alt/Option–4.**

2. If there is a section of music that has incorrect rhythm due to augmentation dots, you can alter durations with the *Mass Edit* or *Selection* tool.

   a. Select the area with the *Mass Edit* or *Selection* tool.

   b. Right-click (**Control–click**) in the highlighted area and select *Change Note Durations.* (In Finale 2008, select *Utilities* menu/*Change Notation.*)

   c. Set values as needed. In the example below all dotted-eighth notes will be changed to eighth notes.

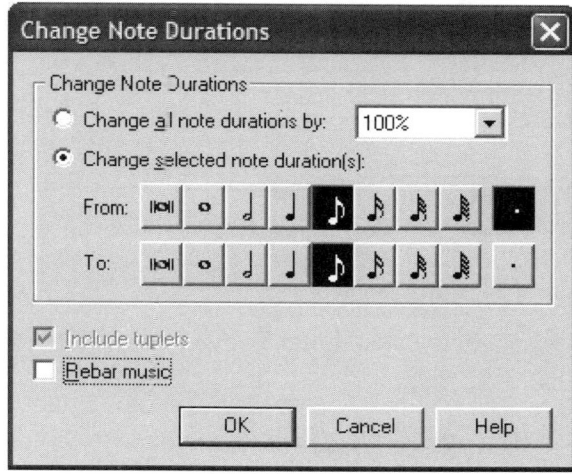

The Change Note Durations dialog

   d. Clear the checkbox next to *Rebar music.*

   e. Click *OK.*

HIDDEN RESTS

Sometimes notes are out of place due to a hidden rest. During scanning recognition, notes not lined up correctly in the original may not align correctly. (This can also happen when a note's duration is changed.) In *Simple Entry* mode, hidden rests appear in lightly screened color (i.e., not solid). If you cannot see hidden rests but suspect they are present, select *View* menu/*Show Hidden Notes.*

Hidden rests are lightly screened

INCORRECT LAYER RHYTHM

As shown above, a hidden rest can alter note placement and rhythm. Lack of hidden rests can alter note placement and rhythm layers as well. Consider the example below. It looks like a complete mess. However, this is easily corrected. The problem is that a half rest on beat 1 is missing. Inserting the rest in Layer 2 pushes the notes to the correct beat.

1. Click on a note value in the *Simple Entry* palette—in this case, the half note value.

2. Select the correct layer (Layer 2 in this case).

3. Type **R** for *r*est. Click on the desired beat to insert the rest.

4. Type **H** to *h*ide the rest if you like.

KEY SIGNATURES

On occasion, pitches may be correct but the key signature is wrong, or the key signature may change in the wrong measure; it may also change for one staff and not others. In this case, it may be best to make key signature changes in the recognized file before copying and pasting it into the newly created document as you did above. To change the key signature without transposing, follow these instructions:

1. Select the *Selection* tool (press **Esc**).

2. Double-click the existing key signature or right-click (**Control–click**) in the measure in which the key signature should change. (This second method must be used if there are no flats or sharps in the key signature, as with C major or A minor.) Select *Edit Key Signature*.

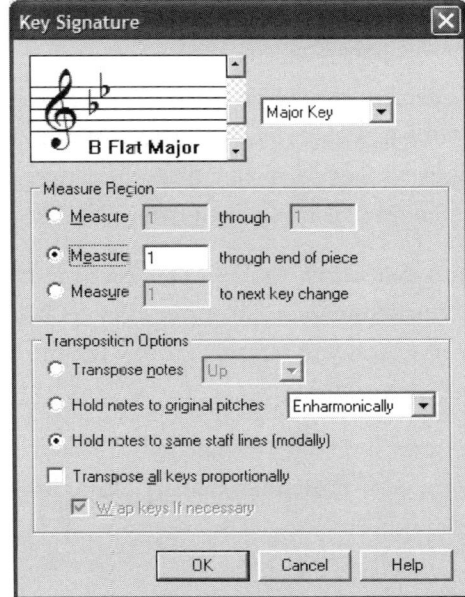

The Key Signature dialog

3. Select the correct key signature.

4. Select the measure range.

5. Click the button next to *Hold notes to same staff lines (modally)*.

6. Click *OK*.

TRANSPOSING INSTRUMENTS

When a score with transposing instruments is scanned, key signatures will be correctly recognized, but Finale will not identify the instrument name. The displayed key signature is considered an independent key not associated with the concert key of the piece instead of a transposed key in relationship to the concert key. After copying and pasting the music from the recognized file into a newly created document, you may notice that key signatures are correct but notes are an octave, fourth, sixth, or other interval off from what is expected. To remedy this:

1. Select the *Mass Edit* or *Selection* tool and click to the left of the staff to be changed.

2. Use the transpose *Metatools* previously created to transpose by octaves or intervals. (In Finale 2008, the preset *Metatools* are down a step (**6**), up a step (**7**), down an octave (**8**), and up an octave (**9**).

TIME SIGNATURES

Incorrect time signatures should be changed before copying and pasting scanned music into a new document. Finale will keep the scanned notes in the correct measure even if the time signature is wrong. Finale defaults to 4/4 when there is no time signature on the first scanned page.

1. Select the *Selection* tool (press **Esc**). Double-click on the existing time signature, or right-click (**Control–click**) in the measure in which you want to change the time signature. Select *Edit Time Signature*.

2. Set the time signature as needed. Do not forget to set the measure range if more than one signature is in the score.

3. Deselect *Rebar Music* so notes will stay in the correct measures. Click *OK*.

BEAMING

As previously discussed, beaming is controlled by the time signature. Generally, scanned music beams correctly. But editing notes after copying and pasting scanned music into a newly created document may cause beaming to change if the time signature beaming is not set correctly.

For example, consider a piece in 9/8. The default beaming for 9/8 is three groups of three eighth notes. SmartScore may calculate 9/8 as nine "groups" of one eighth note each. To correct this, use the instructions above for correcting time signatures and alter the signature's beaming pattern as discussed in chapter 8. You may need to use the *Mass Edit* tool to re-beam if Finale doesn't automatically correct the beaming.

A MESSY MEASURE

Sometimes a measure may be so mixed-up and confused that determining the problem is not worth the time it takes. In that case, it is easier to clear the measure with the *Mass Edit* or *Selection* tool and input it manually.

CREATING A SCORE FROM SCANNED PARTS

Sometimes a conductor's score is quite small and may be difficult to scan. It may be easier and quicker to scan individual parts, then paste each one into a blank score to create the conductor's score. Here are a few things to remember as you do that:

1. Scan the part for the instrument that should appear on the top staff of the conductor's score first, such as the Flute part. Copy/paste it into a new document. From this point on, copy/paste the other parts into the score. The Flute has set the overall layout of concert key, time signature, and repeat endings in the new document, and the remaining parts will follow this lead.

2. In Finale 2006–2007, multi-measure rests are recognized as single measures by SmartScore. To fix this:

   a. Select the *Selection* tool (press **Esc**). Right-click (**Control–click**) in the measure and select *Insert Measures*. (In Finale 2008, select *Insert Measure Stack.*)

   b. Enter the correct number of measures to insert. Click *OK*.

3. SmartScore recognizes full-measure rests as real rests, not Finale's default whole rest. But Finale only includes default whole rests, not real rests, when creating multi-measure rests. A Finale plug-in helps solve this problem.

   a. Select the *Mass Edit* or *Selection* tool. Select the entire score (**Ctrl/Command–A**).

   b. Select the *Plug-ins* menu/*Note, Beam, and Rest Editing/Change to Default Whole Rests.*

USING THE FINALE 2008 MERGE SCORE FUNCTION

In Finale 2008, creating a score from scanned parts is made easier by the new *Merge Score* feature. This loads many files at once and turns them into a single score. However, you will find that it still works best to copy the newly created conductor's score into a new document, created from from a template via the *Setup Wizard*.

1. Scan each part and clean up the scan as described above. Then save each part as a separate file.

2. Select *File* menu/*Merge Score*.

3. Click *Add Files*. Select the files you want to merge.

4. If needed, single-click a file name and use the *Move Up* and *Move Down* buttons to position the files in score order.

5. Click the button next to *Merge These Parts Into One Score*.

6. Click *Merge*.

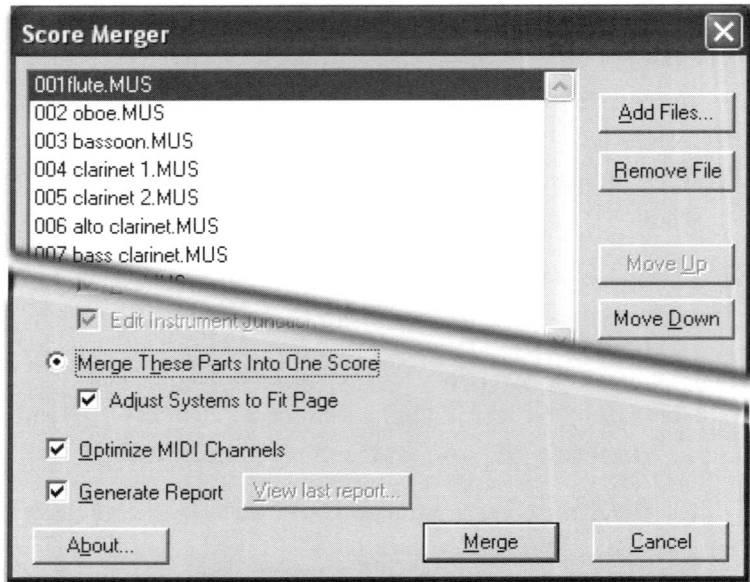

The Score Merger dialog

7. If there are problems with one or more of the files, a dialog displays, detailing the specific file, problem, and measure in which the problem occurs. Most often the problem is that time signatures in the file do not match the score's format, which is created from the first file processed. In the example above, the Flute part is first. If this part does not have time signatures in the correct measures, all other parts will be incorrect and the merge will fail. Fix the problem and try the merge again.

8. Once the new score has been created, you will notice that transposing instruments are not in the correct key. To fix this:

   a. Select the *Selection* tool and select the entire score (**Ctrl/Command–A**). Copy the score (**Ctrl/Command–C**).

   b. Create a new blank score using the *Setup Wizard* with the correct beginning concert key.

   c. Select the first measure of the new blank score and paste (**Ctrl/Command–V**).

SCANNING MORE THAN SIXTEEN STAVES

SmartScore Lite limits systems to a maximum of sixteen staves. If you have a score with more than sixteen staves, scan the first sixteen staves, then scan the remaining staves and paste it all together in Finale.

1. When scanning, remember to always preview the page before scanning.

2. In most scanning software, you can drag the dotted-line box to tell the scanner part of the preview image to scan. This is called cropping. Select only the top sixteen staves of the music.

3. Scan each page, cropping each page to include only the top sixteen staves.

4. When you have scanned each page, select the pages in the *SmartScore* dialog to recognize as explained above.

5. After recognizing these pages, copy/paste the music into a blank score as described above.

6. Now scan the pages again, this time cropping the pages to scan only the bottom staves not previously scanned.

7. After scanning all of the pages in this manner, load the images and recognize the music as before.

8. Now copy/*paste* (do not insert) the music into the appropriate staves in the new conductor score you created which contains the first sixteen staves.

FINALE SOUND SETS, GARRITAN PERSONAL ORCHESTRA AND SMARTMUSIC SOFTSYNTH

Finale comes with two different synthesizer engines which have two separate sets of sounds. The *SmartMusic SoftSynth* is a smaller, less-detailed sound set that will work on most basic computers. The minimum requirements for *SmartMusic SoftSynth* are 256 MB of RAM and an 800 MHz processor.

If you have a more powerful computer, one with a at least 1 GB of RAM and a 2.0 GHz or faster processor, then you might want to try the Garritan Personal Orchestra set that uses the Native Instruments Kontakt player.

The *SmartMusic SoftSynth* (SMSS) is a set of General MIDI sounds that includes the Rowloff® Marching Percussion and Latin Percussion sounds. Finale can play up to 120 pitched sounds and eight sets of non-pitched percussion sounds simultaneously. (A set of non-pitched percussion sounds can include up to a hundred sounds in one set.)

The Garritan Personal Orchestra sounds (GPO) use the Kontakt Player and can play up to any combination of sixty-four pitched and non-pitched sounds. The number of GPO sounds that play simultaneously is based on your computer's limitations. A score for woodwind quartet would play fine on a system with 512 MB of RAM and a 1.6 GHz processor. A larger score, say, with sixteen instruments, would require at least 1.0 GB of RAM and a 2.6 GHz or faster processor.

CHOOSING A SOUND SET

In Finale 2006–2007, you can use either the Kontakt player to play GPO and other Kontakt compatible sound sets or you can use the SMSS sounds, but you cannot use both sets together in the same score.

In Finale 2008, the entire *SmartMusic SoftSynth* was converted to a VST system, so it is possible to have a score with both sets of sounds.

1. Start a new score with the *Setup Wizard.*

2. On the second page of the *Setup Wizard,* click on the pull-down menu at the top to select the synthesizer engine and sound set you want.

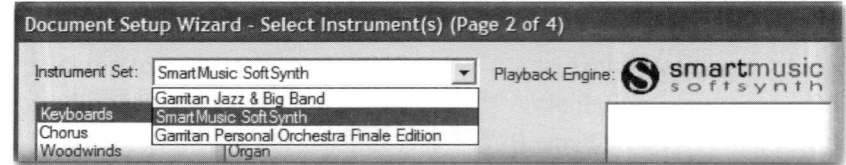

Page 2 of the Document Setup Wizard dialog (Select Instruments)

3. If you have more than one set of Garritan sound sets loaded (for example, the GPO Finale Edition set and the Garritan Jazz and Big Band set), you can use sounds from both sets in the same score because they both use the Kontakt synthesizer engine.

4. Each time you select a new Instrument Set, a new set of sounds are displayed in the *Setup Wizard* showing the available sounds in that set.

5. As you add sounds to the score list in the *Setup Wizard*, Finale automatically assigns a different MIDI channel to each staff, allowing easy individual balance control.

6. Finish creating the blank score with the *Setup Wizard* as you normally would.

GPO LOAD TIME

You may notice that it takes a moment to load GPO sounds into your computer's RAM. This can be time consuming, so you may want to turn off GPO sounds while working on larger scores; then, when you are finished and want to hear the score using the GPO sounds, simply turn on the NI Kontakt Player and Finale will load the sounds at that time.

1. After creating a score using the GPO sounds, save the document.

2. In Finale 2006–2007, deselect *MIDI* menu/*Play Finale Through Native Instruments*. (In Finale 2008, select *MIDI/Audio* menu/*Play Finale Through MIDI*.) This automatically selects the proper SMSS sound for each staff.

3. Once the score has been created, choose one of these methods to turn on GPO sounds:

   a. In Finale 2006–2007, select *MIDI* menu/*Play Finale Through Native Instruments*.

   b. In Finale 2008, select *MIDI/Audio* menu/*Play Finale Through Audio Units*. Finale loads the sounds.

4. You may also need to do one of the following:

   a. In Finale 2006–2007, select *MIDI* menu/*Native Instruments AU Setup/Ambient Reverb* or *MIDI* menu/*VST Setup/Ambient Reverb*.

   b. In Finale 2008:

      i. Select *MIDI/Audio* menu/*Audio Units Setup*.

      ii. Check the box next to *Play Finale File Through Native Instruments Audio Units*.

      iii. In the *Audio Unit* dropdown menu next to *Finale Channel 1–16,* select *Native Instruments: KontaktPlayer2*.

      iv. Check the box next to *Ambient Reverb* at the bottom of the dialog.

ASSIGNING GPO SOUNDS
TO AN OLDER SCORE

You may need to open a Finale score or MIDI file that does not have GPO sounds assigned. You could easily open the score, copy the score, create a new blank score using the *Setup Wizard,* and then insert the copied material into the new blank score. This is the fastest, easiest way to assign instruments to staves. However, if you have already formatted the score exactly as you want and all you want is to take the existing file and assign GPO sounds to it, follow these steps:

1. Select *Window* menu/*Mixer.*

The Mixer

2. Below the volume slider is the *Patch* name; below that is the MIDI channel.

3. Drag the mixer lower on the screen so you can reference it as you open the Kontakt Player.

4. Select *MIDI* menu/*Native Instruments VST setup.*

5. Check the box next to *Play Finale Through Native Instruments VST.*

6. This dialog has dropdown menus for eight sets of Finale channels. Each set can have a different Native Instruments sound set. Each VST instrument represents a different Synthesizer. In Finale 2006 each Kontakt synthesizer can play eight sounds simultaneously. In Finale 2007–2008, the Kontakt synthesizer can play sixteen sounds simultaneously.

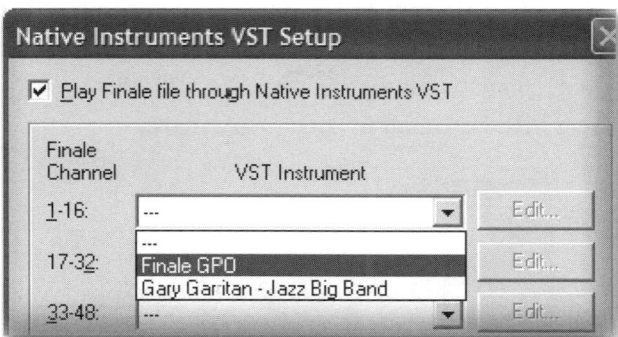

The Native Instruments VST Setup dialog

7. Click on the first dropdown menu to the right of *Finale Channel 1–16*.

8. Select *Finale GPO* (or any other NI Kontakt sound sets you have purchased).

9. Once selected, click *Edit* to the right of the dropdown menu.

10. This launches the Kontakt Player.

KONTAKT PLAYER 1 (FINALE 2006)

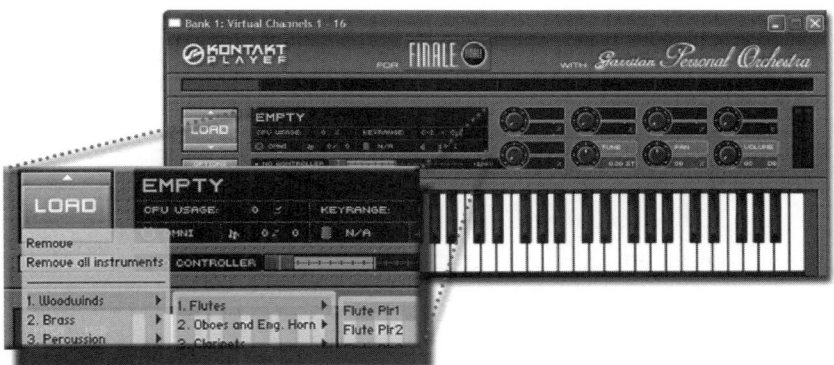

1. Across the top, just below the Finale logo, you will see eight rectangles. One is blue; the others are black. These represent the eight instruments that this synthesizer can play. The first one is selected. Click *Load* to load the desired instrument.

2. After loading the instrument, the name *Empty* changes to the name of the loaded instrument. Below that is the assigned MIDI channel for this sound.

3. Make sure that the MIDI channel listed here matches the channel displayed for that instrument in the *Mixer*. If not, click on the channel number in the Kontakt Player to select the correct MIDI channel for that instrument.

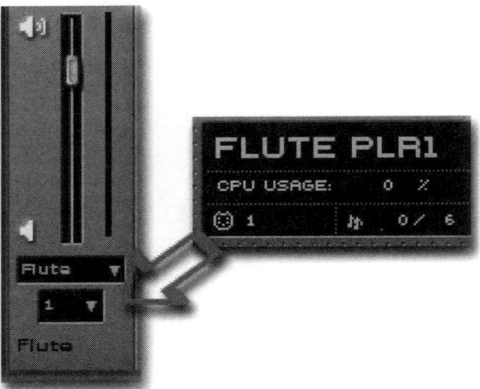

Comparing MIDI channel numbers in the Kontakt Player and Mixer

4. **Note**: If two or more staves in a score share a MIDI channel, you can only load one sound into that MIDI channel. You may want each staff on a separate channel so you have independent control of each. In the choral project, you learned how to create a new MIDI instrument for a staff. If you have more than one staff on the same channel, you may want to create different MIDI instruments for each staff to ensure proper playback and mixer control.

KONTAKT PLAYER 2 (FINALE 2007–2008)

1. The interface for the new Kontakt Player 2 in Finale 2007–2008 looks a bit different, but is similar in function to Kontakt Player 1. Make sure the *Libraries* tab is selected on the left side of the player.

2. Click on the dropdown menu to the right of *Instruments* (left of *Multis*).

3. Select the instrument family, group, and instrument from the submenus. In Finale 2008, you may have two library groups if you upgraded from Finale 2007 on the computer you're using. There are more instruments listed in the *Garritan Instruments for Finale* menu.

The Kontakt Player 2 window

**Two library groups: Garritan Personal Orchestra (Finale edition)
and Garritan Instruments for Finale**

4. Each time you select a new instrument, a new synth module will be added to the rack.

5. In the instrument module that appears after selecting an instrument, the MIDI channel setting is below the instrument name. Here you can change the MIDI channel if needed. Click *MIDI channel* and select from the dropdown menu. You can also simply take note of the MIDI channel assignments and then change the channel in the *Mixer* as discussed below.

MORE THAN SIXTEEN MIDI CHANNELS

As mentioned above, the SMSS can play up to 128 different sounds and the NI Kontakt player in Finale 2006 can play up to sixty-four. The Kontakt 2 player in Finale 2007–2008 can play sixteen channels per port. You may wonder how this is possible, since there are only sixteen

MIDI channels in the MIDI specification. Finale can output sixteen channels per MIDI port.

Recall that the *Native Instruments VST Setup* dialog contains eight synthesizers. In Finale 2006, each synthesizer (synth) can have up to eight MIDI channels assigned to it. In Finale 2007–2008, sixteen channels may be assigned to each synth. Note that the first set of sixteen channels (1–16) is designated for the first Kontakt Player. Virtual channels 17–32 are assigned to the next Kontakt Player. You can access more channels in the Mixer.

When using SMSS, select *MIDI* menu/*MIDI Setup* and note that there are eight different SMSSs listed. (On Windows, click *Advanced* to see this.)

1. In the *Native Instruments VST Setup* dialog, select the next Kontakt Player from the dropdown menu to the right of 17–32.

2. Click *Edit* and select the sounds as described above.

3. When you are finished, close the Kontakt Player and the *Native Instruments VST Setup* dialog to return to the score.

4. With the *Mixer* still open, click on a channel number to reveal more channel options. This channel arrangement is designed to make it easy to match channels in the Kontakt Player(s) with MIDI channels in Finale. For example, to assign the Flute staff to channel 2 of the second Kontakt Player (the player listed next to 17–32 in the *Native Instruments VST Setup* dialog), simply click on the arrow next to the current channel setting; select *2: Finale GPO,* then the channel *Finale GPO 2*. In Finale 2007, this is displayed as *Native Instruments Kontakt 2 2*.

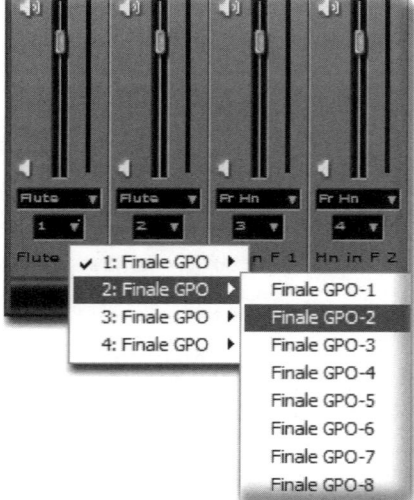

Additional MIDI channel options

The channel assignment will then show channel 18, which is channel 2 of the second set of sounds. Again, all of this is very automated by using the *Setup Wizard.* That is why it is much easier to copy/insert music into a new blank score created by the *Setup Wizard.*

ADDING REVERB

Note that when you select sounds from either the SMSS or from the GPO set, Finale automatically adds reverb to the sounds. The reverb can be controlled in two different ways, depending on the synth engine you select (either SMSS or GPO).

1. **SMSS Reverb Control**. When using SMSS or any General MIDI sound set, you can control the reverb type and amount in the *Mixer.*

2. Select *Window* menu/*Mixer.*

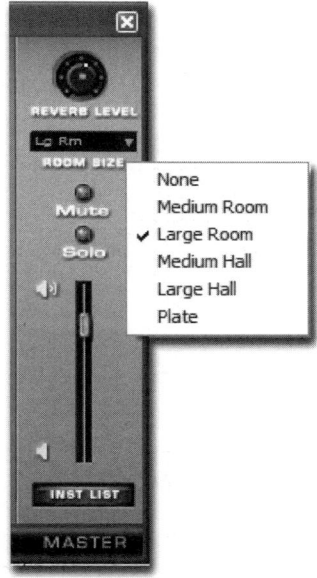

The right side of the Mixer window

3. On the right hand side of the *Mixer* there is a *Master Volume* slider, a *Reverb Type* dropdown menu, and a *Reverb Amount* dial.

4. Click the *Reverb Type* dropdown menu to change this setting.

5. Click anywhere around the *Reverb Level* knob, or drag the pointer on the knob to the desired position.

6. You can click *Play* in Finale and play the score as you make mixer adjustments so you can hear the effect of the *Mixer* during playback.

You will need to access the Garritan Ambience Reverb controls to adjust the reverb of the GPO sounds. On Windows, it is not possible to adjust the reverb of the GPO sounds while playing the score. You will need to stop playback, then call the *NI Setup* dialog to make the adjustments.

1. Select *MIDI Setup* menu/*Native Instruments VST Setup* (on Windows) or *MIDI Setup* menu/*Native Instrument AU Setup* (on Macintosh). Click *Edit* to the right of *Ambience Reverb* at the bottom of the dialog.

The Garritan Ambience dialog

2. Here you will find many types of professional reverb control. If you understand these controls, then adjust them as you like.

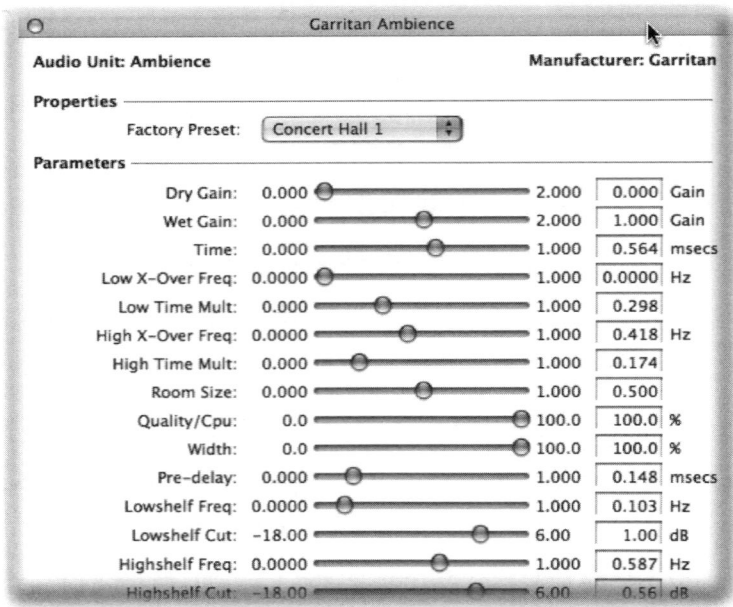

Parameters for a Garritan Ambience reverb preset

3. If you do not care about all of the controls, simply click *Presets* and choose a reverb type.

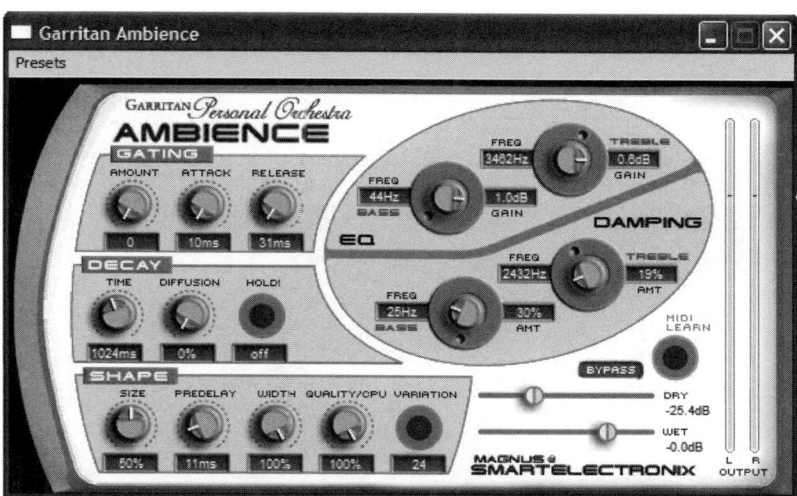

Garritan Ambience presets

4. There are five main controls with which you may want to experiment:

Wet (Wet Gain)
Dry (Dry Gain)
Decay Time (Time)
Shape Size (Room Size)
Quality/CPU settings

a. *Dry* and *Wet* controls adjust the amount of reverb. Increasing the *Dry* amount yields more sound without reverb. Increasing the *Wet* amount gives more sound with reverb. Generally it is not good to set both *Wet* and *Dry* amounts to higher levels.

b. The *Time* knob in the *Decay* section (on Windows; it is simply *Time* on Macintosh) adjusts how long the reverb sustains before dissipating.

c. The *Size* or *Room Size* knob in the *Shape* section adjusts the virtual size of the room. This changes the amount of reverb reflection and character.

d. If your computer is having a difficult time playing GPO sounds, you may want to decrease the *Quality* of the reverb to reduce the demands on the computer's CPU. This is controlled by the *Quality/CPU* adjustment, also in the *Shape* area. The higher this is set, the more CPU processing is required.

5. Close the *Garritan Ambience* dialog by clicking the close box in the corner.

6. Click *Close* to return to the score.

Note: On Intel Macintoshes, *Ambient Reverb* may not work. However, the Kontakt Player 2 allows you to select and edit reverb with the output controls shown in the example below.

Kontakt Player

MIDI AND PLAYBACK CONTROLS (MIDI TOOL AND SPACEBAR PLAY CONTROLS)

To play your score, simply click the *Play* button in the playback controls. Macintosh users have the option to press **Spacebar** for playback. However, there are some other playback controls you may want to know about.

Playback controls

1. On Windows, press and hold **Spacebar,** then click the measure from which you want to play back. Click anywhere on the page to stop. This will play back the notes, but *Human Playback* will not effect playback unless you have applied it with the *Human Playback* plug-in (see below).

a. Also for Windows users: If you want to start playback mid-score *with Human Playback* in effect, you will need to click the *Playback* options icon, then set current counter settings. Now you can enter a measure with which to start playback. Note the *Leftmost measure* setting. This is the setting I use the most. This controls the starting measure for playback by setting the desired measure to the left side of the screen.

Playback settings

2. On Macintosh, you can start playback from any measure by entering the desired measure into the measure text field in the playback controls. Then press **Spacebar** to start and stop playback. The **Spacebar–click** method does not work on Macintosh.

3. Finale has a special playback mode called *Scrubbing*. This is very useful when composing or arranging music, allowing you to manually play, or *scrub* through, any group of notes you like.

    a. Type **Ctrl/Option–Spacebar,** then drag the mouse over the area you want to hear *without* holding down the mouse button. You can drag forward or backwards. You will hear all of the notes in the area over which you drag in the current system.

    b. Add **Shift** to this key combination, making it **Ctrl/Option–Shift–Spacebar.** Now drag over the music and you will hear the notes only for the current staff over which you are dragging the mouse, not the entire system.

MIDI AND HUMAN PLAYBACK

The information that Finale uses to play a score comes from two sources: MIDI information and *Human Playback*. This can be confusing, so consider this explanation.

All information that controls playback is MIDI information. MIDI information comes from the notes in the score and the MIDI info captured in a HyperScribe recording or an imported MIDI file.

MIDI information can be sent directly to a synthesizer, or it can pass through the *Human Playback* filter. This information then passes to the *Mixer* for adjustments controlled by the *Mixer*. Then the information is sent to the synthesizer(s), which could be an internal synthesizer, such as an SMSS, GPO, a computer synthesized sound card, or external synthesizer equipment.

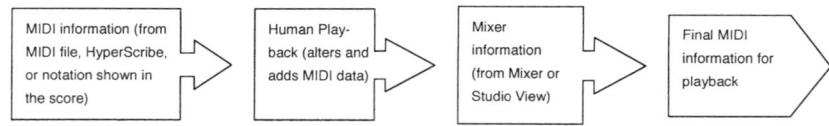

MIDI information flowchart

When importing a MIDI file or recording with HyperScribe, all note information (precise duration, timing, expression, etc.) is captured. But notes manually inputted or scanned all have the same velocity (intensity), and durations are exact.

You can manually alter MIDI information with the *MIDI* tool.

The MIDI tool

You can also alter *Human Playback* settings and edit the playback parameters of articulations and expressions. With no alteration of MIDI information and without applying a *Human Playback* style, a manually inputted score sounds very mechanical on playback.

In Finale 2004, MakeMusic added a feature called *Human Playback*. *Human Playback* intercepts MIDI data, scans and interprets expressions, phrase markings, articulations, and more, then alters and adds to the MIDI information to make playback more human-sounding. You can select different styles for *Human Playback* (HP) on which to base the interpretation. You can also choose whether HP ignores basic MIDI data for timing, duration, velocity, and tempo, uses it instead of the HP settings, or combines HP settings with MIDI data.

Human Playback preferences allow you to control the final MIDI information.

1. Click the *Playback Options* icon (on Windows) or the *Expand* button on the playback controls (on Macintosh).

2. Click *HP Preferences*.

3. In Finale 2007, this screen is organized into selectable sections. Click *MIDI Data* to access these settings.

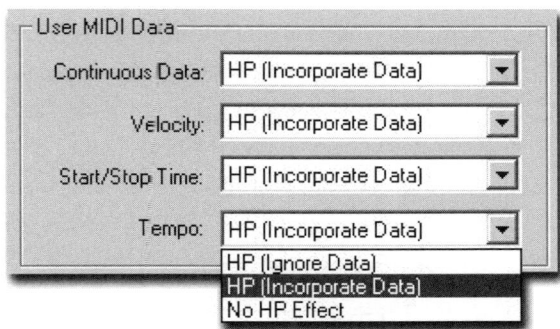

The User MIDI Data controls

4. Here you can select three options for each of the four basic elements of MIDI data (Continuous Data, Velocity, Start/Stop Time, and Tempo):

    a. **HP (Ignore Data).** This setting ignores all MIDI information other than pitch and duration. *Human Playback* will interpret all markings and style and not take into account MIDI data about those elements.

    b. **HP (Incorporate Data).** This alters and adds to MIDI data. It allows you to alter MIDI data manually. Changes will affect playback even with HP turned on.

    c. **No HP Effect.** This turns off HP interpretation for the specified element.

5. The four basic elements of MIDI data are:

    a. **Continuous Data.** This is MIDI information about volume, panning, modulation (vibrato), the sustain pedal, and so forth.

    b. **Velocity.** Note that velocity controls two elements: volume and timbre. This is how hard key on a MIDI keyboard is struck. MIDI keyboards measure this in terms of how fast the key is pressed, thus the term velocity.

    c. **Start/Stop Time.** This setting applies to the timing of a note's attack and release. Humans seldom play exactly on the beat or hold notes for precise durations. *Human Playback* alters attacks and durations to be more human sounding. However, if you used HyperScribe to record your music or imported a MIDI file, you may want it to play back with the feel with which it was recorded. Setting the *Start/Stop Time* parameter to *HP no Effect* prevents HP from altering the feel captured by HyperScribe or an imported MIDI file. If you manually inputted or scanned notes, you will likely want HP to control this element. If you want both, or if you want to manually alter MIDI information, set *Start/Stop Time* to *HP (Incorporate Data).*

d. **Tempo.** HP can alter the tempo slightly so that it is not metronomically strict. It also watches terms such as *ritardando, accelerando,* and fermatas. If you use the Tap feature in Finale. you will want to set *Tempo* to either *HP no Effect* or *HP (Incorporate Data).*

6. In Finale 2007–2008, HP preferences settings can be saved with each document, but in Finale 2006, *Human Playback* settings are global. If you wish to save HP settings with a specific document in Finale 2006, you must run the *Apply Human Playback* plug-in as shown in the example below.

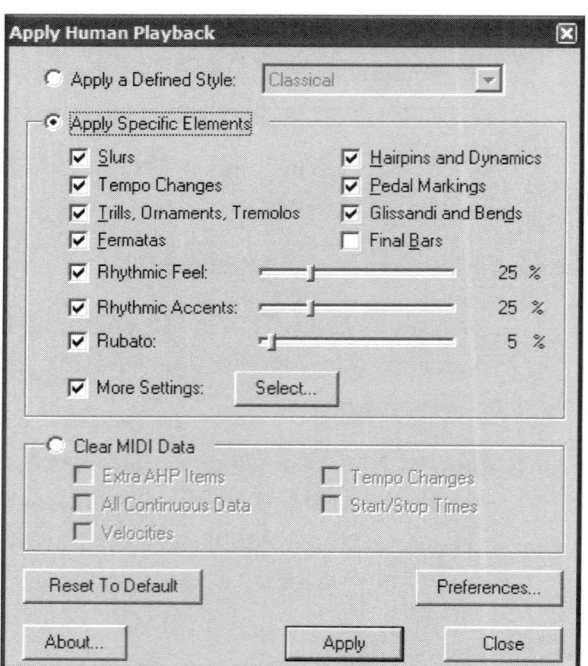

The Apply Human Playback dialog

Now is a good time to take another look at the MIDI information diagram presented above. Note that when you play a Finale score, in general, data tends to go through *Human Playback* settings. You can turn this off by selecting *Playback Controls* window/*Human Playback Style* dropdown menu/*None*.

You may want to apply different HP settings to select sections of a score. You can alter MIDI data to have the same information that HP settings would produce so that Finale can access that information via the MIDI data without having to pass through the HP function.

1. Select *Mass Edit* or *Selection* tool, and then select the area to which you want to apply HP settings.

2. Select *Plug-ins* menu/*Playback*/*Apply Human Playback*.

3. Set the dialog as you like.

4. Click *OK*.

USING NOTEPAD WITH YOUR STUDENTS

Finale is considered the most powerful music notation software by many, but some users may not need all of the power Finale offers. That is why MakeMusic created lighter versions of Finale: Finale Allegro, Finale Print Music, Songwriter, and a free version called Finale NotePad.

NotePad is a free download at www.finalemusic.com that is not shareware; you will not be asked to purchase the program or lose features after a certain period of time. It is a real, free, baby version of Finale. This makes it perfect for students with simple projects who cannot afford the other software products.

NotePad is also a great way for teachers and students to share files with each other, since NotePad and Finale share file formats. NotePad certainly has limitations, but it can open any Finale file regardless of its complexity. It even has the same basic sound set (SMSS) as Finale.

Here are some features and limitations of NotePad.

- no *Chord* tool
- input via clicking or typing, but no MIDI input
- limited articulations with a few dynamics created from articulations
- no *Expression* tool
- maximum of eight staves in a score
- cannot change key or time signatures
- cannot change clefs mid-score
- limited shapes available
- no more than one verse of lyrics
- no page formatting
- text can be added using a basic text tool

The limitations in NotePad are wonderful when creating worksheets and other educational materials for students. You can use items like articulations, lyrics, and text that students can change or edit in NotePad. Worksheet items that are off limits to students can be created in Finale (not NotePad) with the *Expression* or *Chord* tools. You can input notes into Layer 4 and hide them in Finale so students can hear but not see them in NotePad.

Here are a few ideas for using NotePad with students that music educators have shared:

- Have students create their own compositions in NotePad.
- Although NotePad does not allow key and time signature changes, students can be given files that already contain these and other elements of notation that are only available in Finale.
    - *Example:* Create a Finale document with key and time signature changes, repeat endings, etc., but without notes. Students can open this file and enter notes.
- If you need to create a complete rehearsal CD or SmartMusic file for practice, have students create their own part in NotePad, then copy/paste each individual part into a Finale score.
- Create tests, worksheets, and other materials that students can open and complete in NotePad.

The list goes on and on. If you come up with creative ways of using NotePad in your music program, please share them with us by sending an email to tcarruth@makemusic.com or tjohnson@makemusic.com

CREATING SMARTMUSIC FILES

SmartMusic is a complete practice and assessment system by MakeMusic. SmartMusic has access to 30,000-plus accompaniments, 50,000-plus exercises, elementary band and string methods, and it can score, grade, and deliver grades and assessment to teachers. It has become very popular among many music educators of all levels.

Although SmartMusic has many accompaniments and exercises pre-created for you, the time will come when the music you want is not readily available in SmartMusic. Finale allows you to create Ensemble Rehearsal, Solo, Intelligent Accompaniment, and custom Assessable SmartMusic files.

ENSEMBLE REHEARSAL FILES

Ensemble Rehearsal files allow students to:

- play with accompaniment
- control tempo
- set practice loops (for working out difficult passages)
- transpose to any key
- record themselves with accompaniment
- mute any instrument in the accompaniment

INTELLIGENT ACCOMPANIMENT FILES

Intelligent Accompaniment files are like Ensemble Rehearsal files with two differences: individual accompaniment instruments cannot be muted; and SmartMusic Markers can be added to allow the file to follow the performer's rubato interpretation, matching tempo, pausing for breath marks, and more.

ASSESSABLE FILES

Assessable files display as solo instrument parts, but play an accompaniment as well. After playing the music, SmartMusic displays feedback to the student, showing mistakes made. The score, a screenshot of the assessment feedback and an MP3 recording can be sent to the teacher for automatic grading.

In Finale, Ensemble Rehearsal, Intelligent Accompaniment, and Assessable files are created and saved in slightly different manners.

CREATING AN ENSEMBLE FILE FOR SMARTMUSIC

You can start with any file in Finale to create an Ensemble file. Each staff must be on a separate MIDI channel. Starting with the *Setup Wizard* ensures this.

1. Create the score as you normally would.

2. Select *File menu/Save Special/Save as SmartMusic Accompaniment.*

3. A intro screen explaining SmartMusic displays. This can be set to not show again. Click *OK* to go to the *SmartMusic Accompaniment Options* dialog.

4. Check the box next to *Full Ensemble* or *Group.*

5. Make sure that all instruments desired are selected.

6. Click *OK,* name the file, and save it.

CREATING AN INTELLIGENT ACCOMPANIMENT FILE FOR SMARTMUSIC

Intelligent Accompaniment files have a solo staff along with several accompaniment staves. You can attach a Finale notation file to display in SmartMusic, or just save the file as an accompaniment only. You can start with a pre-created score if desired, or you can create a new score in Finale using the *SmartMusic Wizard.* Music can also be scanned and inserted into a blank score created by the *SmartMusic Wizard.*

1. In the Launch Window, click *SmartMusic Wizard.*

2. On page 1 of the wizard, select the first option.

3. On page 2, select *New Solo* and select the solo instrument. Enter title and other info as with the Finale *Setup Wizard.*

4. On page 3, select the instruments you want to accompany the solo.

5. Set pages 4 and 5 as you normally would in the Finale *Setup Wizard.*

6. Input the score, copy notes from a scan, or create the score, including repeat markings and endings, as you normally would in Finale.

7. Input the *SmartMusic Markers.* In Finale 2006, select *Edit* menu/*Add SmartMusic Markers.* In Finale 2007–2008, select *Document* menu/*Add SmartMusic Markers.*

   a. Tell SmartMusic to wait for the beginning or the end of select notes before going on in the score.

   b. Create breath marks, repeat markers, and more.

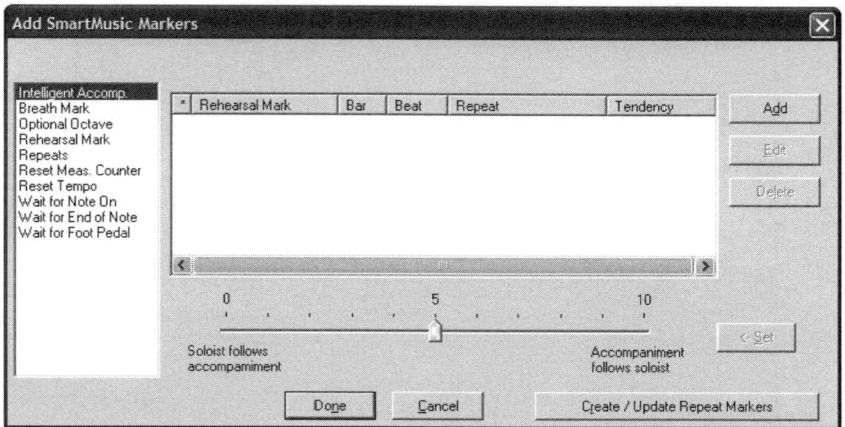

The Add SmartMusic Markers dialog

8. Adding and/or editing these markings in SmartMusic requires the creation of a custom file that must be loaded separately each time the Intelligent Accompaniment file is loaded. Settings made here will be the default settings for SmartMusic when this file is loaded.

    a. **Intelligent Accomp.** This setting tells SmartMusic how closely it should follow the soloist. It can be edited for any measure or beat, since this need will probably change throughout the piece. For example, an accompanist should listen carefully to the soloist during a rubato section, but should have control of the tempo if the soloist has whole notes while the accompanist has a sixteenth-note pattern. In some sections the soloist may want freedom to stray from the notated rhythm without the accompaniment following.

        i. Click *Intelligent Accomp.* in the list on the left of the dialog.

        ii. Click *Add* to the right.

        iii. Select the measure and beat at which to place an IA level.

        iv. Drag the slider to specify how closely the accompaniment follows the soloist. Click *OK.*

        v. You can now add more IA levels to other measures throughout the score.

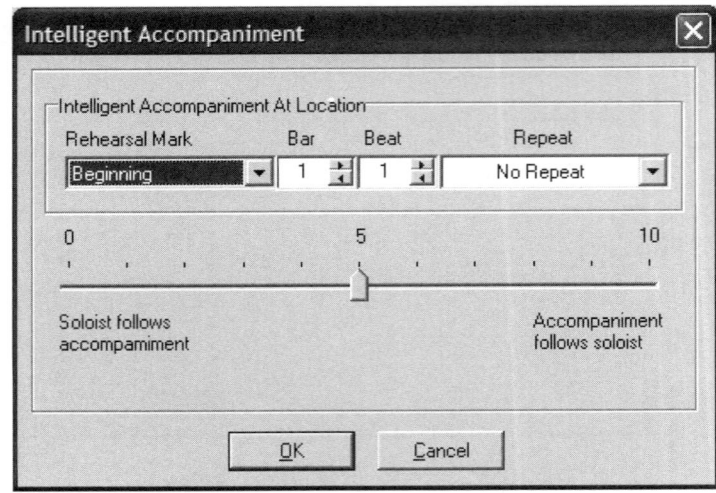

The Intelligent Accompaniment dialog

9. Other settings that adjust Intelligent Accompaniment behavior are *Wait for Note On* and *Wait for End of Note*. The *Wait for Note On* command is placed on a note in the solo staff and tells SmartMusic to stop playing until that note has been played by the soloist. The *Wait for End of Note* command is perfect for fermatas. If the soloist rests after a fermata, then the accompaniment resumes playing after the release of the selected note.

    a. Select *Wait for Note On* or *Wait for End of Note* in the list on the left of the *Add SmartMusic Markers* dialog.

    b. Click *Add*.

    c. Select the measure and note within the measure for which you want to assign a *Wait* command.

    d. Click *OK*.

10. Some SmartMusic Markers are position markers to make it easy in SmartMusic to move to a particular point in the score. *Rehearsal Mark* and *Repeat* markers can display in SmartMusic to allow the user to jump to a point in the score and begin playback.

    a. To add a *Rehearsal Mark,* select from the list on the left of the *Add SmartMusic Markers* dialog.

    b. Click *Add*.

    c. Select the measure for the *Rehearsal Mark*.

    d. Click *OK*.

e. To add a *Repeat* marker, simply click *Create/Update Repeat Markers* at the of the dialog.

11. When all markers have been set, click *Done* to return to the score.

12. You have the option of displaying notation for the solo part in SmartMusic. To do that, extract the solo instrument using Finale's *Extract Parts* feature. Note the directory to which you extract this file.

13. Select *File menu/Save Special/Save as SmartMusic Accompaniment.*

14. Finale pre-selects the proper settings for this dialog if you started with the *SmartMusic Wizard* in the *Launch Window.* If you had not started this way, you would have to select the solo instrument, associated sound, and accompaniment staves.

15. An Intelligent Accompaniment file does not require a notation file to display in SmartMusic, but we have extracted the flute part for this purpose. To attach the extracted notation file to the SmartMusic file, click *Select* under *Select File for Display in SmartMusic.* Find and choose the extracted flute part and click *Open.*

16. Now simply click *OK,* then name and save the file. It is now ready to be opened in SmartMusic.

CREATING A CUSTOM ASSESSABLE FILE FOR SMARTMUSIC

Assessable files can be created from existing or newly created files. If you want Assessable files for each part of an ensemble, each instrument will need to be saved as a separate Assessable file unless each part is in unison. There are certain musical elements and formatting that are not permissible in an Assessable file. Finale will prompt you when you are using a file that has non-assessable elements and formatting.

You may want to create an Assessable file for your ensemble. It is best to create the full score and then extract each part for assessment. Scan or input notes, or create a new blank score and paste individual parts into it to create the full score.

You could even have students create their own parts with NotePad as an extra credit assignment and then copy/paste the score together from these. If you have students create the parts, make sure that they observe the correct number of measures with rests.

Since NotePad does not allow key or time signature changes or mid-score clef changes, use the blank score template method described above and extract parts with multi-measure rests *disabled*. Give students the empty parts and instruct them to input their notes.

To create an Assessable file with accompaniment:

1. Open the file you want to convert.

2. Extract the instrument you want to assess using the *Extract Parts* function described in Chapter 7.

3. Select the *Staff* tool. Select and delete the staff that you extracted if you do not want it to be a part of the accompaniment.

4. Do not overwrite the complete score; instead, save the file with a new filename that includes the word *accompaniment* to distinguish it from the complete score.

5. In the *Launch Window,* select *SmartMusic Wizard.*

6. Select option three: *Create or open a Finale file or exercise that can be assessed and graded in SmartMusic.*

7. Click *Next.*

    a. If you choose *Create a New Document,* you can create the solo instrument for assessment without the accompaniment file as you did when you created the Intelligent Accompaniment file described above. The accompaniment file will need to be created separately. The accompaniment file does not need to follow the same restrictions as the Assessable file, since it is for accompaniment only and will not assessed.

    b. If you choose *Open Existing Document,* you will open only the extracted part for which you want to create an Assessable file, not the entire score.

8. Select *Open an Existing Document.*

9. Under *Select a Solo Instrument,* select the instrument to be assessed (for example, Flute). Click *Next.*

10. Navigate to the extracted file you created in step 2 above. Click once on the filename and then click *Open.* The *Assessment Wizard – File Format Information* dialog displays.

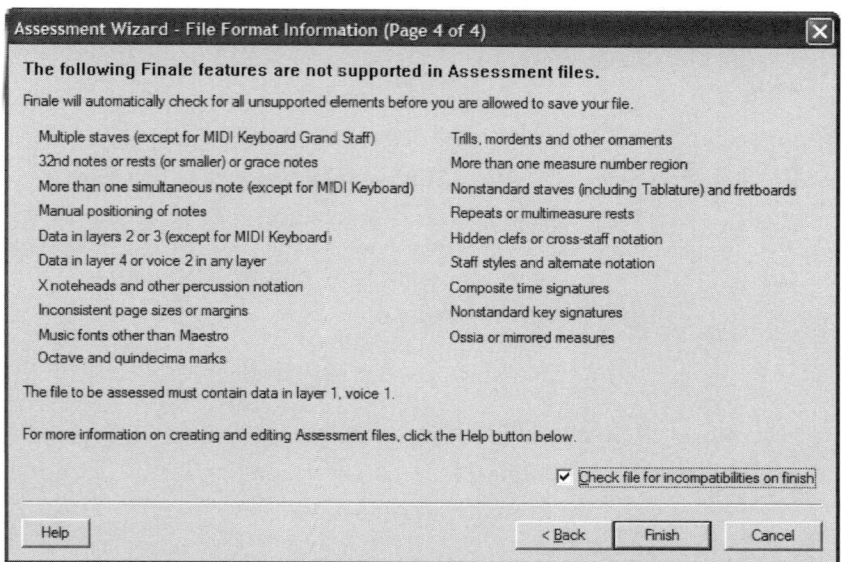

The Assessment Wizard – File Format Information dialog

11. Here you are told that Finale will check for musical elements and formatting not allowed in Assessable files. Remember, this applies only to the instrument being assessed, not the accompaniment. Click *Finish* to open the extracted part.

12. The *Finale Performance Assessment Compatibility* dialog displays if there are issues to be resolved. If needed, alter the score to remove any problems listed. (This dialog can remain open while you deal with problems so that you can refer to the list of issues. Once all are resolved, click *Check Again* in the dialog to see if any remaining problems need attention.)

13. One of the common problems with older files is manually positioned notes (notes that have been moved from the default position, either in *Speedy Note Entry* mode or using *Special Tools;* this does not refer to automatic note spacing). If you have a score with this problem:

   a. Select *Options* menu/*Document Options* or *Document* menu/*Document Options.*

   b. Select *Music Spacing* from the list on the left.

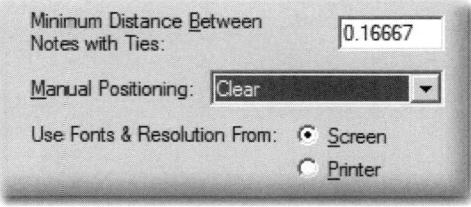

The Music Spacing pane of the Document Options dialog

c. Select *Clear* from the *Manual Positioning* dropdown menu.

d. Click *OK*.

e. Select the *Mass Edit* or *Selection* tool (press **Esc**). Press **Ctrl/Command–A** to select *all*.

f. Type **3** or **4** on the numrow (not the numpad) to execute *Beat* or *Note Spacing*.

g. All manual note spacing is now cleared.

14. Select *File* menu/*Save Special/Save as SmartMusic Accompaniment*. (Although this is not an accompaniment file, this is the proper way to create an Assessable file.)

15. Click *Select Accompaniment File*. Navigate to the file you saved to be the accompaniment file as described above. Click once on the file name, then click *Open*.

16. If there are no additional problems to be fixed, you will be prompted to save the file as a SmartMusic file. If there are further problems requiring your attention, then The *Finale Performance Assessment Compatibility* dialog displays again. As described above, leave this dialog open while you fix problems, then click *Check Again* to see if any remain.

17. Enter a filename and navigate to the location to which you want to save the file.

MusicXML

MusicXML is a file format for exchanging music notation files between programs. Finale uses this file format for two purposes:

1. to import or export files to programs that read or write in the MusicXML format

2. to export a Finale file to an older version of Finale

Note: The Finale file format is not backwards-compatible. This means that a collogue with an older version of Finale will not be able to read files created in a newer version of Finale. MusicXML makes it possible to create a Finale file readable by older versions.

Programs such as SmartScore Pro, Sharpeye, and Finale can write MusicXML files. Sibelius can read MusicXML files, but cannot write them without the Sibelius MusicXML plug-in, which can be purchased from www.recordare.com

MusicXML has been included with Finale for Windows at no charge since Finale 2003. Since MusicXML for Macintosh was not written until 2005 and was not included until Finale 2006. Users of Finale 2003 or older for Windows or Finale 2006 or older for Macintosh need the plug-in to be able to read MusicXLM files.

MusicXLM for Intel-based Macintosh computers was not available until the Finale 2007b maintenance release. You can select *Help* menu/*Check for Finale Updates* or go to www.finalemusic.com to manually find updates.

Saving a MusicXML file is easy. Select *File* menu/*Export MusicXML,* then name and save the file.

To open a MusicXML file in Finale 2006 or higher, select *File* menu/*Import MusicXML.*

To open a MusicXML file in an older version of Finale, start with a blank document and use the MusicXML plug-in.

1. In an older version of Finale, select *Launch Window/Default Document* or *File* menu/*New.*

2. Select *Plug-ins* menu/*MusicXML Import* or *Plug-ins* menu/*MusicXML/Import.* If you do not see anything about MusicXML in your *Plug-ins* menu, you need to purchase the MusicXLM plug-in at www.recordare.com

3. Click *Browse* in the *MusicXML* dialog, select *MusicXML Plug-in,* and click *OK.*

MusicXML will import and/or export all music and page elements. Original page formatting was not retained until Finale 2008. Staff size, number of measures per system, spacing, and more may be different than expected. To preserve the original format:

1. Before exporting the MusicXML file, select the *Mass Edit* or *Selection* tool (press **Esc**).

2. Type **Ctrl/Command-A** to select *all.*

3. Type **L** to lock the systems.

4. Select the *Resize* tool. Click in the top left-hand corner of the page and note the page size. Click to the left of a staff and note the staff size percentage.

5. Open a default document in an older version of Finale, select the *Resize* tool, and set the page and staff sizes to match the original document.

6. Now import the MusicXML file.

CREATING A CADENZA

A common question that is not a part of any of the projects in this book is, "How do I create a cadenza?" Sometimes a cadenza is a single line by itself with nothing else playing. Other times, other instruments are playing while the cadenza is being played. We will discuss how to create both types. Consider the example below.

1. Before inputting notes, you need a measure with a time signature large enough to accommodate all of the notes. If the cadenza plays solo without any accompanying instruments, you can simply change the time signature to something like 19/4 and set the *Time Signature* dialog to display a different time signature using the *Options* or *More Choices* button as we have discussed in other projects.

   a. However, if the cadenza needs a time signature of 19/4, but other instruments need a signature of 4/4, then leave the time signature set to 4/4.

   b. Select the *Staff* tool and double-click the cadenza measure to display staff attributes. Check the box next to *Independent Time Signature*. Click *OK*.

   c. Select the *Selection* tool (**Esc**) and select the measure to hold the cadenza on this staff only. Set the time signature to 19/4 with the option to display 4/4. This will not display a time signature at all unless this is a time signature change for the entire score.

2. Now input the notes for the cadenza. When done, the measure may look something like this:

The Staff tool

3. The notes may be crowded. *Note Spacing* may not fix this even if the next measure is pushed to the next system. Here is a review of the manual *Note Spacing* commands we have learned, along with some new ones.

4. Many times, a cadenza will be notated in smaller notes to make it easier to fit into the desired area. To do this, select the cadenza measure with the *Mass Edit* or *Selection* tool.

The Mass Edit and Selection tools

5. In Finale 2006–2007, right-click (**Command–click**) the measure and select *Change Note Size*. In Finale 2008, select *Utilities* menu/*Change/Note Size*. Set the size to about 85%. Click *OK*.

6. Run the *Note Spacing* command again to see if this fixes the problem (In Finale 2006–2007, type **Ctrl/Command–3** or **–4**, and in Finale 2008, type **Ctrl/Command–4** or **–5**).

7. You may want to change the measure width. If you want to retain the same number of measures on the system, consider locking the system before changing the measure width. To do this, select a measure in the system and press **L** (on Windows) or **Command–L** (on Macintosh).

8. Select the *Measure* tool. Click the cadenza measure. Drag the top handle on the right barline to adjust measure width.

9. You can also right-click (**Command–click**) the measure and select *Beat Positioning Chart* as we did in the choral project, or, with the *Measure* tool, click the bottom handle on the right barline. The *Beat Positioning Chart* appears above the staff.

10. Drag a lower handle to reposition a single beat, or press and hold **Shift** and drag a lower handle to reposition that beat and all beats to the right.

The Special Tools tool

The Note Positioning tool

The Accidental Positioning tool

11. Use the *Beat Positioning Chart* if music in other instruments must vertically align with beats in the cadenza. If this is not important, use the *Note Positioning* tool in the *Special Tools* palette instead.

12. Select the *Note Positioning* tool. Click in the cadenza measure to display handles above each note. Drag a handle to reposition a note.

13. You can also marquee more than one note and move the group by dragging or using arrow keys.

14. You may need to move accidentals closer to noteheads to create a cleaner look. Select the *Accidental Positioning* tool in the *Special Tools* palette.

15. Click in the measure to activate the *Accidental Positioning* handles.

16. Click to select a single handle, or **Shift–click** to select multiple handles and drag or move using arrow keys. Zooming in may make it easier to perform this action.

U, V, W, Z

About the Author

TOM CARRUTH is a MakeMusic Clinician and Product Specialist for Finale, MakeMusic's premier music notation program, and SmartMusic learning software for band, orchestra, and choir. He regularly creates supplementary educational materials for these programs, and participates in their future design.

Carruth is a graduate of Weber State University with a BA in Piano Performance and a minor in Computer Science. His fifteen years in music retail and specialization in software and hardware for the music education and production markets provide a deep background that informs his work as the leading instructor of Finale.

His three years as a composer and sound engineer for Wyvern Studies gave him a solid, hands-on experience at producing music and sound for a variety of projects, including video games, independent film, animation, and virtual rides.

He is a published composer with two compact discs of his original compositions, and has lectured on electronic music and software at colleges and universities throughout the United States.

This wealth of experience gives Carruth a solid base on which to educate Finale users, newcomers and seasoned veterans alike.